Four Gospels, One Christ

Four Gospels, One Christ

The Public Ministry of Jesus

MICHAEL HOOTON

RESOURCE *Publications* · Eugene, Oregon

FOUR GOSPELS, ONE CHRIST
The Public Ministry of Jesus

Copyright © 2016 Michael Hooton. All rights reserved. Except for brief quotations in critical publications or reviews, no part of this book may be reproduced in any manner without prior written permission from the publisher. Write: Permissions, Wipf and Stock Publishers, 199 W. 8th Ave., Suite 3, Eugene, OR 97401.

Resource Publications
An Imprint of Wipf and Stock Publishers
199 W. 8th Ave., Suite 3
Eugene, OR 97401

www.wipfandstock.com

PAPERBACK ISBN: 978-1-4982-8112-6
HARDCOVER ISBN: 978-1-4982-8114-0
EBOOK ISBN: 978-1-4982-8113-3

Manufactured in the U.S.A.   05/16/16

Scripture quotations are taken from the HOLY BIBLE, NEW INTERNATIONAL VERSION ®, Copyright © 1973, 1978, 1984 by International Bible Society. Used by permission of Zondervan. All rights reserved.

Contents

Preface | vii

1 **Four Gospels** | 1
2 **The baptism** | 37
3 **The temptation** | 61
4 **Going public** | 71
5 **Announcing the Kingdom** | 88
6 **Teaching the Kingdom** | 101
7 **Demonstrating the Kingdom** | 125
8 **Controversy** | 145
9 **Training the Twelve** | 158
10 **The Kingdom and the Gentiles** | 173
11 **The Kingdom and the cross** | 186
12 **The Kingdom and the poor** | 202

Bibliography | 217

Preface

"It seemed good also to me to write..." (Luke 1:3)

A much respected preacher, within a few years of his retirement, was asked, if you could start your time in ministry all over again, what would you do differently? After a moment's reflection, he replied, "I would preach less from the letters, and more from the Gospels."

That comment would not have been intended as a relegation of the New Testament letters to second-class status. But it does perhaps reflect the fact that the doctrinal study of the letters has often seemed to appeal more to the western delight in analysis and argument than the personal story of the Gospels. There are those who would prefer the old children's hymn "Tell me the stories of Jesus" to be re-worded as "Expound to me the doctrines of Jesus"; it might not fit the tune as well, but it would suit the somewhat cerebral approach to faith that traditionally has tended to characterize parts of the western Protestant church since the enlightenment, and to some extent continues into our own day.

But it is fundamental to our Christian faith that doctrine comes wrapped in flesh and blood: the Word became a human being and lived among us. Truth is not propositional, but personal: Jesus said, "I *am* the truth." If Jesus is the very heart and soul of all that it means to be Christian—and he is—then it is in the Gospels that that heart is revealed. We urgently need the exposition of Christian truth in the letters; but we need at least as urgently to be confronted regularly and often with the one who *is* that truth, as we find him in the Gospels.

I should perhaps start by saying what this book is *not*. First, it is not a commentary. It does expound and comment on a number of passages, but it makes no attempt to cover the whole text of the Gospels systematically.

Second, it is not a harmonization of the Gospels. Whilst the general shape of Jesus' life and ministry is clear, and a great deal of the specific detail within that overall shape is equally clear, it is not always possible or, I suggest, necessary to know in precisely which order all the narrated events happened. The Gospels, especially Matthew and John, sometimes seem to arrange their material thematically rather than purely chronologically. That in no way undermines their reliability as history—it is a perfectly valid way of writing a historical account—but it does mean that when, for example, Luke seems to place an incident in Jesus' life earlier or later than Matthew, the time we might spend wondering which of them is chronologically more "accurate" could be more usefully spent reflecting on the themes that Matthew and Luke are inviting us to draw out of the incident.

Third, it is not an "introduction" to the Gospels; that is, it does not aim to discuss at length such matters as the authorship, date of writing, and intended readership of the Gospels. For example, I accept the traditional view that the authors of the Gospels are Matthew, the disciple and former tax collector; John Mark, the young missionary who went with Paul and Barnabas from Jerusalem back to Antioch (Acts 12:25) then accompanied Paul on his first missionary journey as far as Pamphilia (Acts 13:5,13), and who is mentioned in Colossians 4:10 as the cousin of Barnabas; Luke, who also accompanied Paul on some of his missionary journeys and to whom Paul refers in Colossians 4:14 as "our dear friend Luke, the doctor"; and John, the disciple and brother of James—and I accept it not simply because it is traditional, but because I have never found the reasons put forward for doubting it to be either necessary or convincing. But those who want to explore the arguments for and against the traditional view of authorship will need to look elsewhere. Whether they will be spiritually enriched by so doing is, at best, a moot point. So my general comments in chapter 1 are not intended to give a full background introduction to the Gospels, but to suggest the particular character and "flavor" of each one. The four Gospels are not bland and featureless repetitions of the same story; each highlights different facets of the person of Christ, and chapter 1 is a simple attempt to characterize the four complementary accounts of Jesus.

We can divide the story of Jesus in the Gospels very roughly into three sections. The composer Robert Schumann wrote an orchestral work, which is often regarded as a three-movement symphony in all but name, which he called *Overture, scherzo and finale*; and we might in an analogous way regard the story in the Gospels as a three-movement symphony: the "overture," comprising the introductory material (for example, the prologue in John 1:1–18, and the story of the birth of John the Baptist in Luke 1) and the birth story (which is narrated only in Matthew 2 and Luke 2); then the central "scherzo," the public ministry of Jesus, starting with his baptism by John, and concluding just before his triumphal entry into Jerusalem riding on a donkey—though bearing in mind that the literal meaning of the word "scherzo" is "joke," that is perhaps not quite the best term: the public ministry of Jesus was certainly no joke!; and then the grand "finale," the last week—which is in the liturgical tradition of the church called "Holy Week"—leading up to the cross and resurrection.

This book focuses on the central movement, the three years of Jesus' public ministry.[1] Of course, everything in the Gospels is important for our faith; but there is at least one thing that is characteristic about Jesus' ministry, which distinguishes it from the birth story and the account of his death and resurrection. Both Jesus' birth and his death were unique: his entry into this world was by a one-off miracle, the virgin conception; and his death was a unique and unrepeatable sacrifice to atone for sin. That does not mean that the accounts of Jesus' birth and death do not have any lessons for our own life and faith: but they are first and foremost about Christ himself, who he is, and why "salvation in found in no one else, for there is no other name under heaven given to men by which we must be saved" (Acts 4:12). But the ministry of Jesus, whilst it is a significant part of the biblical portrayal of who Jesus is, is also a model of how we are to live as his disciples. Jesus himself said that those who believe in him are called to do the same works that he did (John 14:12), and John says that "whoever claims to live in him must walk as Jesus did" (1 John 2:6). His life is the pattern for our lives, and his ministry is the prototype of our ministry.

In John 12:21 we are told that some Greeks once approached Philip with the request, "Sir, we would like to see Jesus." This book is for ordinary Christian believers, rather than theological specialists, who share the same desire; but who, as well as seeing him, would like to think through the implications of what they see. Of course it is the Gospels themselves that introduce us to Jesus; this book, or any other, can at best be a help towards discovering more of what the Gospels themselves have to say to us. It is an attempt to explore the themes that arise from the story of Jesus as it is told

---

1. The conventional assumption that Jesus' ministry lasted three years is admittedly based not on any explicit statement in the Gospels, which do not contain a clear timetable of Jesus' life, beyond the fact that he began his public ministry when he was "about thirty years old" (Luke 3:23), but on the fact that John mentions Jesus being present at three annual Passovers (John 2:13, 6:4, 11:55; it is to be assumed that the Passover mentioned in 11:55 is the same as that in 12:1 and 13:1, when Jesus shared the Last Supper with his disciples). That tells us that Jesus' ministry lasted *at least* three years; whether it was longer is not easy to tell, in the light of John's comment that Jesus did many other things "which are not recorded in this book" (20:30). But three years is a reasonable estimate in view of the facts recorded in the Gospels.

in the four Gospels, a series of reflections on Jesus' life and ministry, and on the various threads and themes that run through the four-fold Gospel. It aims to outline some of the lessons that we can learn from the life and ministry of Jesus, which can then shape our own thinking and our own lives and service.

There are for obvious reasons a great many references to texts in the Gospels; where it seemed appropriate I have often quoted the actual words of the Bible, but I have normally also added the reference in brackets. These references are not simply my attempt to show that everything I have written is rooted in the Bible, but are intended to encourage the reader continually to go back to the Bible itself, just as the people of Berea "examined the Scriptures every day to see if what Paul said was true" (Acts 17:11). Where parallel verses or passages in different Gospels are listed, I have used the common convention of separating them by slanting parallel lines: so "Matthew 12:50//Mark 3:35" means that those two verses are Matthew's and Mark's record of the same saying, even if the actual wording may occasionally differ slightly.

There are also a substantial number of footnotes. Whilst I do not feel compelled exactly to apologize for these, I should perhaps say why they are there. Some are identifying sources of quotations or references; some are defining terms that may not be widely understood. But many are simply additional comments—the literary equivalent of a conversational "Oh, and by the way . . ."—which I felt would have interrupted the flow of the main text. No one is obliged to read them; but if any of them prove of interest, I will feel that their presence is justified.

Unless otherwise stated, Scripture quotations are taken from the *New International Version* (International Bible Society, 1973, 1978, 1984); I have used the 1996 edition (Zondervan, Grand Rapids, Michigan).

1

Four Gospels

"Many have undertaken to draw up an account..." (Luke 1:1)

Paul tells us in 1 Corinthians 12 that the various members of the church together make up the Body of Christ. No single person can adequately represent Jesus to the world. "You are to be Christ to the world" is a perfectly proper challenge to discipleship and service, provided that we remember that the "you" is plural; it is *you*, the church together, not just *you*, the individual believer, that are the hands, the feet, the lips of Jesus. The ministry of Jesus is so multi-faceted that no individual can truly fulfill it.

In a similar way, the *person* of Jesus is so multi-faceted that no single account of him can possibly do him justice. God could have ensured that we had in the Bible a record of Jesus' life, works and words. But in his generosity he has left us four. In fact, as John reminds us, even with these four we have still only scratched the surface, because if everything about Jesus were to be written down "I suppose that even the whole world would not have room for the books that would be written" (John 21:25). However, four is four times better than one.

All four Gospels are selective; they show us complementary aspects of the person of Jesus. They have a certain amount in common; but each has its distinctive emphasis. They are like the four large pieces of a jig-saw; and even if they still do not tell us absolutely everything that could possibly be said about Jesus, they do show us everything that God in his wisdom has decided that we need to know. True, we see at present "but a poor reflection"

(1 Corinthians 13:12); but the four Gospels together do at least give us a better and fuller reflection than any one of them could have done on its own. And we have the assurance that, when Jesus returns in person, "we shall see face to face."

Until then, we have Matthew, Mark, Luke and John to give us the authoritative account of Jesus' life and ministry, as well, of course, as his death and resurrection, which are not specifically discussed in this book. Each has its own characteristic features; so before we come to the story of Jesus' ministry as it is reflected in the four Gospels, it is worth summarizing the qualities that are most likely to strike the reader as distinctive about each, and what they say about who Jesus is and how we are to think of him.

Mark

The story

We start with Mark, because, although in our English Bibles it comes after Matthew, it is generally agreed that Mark's was probably the first Gospel of the four to be written, and the one on which Matthew in particular was to draw for his own work. It is by far the shortest and simplest Gospel. It seems to be based primarily on the recollections of Peter. In 1 Peter 5:13 Peter mentions Mark and calls him "my son," meaning "my disciple"; Jewish Rabbis often called their disciples "son." This suggests that Mark was an assistant to Peter in the latter years of Peter's life. As one Bible commentator has put it, "even if the hand be Mark's, the voice is Peter's."[1] This connection with Peter not only gives the book its authority as an apostolic Gospel, but also accounts for its distinctive quality. More than any other Gospel, except, in a different way, John's, it has the character of an eye-witness account. But the interesting thing is that the events in which Peter was involved are told with vivid detail, often using very colorful language, just as Mark might have heard Peter telling the story using graphic illustrations to paint a word-picture of the scene. So for example in 6:39 he even mentions that the people sat down on "the green grass"; and in 9:3 he uses the striking phrase of Jesus' appearance in the transfiguration that his clothes were "whiter than anyone in the world could bleach them." On the other hand, the events in which Peter was not involved personally, such as the temptation (1:13), are merely mentioned in passing. Peter would know that it had happened, from the things Jesus had said, but because he was not at the scene, he does not describe it. So Mark's Gospel has nothing of the birth and childhood

---

1. R. A. Cole, in his article on "Mark, Gospel of" in *New Bible Dictionary*, 728.

narratives. It starts with the baptism of Jesus, at which Peter was probably present; or, even if Peter himself was not there, his brother Andrew, who was a disciple of John the Baptist (John 1:35,40), almost certainly would have been. It then speaks of the calling of the first disciples, of whom Peter was one. It focuses on the Galilean ministry of Jesus around Capernaum, Peter's home. It is noteworthy, and a tribute to Peter's humility, that the incidents which would present Peter in a more positive light, such as the blessing pronounced on him at Caesarea Philippi (Matthew 16:17–19) or his walking on the water (Matthew 14:28–29), are omitted from Mark; but those which show his human frailty, especially the denials, are highlighted (14:29–31, 14:66–72).

Of all the Gospels, Mark's is the most descriptive; it is the Gospel, not simply of recorded history, but rather, in the full sense of the word, of *storytelling*, of vividly describing what happened so that the reader can picture the scene. Mark uses more adjectives, adverbs and descriptive phrases than the other Gospel-writers, in order to describe scenes that clearly made a powerful impression on Peter. These are part of what the other writers cut out of their Gospels: they record the essential facts, but without the same vivid sense of painting a picture. It is generally true that, whilst Mark does not include nearly so much material as Matthew and Luke, his language is more expansive. He includes a lot of secondary descriptive detail, which Matthew and Luke leave out; they trim down Mark's accounts to the essentials in order to make room for the extra material that they are going to add, whereas Mark describes events and scenes at greater length. To cite one typical example: in the account of Jesus' healing of the woman who was subject to bleeding (Matthew 9:20–22//Mark 5:25–34//Luke 8:43–48) Matthew tells the story, in the original Greek of the New Testament, in forty-eight words; Luke, who like Mark includes the dialogue about "who touched me?," which Matthew omits entirely, uses 105; and Mark's version takes 154. Mark, more than the other Gospels, will often typically describe Jesus' looks (for example, 3:34, "he looked at those seated in a circle around him"; 5:32, "Jesus kept looking round to see who had done it"), his acts and gestures (9:35–36, "Sitting down, Jesus called the Twelve . . . He took a little child and had him stand among them. Taking him in his arms, he said . . ."), and his emotions and feelings (3:5, ". . . in anger and deeply distressed"; 7:34, "He looked up to heaven and with a deep sigh said . . ."). Reading this, one can imagine Mark having heard Peter re-telling the stories, probably using lots of body language, maybe re-enacting Jesus' gestures and actions, and saying to his hearers, "And this is what it was like!" There are many other examples of small details which contribute to the vivid picture being painted: the description of the breaking up of the roof of a house to let down a paralyzed man (2:4); or of Jesus asleep in the boat, with his head on a pillow (4:37–38), and in a later scene on the lake, the description of the disciples "straining at the oars" because of the storm (6:48); the actions of Jesus in healing a deaf and dumb man, by putting his fingers in his ears and touching his tongue (7:33); the picture of Peter in the high priest's palace as "he sat with the guards and warmed himself at the fire" (14:54); and many others.

Mark's is the shortest Gospel, largely because he leaves out most of the teaching material in the other three Gospels: 41.4 percent of the verses in Matthew contain the teaching of Jesus; 34.7 percent of Luke; but only 16.9 percent of Mark. Mark's is the Gospel of actions rather than words, of story rather than doctrine; he concentrates on painting a picture of the events of Jesus' ministry. And his style is simple and fairly unpolished; it reflects the popular language of preaching, rather than the cultured language of the literary classes, and makes his book sound more like that of a story-teller than a literary historian. Mark writes in the style of "the man in the street." C. E. B. Cranfield, in his commentary on Mark, says: "Often, when the language of Matthew and/or Luke differs from that of Mark, it will be seen that it represents a grammatical or stylistic improvement."[2]

And his Gospel is dramatic. One of Mark's favorite words is the Greek term *euthùs*, which he uses forty-one times—eleven times in chapter 1 alone—and which is sometimes translated as "immediately," or similar words; at other times, it is left untranslated. This frequent use of "immediately" stresses the dramatic quality of Mark's narrative; we go straight from one vivid scene or event to another, with scarcely a pause for breath—at least in the first half of the Gospel.

The Son

The key phrase which Mark uses to summarize his message is that Jesus is "the Son of God." He is affirmed as God's Son in the opening verse of the Gospel, which is a kind of heading for the whole book. At his baptism, the voice of the Father from heaven declares him to be the Son of God (1:11). Demons recognize him as the Son of God (3:11, 5:7). At his transfiguration, the Father again declares him to be the Son (9:7). At his trial, Jesus says that he is the Son of God (14:61–62). At his death, the centurion declares that Jesus is the Son of God (15:39).

For Mark, the Sonship of Jesus is seen in two ways. First, it is demonstrated in mighty works of power. Jesus is the "man of action," the Son of God who comes to perform the works of God in the world. But second,

---

2. Cranfield, *Mark*, 7.

and very importantly for Mark, it is understood in the light of the cross. It is significant that the only affirmation of Jesus as the Son of God from *human* lips comes right at the end, when, at the cross, the centurion declares that this was the Son of God. Mark can use "Son of God" as part of his overall title; the Father, in the baptism and transfiguration, calls Jesus his Son; the demonic powers recognize from the outset that Jesus is the Son; but men can see Jesus as the Son of God only when they stand at the cross, as the centurion, quite literally, did. The wording of 15:39 is very important; it was when the centurion "stood there in front of Jesus" (on the cross), and "saw how he died" that he made his confession of Christ as the Son of God.

The other main title of Jesus, and Jesus' own preferred way of referring to himself, is "Son of Man." Though it occurs more often in Matthew (thirty times) and Luke (twenty-five times), it is also noticeable in Mark, who uses it fourteen times. Sometimes "Son of Man" refers to the ordinary human life of Jesus, though not particularly in Mark: it is Matthew and Luke who give us most of the "Son of Man" sayings about the common humanity of Jesus: for example, "the Son of Man came eating and drinking," Matthew 11:19// Luke 7:34; "the Son of Man has no place to lay his head," Matthew 8:20// Luke 9:58. At its simplest "Son of Man" just means man, human being; it stresses Jesus' humanity. It may also carry the sense, not just that Jesus was "a man," but that he was *the* archetypal man, Man *par excellence*. In the closing lines of Shakespeare's *Julius Caesar*, Antony sums up Brutus' character in the words, ". . . Nature might stand up and say to all the world 'This was a man!'" If that could be said of Brutus, the Gospel writers, including Mark, want us to know how infinitely more it can be said of Jesus, who is truly Man as God always intended.

But most of the "Son of Man" sayings of Jesus, and almost all of the ones found in Mark, refer to two paradoxically different aspects of his work. Some speak of the future glory of Jesus as the King of heaven; Matthew and Luke in fact include far more such sayings than Mark, who has only three: "If anyone is ashamed of me and my words in this adulterous and sinful generation, the Son of Man will be ashamed of him when he comes in his Father's glory with the holy angels" (8:38); "At that time men will see the Son of Man coming in clouds with great power and glory" (13:26); and "You will see the Son of Man sitting at the right hand of the Mighty One and coming on the clouds of heaven" (14:62). The background to the phrase "Son of Man" in this sense is in Daniel 7:13–14, where, at the end of the ages, "one like a son of man" comes in the clouds of heaven, and is given an eternal kingdom over which he shall reign for ever and ever.[3] By calling himself

---

3. Daniel's vision is usually assumed to be a prophecy of the second coming of Jesus,

"Son of Man," Jesus is saying that he is the one Daniel saw, the one who will reign over God's eternal Kingdom.

But many other "Son of Man" sayings, and most of those in Mark, speak of Jesus' betrayal, suffering and death: e.g. "[Jesus] then began to teach them that the Son of Man must suffer many things and be rejected by the elders, chief priests and teachers of the law, and that he must be killed . . ." (8:31). For Mark, the most important thing about the Son of Man was that he would suffer and die; we will return to that vital truth shortly, as we summarize the specific benefits of reading the Gospel of Mark.

Reading Mark

So how can reading Mark's Gospel in particular be of help to us? Primarily in two ways.

The dramatic story

Mark's is the most *striking* Gospel. It is an ideal introduction to the person who wants to find out about Jesus. It tells the story of Jesus in a way that can appeal to the imagination; it presents a Jesus who is both a remarkable man and the Son of God.

For this reason, Mark is probably the best Gospel to give to the person who is interested in, but largely uninformed about, Jesus. Of course, any Gospel—indeed, any part of Scripture—can be the means by which God speaks to people, and no part of the Bible is any less the inspired Word of God than any other. But the various books of the Bible were all written for some specific purpose; and part of the purpose of Mark is clearly to present the story of Jesus in the most straightforward way. It is therefore ideally suited to the needs of a generation that is often more receptive to story-telling

---

when he returns at the end of human history in clouds of glory with his angels, as described in Matthew 24:30//Mark 13:26//Luke 21:27; and that is certainly what Jesus is speaking of in the verses in Mark quoted above. In fact the language of Daniel 7:13 makes it more likely that what is being described is the ascension of Jesus: he "approached" God on his throne and was led "into" his presence. Jesus' ascension was his glorious and triumphant return to the throne of heaven, following the completion of his earthly ministry; and it is the ascended and enthroned Christ who is given authority over the eternal Kingdom of God (Revelation 5:9–10). That Jesus uses the language about the Son of Man coming on the clouds to refer to his coming again in glory at the end of history is not in conflict with that understanding of Daniel's phrase; after all, the angels at Jesus' ascension said that he would come back "in the same way you have seen him go into heaven" (Acts 1:11).

and to the visual than to the doctrinal, and in which many are unaware of, or have quite misleading and misinformed ideas about, who Jesus really was and what he actually did. Of course there is doctrine in Mark, as the above comments about the presentation of Jesus as Son of God and Son of Man demonstrate. But in Mark, even more than in the other Gospels, doctrine comes dressed in story; it is doctrine *incarnate*, doctrine that is *enacted* in the life of a person who went about doing things that demonstrate who he is. In Mark, people can encounter in a vivid and memorable way the essential personality of Jesus.[4]

The passion story

Mark in particular stresses the absolute centrality of the cross; and, as we saw above, that is the focus of most of Mark's sayings about Jesus as the "Son Man," the one who will suffer at the hands of men and die on the cross. The first half of Mark is, as we have said, a brisk jog-trot through the three years of Jesus' public ministry; Mark's favorite word "immediately" occurs regularly, as we move at top speed from one dramatic story to another. But as soon as we come to the start of the last week of Jesus' ministry, the triumphal entry into Jerusalem on Palm Sunday (11:1–11), the pace suddenly slows down. We get far more detail, as we move towards the cross. Of the whole of the text of Mark, a higher proportion is given to the passion story than in any of the other Gospels: 37.3 percent of all the verses in Mark are the account of the last week, leading up to the cross and resurrection. Of course the cross and resurrection are vital in all the Gospels, and indeed in the whole New Testament; but Mark more than any other arranges his Gospel so that we cannot fail to see that the really essential thing about Jesus is that he came into this world to die on the cross. That is the significance of the confession of the centurion, who, "when [he] . . . stood there in front of Jesus . . . and saw how he died, he said, 'Surely this man was the Son of God!'" We cannot really know who Jesus is until we spiritually stand before the cross, and see him, not just as the doer of mighty works, but as the crucified one. Leon Morris quotes the perhaps somewhat fanciful analogy that Dennis Nineham used to use with his students:

4. The dramatic and narrative quality of Mark was celebrated in the 1970s in the remarkable one-man stage show by the actor Alec McCowen, whose solo performance of the complete text of Mark was widely acclaimed by both theater critics and audiences. Whilst few of us could emulate Mr McCowen's acting skills, the text itself clearly had and still has that quality of being able to impact people powerfully as an engrossing drama; and it is ideally suited for reading aloud to others, for those in a position so to use it, and having the necessary story-telling gifts.

"[Mark] is rather like a tadpole—a large head with a comparatively short tail. The head of the Gospel is what theologians call the Passion Narrative—the account of the last few days in Jerusalem when Jesus suffered and died . . . Not only has Mark given to the passion the position of pre-eminence and climax in the Gospel—he has so selected and arranged the rest of his material that, for all its importance, it is seen to be subordinate to what happened in Jerusalem. If you read the earlier part of the Gospel attentively, you will see that practically everything in it is in some way introductory to the passion of Jesus; the aim throughout is quite single-minded—to help the reader to see Jesus on the cross."[5]

That is why the contemporary church needs Mark. It is dangerously easy to allow all sorts of things to replace the cross at the heart of our faith in Christ, things that are perfectly true and valid, but which are the *concomitants* of salvation rather than the *crux* of salvation: Jesus as the healer of sickness, the giver of peace of mind, the befriender of the lonely, the overcomer of demonic powers. Jesus is all those things, and much more. But he is above all else the Son of God crucified for our sins; and unless we know him first and foremost as the crucified and risen Savior, we have not truly grasped the essence of the Gospel. Mark confronts us with what P. T. Forsyth neatly termed "the cruciality of the cross";[6] he reminds us, just as much as Paul in 1 Corinthians 1:23, that "we preach Christ crucified."

Matthew

Matthew was one of Jesus' twelve disciples. His call to be a disciple is recounted in Matthew 9:9//Mark 2:14//Luke 5:27–28. In Mark and Luke he is called by his Jewish name, "Levi," rather than his Greek name, Matthew.

Matthew was a tax collector when Jesus called him. That means that he would be seen by his fellow-Jews as a collaborator with the Roman occupying powers, and that he would be enjoying the protection of Rome, and probably also considerable financial benefits, for taking large sums of money from his compatriots to give to the Romans. As a result, he would

---

5. Morris, *Cross in the New Testament*, 14–15.

6. Forsyth's outstanding book of that title appeared in 1909. The title is of course a play on words: in modern English "crucial" just means "essential," but it was originally the adjective from the Latin word *crux* ("cross") and so means "cross-shaped" or "having to do with a cross"; "crucial" is defined in *Chambers Twentieth Century Dictionary* as "decisive, as if of the nature of a finger-post at a cross-road."

be hated and despised by his fellow-Jews. It is interesting that this former traitor is the man who ends up writing the most "pro-Jewish" Gospel of all.

We could list a number of characteristics of Matthew, and themes that run through his Gospel; but we will focus on just two of the most obvious.

Jesus, the Teacher

If Mark is the Gospel of story-telling, Matthew is the Gospel of *instruction*. His accounts of the stories of Jesus are shorter than Mark's, and he cuts out a lot of Mark's descriptive details; but he includes far more of the teaching of Jesus. If Mark wrote his Gospel, so to speak, in answer to the request to "tell me the stories of Jesus," Matthew wrote his to provide the church with a resource for its teaching ministry, a manual of systematic instruction for church members about the life of God's Kingdom, and how to follow Jesus.

Most of the instruction in Matthew is gathered into five main blocks of teaching. They are: the *character* of the Kingdom (chapters 5–7, the Sermon on the Mount); the *mission* of the Kingdom (chapter 10, Jesus' instructions to his disciples before sending them out on mission); the *growth* of the Kingdom (chapter 13, the parables of the Kingdom); the *community* of the Kingdom (chapter 18, instructions on church life); and the *consummation* of the Kingdom (chapters 24–25, teaching and parables about the end of the world). A similar formula concludes each of these five sections: "When Jesus had finished saying these things . . ." (7:28, 11:1, 13:53, 19:1, 26:1), and the last of the five includes the significant word "all" ("When Jesus had finished saying *all* these things . . ."), which marks the end of the last block of teaching in the book.

It is often suggested that these five teaching sections are a kind of New Testament equivalent of the five books of the law in the Old Testament, Genesis, Exodus, Leviticus, Numbers and Deuteronomy. This is a valid comparison, though there is really no parallel with the character of the five sections of teaching and the five books of the law. Matthew shows us Jesus giving his disciples the basis of the new Kingdom of God, just as the law gave the Jews the basis for the Old Covenant.

Jesus, the King

The other obvious feature of Matthew is his "Jewishness." Matthew is above all else—in a sense that we shall qualify shortly—the Gospel for the Jews; Jesus is presented as the King of the Jews. This Jewish emphasis is seen in a number of ways, starting from the very first page of the Gospel with the *genealogy* (1:1–17), representing Jesus as the descendant of David and Abraham (verse 1), and therefore as the fulfiller of the promises to Old Testament Israel. The very opening words of Matthew (NIV, "A record of the genealogy . . ."; in Greek this is just two words: *bíblos genéseōs*) are full of Old Testament significance. In the Greek translation of the Old Testament that was used in Jesus' day, *bíblos genéseōs* —literally "book of origins" or "of [the] ancestry"—occur in only two places, Genesis 2:4 and 5:1, which talk about the creation of the world and of the human race respectively. Matthew starts the New Testament just as Genesis starts the Old; the coming of Jesus is a new beginning, a new Genesis.

There are also in Matthew a great many *Old Testament quotations*. Matthew, far more than any other Gospel, repeatedly points out how Jesus fulfills the prophecies of the Old Testament Scriptures; thirteen times he quotes from the Old Testament, showing how Jesus fulfilled a particular promise.[7] In addition, he records twenty-six instances of Jesus quoting the Old Testament in his teaching;[8] and there are a number of other passages, which, although they are not introduced as "quotations," are clearly borrowed from or allusions to the Old Testament.[9] This emphasis on the Old Testament shows that Jesus is the one in whom all the promises and prophecies of the Old Testament are fulfilled, and that the ministry and teaching of Jesus are not at variance with the Old Testament, or independent of it, but rather arise directly out of it.

Matthew particularly stresses the Jewish *titles of Jesus*, especially those which are to do with the Kingship of Christ. He is the King of the Jews (seven times), the Son of David (nine times), that is, the special King who will inherit the throne of David, and the Christ, that is, "the Messiah" (ten times). He frequently refers to the *Jewish law*, and to *Jewish practices* like almsgiving (6:1–4), fasting (6:16–18), bringing gifts and sacrifices (5:23–24)

---

7. The reference in 2:23 ("He will be called a Nazarene") is not to any specific Old Testament text. Matthew's phrase, "that what *the prophets* [not any particular prophet] said might be fulfilled" suggests that he is not so much quoting a reference, but rather alluding to a general theme in Jewish prophecy. Many prophecies speak of how the Christ would be of lowly origin, and would be despised and rejected by men; and as John 1:46 shows, people from Nazareth, an unimportant and unimpressive little northern town, were somewhat despised and disregarded. That more general interpretation of Matthew's words makes complete sense, whereas the attempt to tie "Nazarene" to a specific Old Testament phrase invariably seems somewhat forced and artificial.

8. 5:33 is not an exact quotation, but the sense is identical, and some of the wording very similar, to Numbers 30:2 and Deuteronomy 23:21.

9. For example: 10:35–36 (Micah 7:6), 11:5 (Isaiah 35:5–6), 18:16 (Deuteronomy 19:15), 21:33 (Isaiah 5:1–2), 26:15 (Zechariah 11:12), 26:64 (Daniel 7:13), 27:34–35 (Psalm 69:21, 22:18), 27:46 (Psalm 22:1).

and tithes and offerings (23:23), the temple and the altar (23:16–22), and the paying of temple tax (17:24–27). He uses lots of specialist *Jewish expressions* like "phylacteries"[10] (23:5), "whitewashed tombs" (23:27), and Jewish words like *racá*[11] (5:22), *korbanâs* (translated as "treasury" in 27:6), and "jot" and "tittle" (5:18),[12] which are, respectively, the smallest letter of the Hebrew alphabet (the equivalent of our letter i), and part of the tail of a letter, like the final horizontal stroke on the tail of an English q. The reference in 5:41 to someone who "forces you to go one mile" is a reflection of the privileges of Roman soldiers in an occupied country like Israel; a soldier could require a Jew to go with him and carry his pack for one mile. Jesus says, rather than resenting this as a terrible imposition, go a second mile as a sign of grace. But the saying is clearly directed at the Jewish people whose land is occupied, not at the Romans who were the occupying power. And Matthew usually speaks of the "Kingdom of heaven" rather than the "Kingdom of God," which is Mark's normal phrase: Jews would often use "heaven" as a way of referring to God without actually speaking his sacred name.

The Jewish character of Matthew is, in a sense, obvious. But alongside this, there are a number of ways in which the Gospel also demonstrates that the Kingdom is not just for Jews, but also for Gentiles; it highlights the Old Testament background to the coming of Jesus, but right from the outset, it shows Jesus to be the King who comes from *amongst* the Jews to be the King *of* all people. This starts from the opening *genealogy* (1:2–16), which in a most remarkable way stresses the grace of God to Gentiles. There are four women mentioned in the genealogy, apart from Mary herself, and of these four, three—Tamar (verse 3), Rahab (verse 5), and Ruth (verse 5)—were Gentiles, who are specifically mentioned as standing in the line of the Jewish Christ.

---

10. A phylactery was a small box or tube made from the skin of clean animals, worn on a strap round the forehead or on the wrist, and containing small pieces of parchment on which were written words of Scripture: traditionally, Exodus 13:1–16 and Deuteronomy 6:4–9 and 11:13–21, and sometimes also the Ten Commandments. Pious Jewish men wore them in particular at the hours of prayer.

11. *Racá* is a term of contempt, which various commentators define as the Aramaic equivalent of "fool," "blockhead," or "good-for-nothing." Its use was considered serious enough to be the grounds for action by a Jewish local court as a form of slander. Interestingly, it is probably derived from the Hebrew word *rēyq*, which is what Michal accused David of being when he danced before the Ark of the Covenant in what seemed to her to be an unseemly way (2 Samuel 6:20); so *racá* could apparently be used to imply not merely "stupid," but also spiritually unworthy—presumably by those who thought that they themselves were spiritually worthy!

12. The NIV translates as "the smallest letter . . . the least stroke of a pen," rather than the technical terms which Matthew actually uses, "jot" and "tittle."

In the birth story, Matthew focuses on *the Magi* (2:1–12) who came to visit Jesus. It is generally assumed that the Magi were not Jews, but came from a background in eastern religion. The word "Magi" was originally used to refer to a caste of Zoroastrian priests in Persia, which is probably where these Wise Men came from. The first people to affirm Jesus as the King of the Jews were not themselves Jews; but they come to kneel before and worship the King. They are an early and partial fulfillment of the Old Testament promise of people coming from many lands and from many religious backgrounds to worship the God of Israel.[13] And in Matthew's account of *the infancy* (2:13–15) of Jesus, when he is in danger, it is within a foreign land, Egypt, that he finds refuge. We need to try and grasp how shocking this would be for Jews to accept. Ever since the time of the exodus, they had thought of Egypt as the place *out of* which God's people are delivered from danger and into the place of safety. But the infant Jesus is in danger in Israel, and finds safety and refuge *in* Egypt.

The Gospel ends (28:18–20) with *the commission* to "make disciples of all nations." Moreover 10:18 says that the disciples will be witnesses to the Gentiles; 15:31 reports that Gentiles, when they saw the works of Jesus "praised the God of Israel"; and in 26:13 Jesus anticipates the time when "this Gospel is preached throughout the world." And the fact that the Gospel will be proclaimed throughout all nations is stated in parable ("the field is the world," 13:38) and prophecy ("this gospel . . . will be preached in the whole world as a testimony to all nations," 24:14). The rejection of unbelieving Jews in favor of Gentiles is reflected in 8:11–12 and 21:43.

In the light of this, we need to understand rightly the sense in which Matthew is "the Jewish Gospel." Matthew's Gospel *is* Jewish in style and cultural and religious background, but it does not endorse Jewish nationalism or exclusiveness: his concern is to show how completely Jesus fulfills the promises of God in the Old Testament that he would one day send the one who would be a light to the Gentiles.

Reading Matthew

If Mark is, as we suggested, the most striking Gospel, Matthew is the most *systematic* Gospel. It is *the* teaching Gospel *par excellence*, which provides a manual for discipleship, the ideal material for Bible studies, nurture groups

---

13. The traditional liturgical term "epiphany," which is the name of the annual commemoration of the visit of the Magi, celebrated on 6th January, is a word meaning "revelation," and refers to the revelation of Christ to the Gentiles in the story of the Wise Men.

and new disciples' classes. That is most famously true of the Sermon on the Mount (chapters 5–7), Jesus' presentation of the life of the Kingdom of God; but it is equally true of the other significant blocks of teaching that Matthew gathers together. No preacher who is concerned to instruct his flock in Christian life and faith could ever run out of material for sermons, even if he had only Matthew's Gospel to draw on. If we read Mark in order to be confronted with the person of Jesus, we read Matthew in order to be taught how to live for the Kingdom of Jesus.

Matthew's emphasis on Jesus as the fulfiller of the Old Testament needs to be rightly understood. There will be some who find it hard to relate to Matthew's "Jewishness," and who may be somewhat disconcerted when, having turned from the Old to the New Testament, they find themselves confronted on the very first page with one of those obscure Jewish genealogies that they thought, and no doubt hoped, they had now left behind. Much—though by no means all—of the cultural and spiritual atmosphere of Matthew can seem, more than in any of the other Gospels, to belong to a different world than that of twenty-first-century Western Europe.

Fortunately, the Jewish details that can seem alien to us are relatively unobtrusive—primarily some words and references that might need clarification—and should not distract most people from the key teaching in Matthew. But we do need to learn from Matthew's presentation of Jesus as the fulfiller of the Old Testament. He clearly sees it as important to stress this: "This took place to fulfill what was spoken through the prophet," or words very similar, occur thirteen times in Matthew. Jesus' own words in 5:17 are vital: "Do not think that I have come to abolish the law or the prophets; I have not come to abolish them, but to fulfill them."

The key word is "fulfill." There are two things which Jesus does *not* do. One is plainly stated: he does not abolish the law and the prophets. He does not set aside or make redundant the Old Testament. But the other thing is equally important: he does not merely re-state and re-affirm the Old Testament on its own terms. Rather, he *fulfills* it.

The word translated "fulfill" can have a number of senses. First, it can mean to fulfill a prophecy, to be the one who accomplishes in reality what others had predicted. In that sense, Jesus is the one whose coming the prophets had foretold. That is the sense of the verb "fulfill" in thirteen out of its fifteen occurrences in Matthew, where he says that the things Jesus did were in fulfillment of various Old Testament prophecies. Second, it can mean to complete or fill out: so the sense would be that the Old Testament law was partial, and Jesus brings the completion. Matthew uses the verb in that sense in 23:32, where Jesus says to the Pharisees, "*Fill up*, then, the measure of the sin of your forefathers"; in other words, if you kill me, you will be completing what your ancestors started. And Jesus certainly does, in the Sermon on the Mount, extend and deepen some aspects of the law; in particular, he says that the Old Testament laws prohibiting murder and adultery are to be taken, by those who are disciples of the new Kingdom, as referring not merely to outward physical acts, but also to harboring anger or lust in the heart (5:21–30). Third, it can mean to fulfill in the sense of fulfilling an obligation or completely satisfying a requirement. At least something of that sense lies behind Jesus' words to John the Baptist in 3:15 ("It is proper for us to do this [= for John to baptize Jesus] to *fulfill* all righteousness"). Jesus lived a life that in every way fulfilled the righteous requirements of God's law.

In all those senses Jesus fulfilled the law. But the over-riding meaning of "fulfill," the sense that gathers all those other senses together and is taught through the rest of the New Testament, is the principle of *consummation*. Jesus brings the full reality of which the Old Testament was merely the foreshadowing. As Hebrews 10:1 says, "The law is only a shadow of the good things that are coming—not the realities themselves." Jesus is "the reality itself." Jesus "fulfills" the Old Testament in the sense that he is the one who, through his death and resurrection, brings the fullness of which the law and the prophets were a partial foretaste.

Matthew repeatedly shows us how Jesus fulfills the Old Testament. The predictions of the prophets come to pass in Jesus' ministry; characters and events in the Old Testament are small-scale foreshadowings of Christ; the life expected of God's people in the Old Testament is a pattern of the new life that Jesus will make possible through his gift of the Holy Spirit. So the Christian way of handling the Old Testament is neither to ignore it—to see it as outdated religious history—nor to see ourselves as bound by what it says *on Old Testament terms*. It is rather to ask, what does this show us about Jesus? In what way does this foreshadow Jesus or shed light on what Jesus did? Matthew makes a significant contribution to our understanding of Jesus as the one who fulfills and consummates the Old Testament, who brings the reality which it prefigured. His Gospel can help us to learn the lessons of the Old Testament, but it also reminds us to apply them in a New Testament way.

Luke

Luke's is the fullest account of the life of Jesus, and in many ways the most human, which may be one of the reasons why Luke, for many people, is their favorite Gospel.

The human story

Luke's Gospel includes a lot of historical material that is not found elsewhere, just as Matthew includes more teaching material. It is Luke who gives us the fullest account of the birth and childhood of Jesus: the announcement by the angel of the future birth of John the Baptist (1:5–25); the similar announcement to Mary about the birth of Jesus (1:26–38); the visit of Mary to Elizabeth (1:39–56); the birth of John the Baptist (1:57–80); details about the actual events around the birth of Jesus (2:1–20); the dedication and presentation in the temple of the infant Jesus (2:21–40); and the visit by Jesus as a twelve-year-old to the temple (2:41–52), which is the only recorded incident between the birth and the public ministry of Jesus.

In addition, Luke records far more of the teaching of Jesus on the final journey to Jerusalem, and includes a number of other incidents which are not found elsewhere, such as Jesus' preaching in Nazareth and the people's response to it (4:16–30), the raising of the widow of Nain's son (7:11–17), the healing of the ten lepers (17:11–19), and many others.

As well as the fullest accounts of the human life of Jesus, Luke has a great interest in all sorts of people. He gives us the most fascinating *descriptions of people*, which give his Gospel its tremendous human interest: for example, the elderly Zechariah and Elizabeth (1:5–25,57–66), Mary's visit to Elizabeth (1:39–56), Mary and Martha (10:38–42), Zacchaeus (19:1–10), Cleopas and his friend (24:13–35), and many more. Luke's Gospel is like a portrait gallery of real human beings in real situations. The same is true of many of the *parables* in Luke: whereas Matthew's parables tend to be symbolic illustrations of the Kingdom of God, Luke records far more parables which are realistic stories about people. He even gives a name to one character in a parable (Lazarus, in 16:20).[14] Examples of these kinds of parables as human stories are the good Samaritan (10:30–37), the visitor at midnight (11:5–8), the rich fool (12:16–21), the prodigal son (15:11–32), the shrewd manager (16:1–9), the rich man and Lazarus (16:19–31), the persistent widow and the judge (18:1–8), the Pharisee and the tax collector (18:9–14), and the king and his servants (19:11–27).

Luke, more than any other Gospel, stresses Jesus' ministry to *the poor*, the needy, those who are outcasts from or on the margins of society. At the birth, it is to poor shepherds (a despised class in Israel) that the angels announce the Good News (2:8–20). Luke stresses the poverty of Jesus' family: the offering made by his parents after the birth was that designated for the poor (2:23–24; see Leviticus 12:8). Jesus is anointed by "a woman who had

---

14. The traditional "name" for the rich man in this parable, "Dives" (pronounced "die-vees"), is not actually a name: it is simply a Latin word for "rich man."

lived a sinful life," and defends her against the attacks of the Pharisees (7:36–50). Luke records how many tax collectors and sinners gathered around Jesus to hear him (15:1). The heroes of many of Jesus' parables are socially disreputable: the two debtors (7:40–43), the prodigal son (15:11–32), the tax collector (18:9–14). Zacchaeus was another social outcast welcomed by Jesus (19:1–10). Luke alone records the repentance of the criminal crucified with Jesus, and Jesus' promise to him of salvation (23:40–43).

This interest in the socially marginalized extends to *women*. Luke has a particular interest in women, and gives them an honored place in his Gospel. Women were a despised underclass in first-century society. But Luke shows how prominently they figured in the life and ministry of Jesus. He mentions thirteen women who are not mentioned elsewhere in the New Testament, such as Elizabeth, the mother of John the Baptist, the elderly prophetess Anna (2:36–38), the widow of Nain (7:11–17), and the unnamed woman in the home of Simon the Pharisee who had "lived a sinful life" (7:36–50). But Luke does not only tell stories about women: he clearly affirms their spiritual value alongside men. In the story of Mary and Martha (10:38–42), the phrase in verse 39, that Mary "sat at the Lord's feet," is particularly significant: this was a technical term meaning to be the disciple of a Rabbi—in Acts 22:3 Paul says that he sat, literally, "at the feet of Gamaliel"; the NIV translates as "under Gamaliel I was thoroughly trained…."—and in Jesus' day, women were not allowed to be disciples of a Rabbi: that was only for men. That is the reason for Martha's disapproval (verse 40)—Mary is not in her rightful place. But Jesus defends her, and affirms her equal right with men to sit at his feet as a disciple. Luke also stresses that women were the first witnesses of the resurrection (24:1,10). Again, this was very revolutionary for its day. As well as not being allowed to be disciples of a Rabbi, women were not allowed to give evidence in court: they could not act as witnesses, but Luke stresses that these women were witnesses of the risen Christ to the apostles (verse 9).

Similarly, Luke has an interest in *children*. He alone records the childhood of John the Baptist (1:57–80), and says anything about the childhood and growing up of Jesus (2:21–52). Three times he mentions that people he is talking about had an "only child" (7:12, 8:42, 9:38). In his account of the mothers who brought their children to Jesus (18:15–17), Luke uses the Greek word *brépsē*, meaning "infants," "babes," whereas Matthew and Mark both use the more indeterminate word *paidía*, meaning "children" (of any age).

Luke depicts Jesus in the context of *social relationships*. Three times he records Jesus dining with Pharisees (7:36–50, 11:37–44, 14:1–4); he speaks of Jesus' social life at Bethany (10:38–42), at Zacchaeus' home (19:1–10), and at Emmaus (24:13-32). He often uses very homely illustrations: the innkeeper looking after the wounded man (10:35), the unexpected visitor needing food (11:5-8), the lost coin and the search through the whole house for it (15:8-10), the party at the prodigal's return (15:22-32). More than any other Gospel, Luke shows Jesus living in the recognizable social world of common humanity; if I may so phrase it, without implying anything disrespectful, the Jesus of Luke's Gospel is the Jesus whom we can most easily imagine wearing jeans and a T-shirt.

The universal Gospel

Luke stresses even more than the other Gospels that Jesus has come for all people. The angels' announcement of the birth of Jesus declares the good news to be "for all the people" (2:10).[15] Simeon, in the temple, says that Jesus will be "a light for revelation to the Gentiles" (2:32). When John the Baptist is described in the quotation from Isaiah 40 as "a voice of one calling in the desert," Luke alone continues the quotation to include the words "and all mankind will see God's salvation" (3:4-6). His genealogy of Jesus goes back, not just to Abraham, but to Adam; in other words, to the start of the whole human race (3:23-38). He records Jesus using illustrations from the Old Testament of how God blesses non-Jews (4:25-27). Jesus invites Samaritans to receive him, and refuses to call on God to punish them when they do not (9:52-56); in other words, he does not side with the Jews in seeing the Samaritans as, at best, God's second-rate people. Samaritans are seen in a very positive light in a parable (10:30-37) and a miracle story (17:11-19).

Having said that, Luke does also have a great deal of interest in Jerusalem and the temple. His Gospel begins (1:5-10) and ends (24:53) at the temple (unlike Matthew, the most Jewish Gospel). Luke alone records the presentation of Jesus at the temple (2:22) and his visit there at the age of twelve (2:41-49). Luke contains a major section, most of which is not in Matthew or Mark, about Jesus' last journey to Jerusalem (9:51—19:45), and he frequently stresses that Jerusalem is his destination (9:51,53, 13:22, 17:11, 18:31, 19:28). Overall, Luke refers to Jerusalem thirty-one times, as opposed to thirteen times in Matthew, ten times in Mark, and twelve times in John.

---

15. In fact, "all *the* people" refers to the whole nation of Israel; bearing in mind that this announcement is made to a group of people—shepherds—who were regarded as outsiders to the respectable religious community of Israel, that stresses the inclusiveness of Jesus' ministry: he has come for all, not for a social and spiritual *élite*.

So it is not quite true to say that Matthew is the Gospel for Jews and Luke is the Gospel for Gentiles. Both stress that Jesus has come for both Jews and Gentiles. However, Luke does certainly have a special interest in the universal application of the Gospel; maybe his stress on Jerusalem is his attempt to urge non-Jews to identify with the work of salvation that God accomplished there.

The social concern

Linked with Luke's interest in people, and especially in ordinary and poor people, his Gospel has a particular stress on the moral, social and financial implications of the Gospel. He is interested not only in social relationships but also in *social responsibility*. In the *Magnificat*, Mary sings that the hungry are filled with good things, and the rich sent away empty (1:53). John the Baptist challenges people about social and financial integrity and generosity: people who want to be baptized should share with others, tax gatherers must avoid extortion, and soldiers must be content with their pay (3:10–14). In Nazareth Jesus proclaims good news to the poor (4:18). In the Sermon on the Plain[16] he pronounces a blessing on the poor (6:20; unlike in Matthew's Sermon on the Mount, he does not qualify it with "in spirit": Luke's sermon much more clearly refers to the literally poor), and pronounces a woe (a curse) on the rich (6:24). Jesus says to John the Baptist's messengers that he brings good news to the poor (7:22). Many of Jesus' parables in Luke deal with money matters: the two debtors (7:40–43), the rich fool (12:13–21), the tower builder (14:28–30), the lost coin (15:8–10), the shrewd manager (16:1–15), the rich man and Lazarus (16:19–31), the "minas"[17] (19:11–27).

---

16. The teaching in Luke 6:17–49 is conventionally referred to as the Sermon on the Plain. It contains a certain amount of material similar to Matthew's Sermon on the Mount, though there are a number of differences in emphasis as well as in content. The title "Sermon on the Plain" arises from the introduction in verse 17, which says that Jesus went with his disciples and "stood on a level place," where he gave the teaching that follows. This different setting suggests that Luke 6 is not merely Luke's version of Matthew 5–7; but whether either or both of these sermons are records of single addresses, or whether they are compilations of teaching given at different times, is a question that need not detain us if our aim is to understand and follow Jesus' teaching as given in the biblical text. For what it is worth, I can think of no reason why Jesus should not have given similar teaching on different occasions and in different places, but with some changes of content and emphasis as he felt appropriate and necessary.

17. A "mina" was a Greek coin worth one hundred drachmas; in the first century it was about a quarter of the annual pay of an agricultural laborer, in other words, a fairly modest amount. There is a similar parable to that of the ten minas in Matthew 25:14–30, the better-known parable of the talents; the main lesson of the two parables is the same, though the details, including the number of servants and the amounts of

Jesus urges his followers to show special concern for the poor and needy (14:11-13,21). The Pharisees are described as people "who loved money" (16:14). And many stories contain warnings to the rich: Zacchaeus (19:1-10), the rich young ruler (18:18-27), the widow's mite (21:1-4).

The spiritual themes

It is clear that Luke, more than any other Gospel writer, wants his readers to see the human Jesus and to understand the social challenges of following him. But, lest anyone think that Luke's vision is merely social or even secular, it is very noticeable that, hand in hand with its *social realism*, his Gospel also stresses *spiritual reality*. There is a major emphasis, for example, on *prayer*; Luke records nine prayers, or occasions of prayer, in the life of Jesus, seven of which are found only in this Gospel. Three of the parables which are unique to Luke deal with prayer: the friend at midnight (11:5-8), the unjust judge (18:1-8), and the Pharisee and the tax collector (18:9-14). And Luke alone records that Jesus prayed for Peter (22:31-32); that he exhorted his disciples to pray in Gethsemane (22:40); and that he prayed for his enemies (23:34) and for himself (22:41). Jesus tells his disciples to pray for their enemies (6:28), and commends prayer as a safeguard against temptation (22:40,46).

Prayer goes hand in hand with *praise*. Luke includes a number of songs that have become prayers of praise in the church. In the liturgical tradition, these are invariably known by their opening words in Latin: the *Magnificat* (1:46-55)—literally, "magnifies," in the sense of "extols" or "praises"; the *Benedictus* (1:68-79)—literally, "blessed [be the Lord]"; the *Gloria in excelsis* (2:14)—literally, "glory in the highest"; and the *Nunc Dimittis* (2:29-32)—literally, "now dismiss." Often, people who receive benefits from Jesus praise and glorify God: the shepherds who visit the baby Jesus (2:20), the crowd that saw Jesus raise the widow of Nain's son from the dead (7:16), the woman healed of curvature of the spine (13:13), the Samaritan leper (17:15), and the blind beggar outside Jericho (18:43).

---

money they received, are different. A "talent" was a much more substantial sum of money than a "mina": whereas a mina was a coin worth one hundred drachmas, a talent was not a single coin but a unit of monetary reckoning: it was the equivalent of six thousand drachmas. The moral lesson of both parables is clear: what matters in Christian life is not how much you have, but what you do with it; rather than assessing whether we have, or anyone else has, more or fewer gifts, opportunities, or blessings than others, our calling is to use in God's service whatever resources we have been given, whether many ("five talents") or few ("one mina").

Linked with praise is Luke's recurring motif of *joy*. He uses the words for "joy" and "rejoice" twenty times; there are also phrases about leaping for joy (6:23), laughter (6:21), gladness (19:6) and celebration (15:23,32). Luke contains three special parables about the joy in heaven over those who repent (chapter 15). His Gospel begins (1:47) and ends (24:52–53) with rejoicing.

Luke has as much to say about *the Holy Spirit* as John. In Matthew, there are ten verses explicitly about the Holy Spirit; in Mark, five; in Luke, twenty-four; and in John, twenty-four, many of which are the sayings in the upper room in chapters 14–16, which are only in John. We should also bear in mind that Luke wrote Acts, in which the coming of the Spirit is a major theme.

The birth of Jesus is characterized by a new outburst of the Spirit's activity. This is significant, following, as it does, a period of three hundred years or more when there had been little or no spiritual activity, certainly of a prophetic kind, in Israel. Then, suddenly, in anticipation of the coming of Jesus, there is a rapid increase in people's experience of the Spirit. John the Baptist will be filled with the Spirit from birth (1:15), Mary will be overshadowed by the power of the Spirit (1:35), Elizabeth is filled with the Spirit (1:41), as are Zechariah (1:67) and Simeon (2:25–26).[18] The Spirit comes on Jesus in his baptism (3:22); Jesus is described as "full of the Holy Spirit" (4:1), is led by the Spirit in the desert (4:1), and returns from the desert in the power of the Spirit (4:14). In Nazareth, Jesus declares from Scripture that the Spirit of the Lord is on him (4:18); he rejoices in the Spirit (10:21); in his teaching about prayer, Jesus promises the gift of the Spirit to those who ask (11:13); he promises the inspiration of the Spirit for those who find themselves "put on the spot" and required to defend themselves (12:12); and he tells his disciples to stay in Jerusalem until they receive "power from on high" (24:49).

Finally, Luke has a characteristic way of using the vocabulary of *salvation*. Alone amongst the four Gospel writers, Luke sets the coming of Jesus in its historical context (2:1–2, 3:1–2): he is interested in the historical fact of the coming of salvation. The word "salvation" is not used at all in Matthew or Mark, and only once in John, but is found six times in Luke. He

---

18. The reference in 1:80 to the young John the Baptist growing to become "strong in spirit" is almost certainly intended as a reference to his human personality; the word "spirit" has no definite article (that is, not "in *the* Spirit"), which would be more normal if Luke was speaking of the Holy Spirit of God. Having said that, bearing in mind that it was prophesied that John would be filled with the Spirit from birth (1:15), Luke would doubtless intend us to understand also that John's development was under the guidance and inspiration of the Spirit.

uses the verb "to save" more than any other Gospel writer; and twice he calls Jesus "Savior." The key text summing up the message of salvation in Luke is 2:11: "Today . . . a Savior has been born . . . he is Christ the Lord."

It is a particular feature of Luke's Gospel that he stresses how salvation has become a present reality in Christ by the use of the adverbs "now" (fourteen times; compare four times in Matthew, three times in Mark) and "today" (eleven times; compare eight times in Matthew and once in Mark). 4:21 is the classic statement: right at the beginning of his public ministry, Jesus declares, referring to the Old Testament promises of a future era of salvation, "Today this scripture is fulfilled in your hearing." In these words, Jesus is saying what Paul said in 2 Corinthians 6:2: "Now is the day of salvation."

Reading Luke

If Mark is the most striking Gospel, and Matthew is the most systematic Gospel, we might say that Luke is the most *sympathetic* Gospel. Here is the most fully rounded, human portrait of Jesus. We may feel, rightly, that in our own day the greatest need is to proclaim Christ as Lord and God, since in the secular world he is normally treated as, at best, a good man. But true though that is, we must never allow it to make us forget that Jesus *was* actually a man—a real man, a flesh-and-blood man, and, yes, the supremely good man. All people need a Savior; but in our world they also need a role-model, and there cannot be a better one than Jesus. After all, his invariable challenge to those whom he called to be his disciples was "Follow me!" Not once did he call a disciple using the words "Accept a theology about me!"

I am not for one moment suggesting that holding a fully biblical theology of Jesus as Savior and Lord is not supremely vital. Jesus himself said (John 8:24), "If you do not believe that I am the one I claim to be, you will indeed die in your sins"; the wording is literally, "If you do not believe that 'I am,' you will indeed die in your sins," a phrase pregnant with theological significance. Those who, like myself, stand firmly in the evangelical tradition of the church can be deeply distressed and angered by that strand of liberal thinking that reduces Jesus to being a good teacher and example. Unfortunately, in our zeal to declare that Jesus is, in Thomas' words, "my Lord and my God" (John 20:28), we evangelicals can be guilty of forgetting that he *is* also our Teacher and Example. If we want to be taken seriously when we declare the Jesus of John's Gospel to be Lord and God, then we need ourselves to take seriously the challenge to follow faithfully in the footsteps of the Jesus of Luke's Gospel. "Either/or" is not an option.

All the Gospels, but perhaps most especially Mark and Luke, show us the Jesus who is the man we can follow. They also show us that he is more than that—but he is certainly not less. There are those for whom encountering the fully human Jesus in Luke's Gospel can be the best starting point.

And for the Christian church—and, if I dare say, in particular for the modern evangelical church—Luke adds a much-needed strand to our all-round understanding of what Christian life and Christian service are about. His consistent theme of the moral, social and financial challenges of discipleship is one that the western church, living as it does in what is, recession notwithstanding, still a remarkably affluent society, may not always find comfortable. But that is all the more reason why we need to read Luke, who poses a serious challenge to the prosperous western church, which so often seems to think it is "out of touch" unless it is seen to operate in the same way as a successful business enterprise.

But the fact that Luke is also the Gospel of joy, of praise, of the Holy Spirit, is a warning to those who would drive a wedge between the social and the spiritual. For some, Christian life is all about celebration, praise, being filled with joy in the Lord, praying in the Spirit—but where is Luke's concern for the poor and the socially marginalized? There are others who have a deep concern for social action, but who do not feel that they are "into" the things of the Spirit; Luke would say to them, look at Jesus—for him, social responsibility and spiritual experience were the two sides of the same Kingdom coin.

John

If Luke's Gospel gives us a picture of "the most human Jesus," John's gives us a revelation of "the most heavenly Jesus." For this reason, just as Luke is many people's favorite Gospel, so John is the favorite for many others.

The same story?

John, let's face it, is different from the other Gospels. It contains a high proportion of material that is not in the others, and it leaves out most of what *is* in the others, apart from the cross and resurrection. Traditionally, a major distinction has been drawn between John and the other three so-called "synoptic" Gospels: the word "synoptic" means "eye-witness" (literally, "with the eye"). That John has a different character is beyond dispute. But the difference is not as great as is often stated, and, in particular, we should never say (though many people do) that the first three "synoptic" Gospels are "historical" whilst John is "theological" (which, by implication, is assumed to mean not a proper historical record). John's Gospel itself claims to be an eye-witness account (19:35, 21:24); in that sense, it is a truly "synoptic" Gospel—in fact, John is ironically the only Gospel in which the writer actually claims to have been an eye-witness of the events he is recording; yet it is Matthew, Mark and Luke that are collectively referred to as the "synoptic" Gospels! John records what he saw; what he says in his first letter (1 John 1:1), ". . . which we have heard, which we have seen with our eyes, which we have looked at and our hands have touched, this we proclaim . . . ," could be said equally of his Gospel. And John contains many of those small and apparently insignificant historical details that are typical of an eye-witness account: for example, the reference to Jesus being tired and needing to sit down for a rest by a well (4:6), the description of Jesus "doodling" with his finger in the dust (8:6), the reference to how Jesus wrapped a towel round his waist before washing his disciples' feet (13:4), the record of the blood and water issuing from the side of the crucified Christ (19:34), the description of the fire of burning coals with fish cooking (21:9). These are typical hallmarks of the personally recollected account; John describes what happened, because he saw it happen.

It should also be pointed out, in the light of the fact that many people say that John lacks the kind of factual and historical references that we find in the other Gospels, that John actually agrees with the others in a number of small and precise details. For example, both Mark and John note the fact that the bread required to feed the five thousand would cost "two hundred denarii" (Mark 6:37, John 6:7; the NIV translates as "eight months' wages"), and that the oil with which Jesus was anointed was worth "three hundred denarii" (NIV, "a year's wages": Mark 14:5, John 12:5); and both Luke and John mention the characters of Mary and Martha (Luke 10:38–42, John 11:1) and the high priest Annas (Luke 3:2, John 18:13,24).

It would also be quite wrong to say that the first three Gospels are less "theological" than John. Just as John is as historical as they, so they are clearly as full of a theology of Jesus as John. This is seen, for example, in the significance for Matthew of Jesus as the Christ, the King of the Jews, the fulfiller of Old Testament prophecy; or in Mark's theme of Jesus as the Son of God, and in the centrality of the cross in Mark; and in Luke's emphasis on Jesus as the light to the Gentiles, the giver of the Holy Spirit, and the one who comes to bring good news to the poor.

In other words, John, though in ways that are different from the other three, is, like them, a historical account of the person of Jesus, which contributes a further piece of the theological jig-saw, giving us an all-round picture of the nature of Christ.

It is however true that John leaves out most of the key events that the other Gospels focus on: the birth, the baptism, the temptation, the Galilean ministry, the parables of the Kingdom, the transfiguration, the Last Supper. It seems, in fact, that John has hardly included anything that the other Gospels mention, except of course the trial, death and resurrection of Jesus. The only miracles in John to appear in the other Gospels are the feeding of the five thousand and the walking on the water (6:1–14,16–21). The first historical events which John mentions that are also in the other Gospels are those that herald Jesus' arrival in Jerusalem, and the start of his passion: the triumphal entry (12:12–19) and the anointing at Bethany (12:2–8). After that John includes none of the events of the last week (such as the controversies with the Pharisees), until we come to the arrest and trail, and the death and resurrection of Jesus.

A number of things are worth saying about these omissions.

1. Although John may not recount an event, it is nonetheless often the case that it is clearly assumed or alluded to as happening or having happened. For example, although John does not describe the baptism of Jesus, the ministry of John the Baptist is stressed (1:1–34), and John's testimony to seeing the Spirit descend on Jesus immediately after his baptism is included (1:32–34). John does not recount the arrest of John the Baptist as the event that triggered Jesus' public appearance in Galilee, but he does allude to the arrest (3:24) as a known fact. John does not record the rejection of Jesus in Nazareth (Mark 6:1–6), but he refers to it in passing (4:44). Although John does not record the Last Supper, he does speak of the ministry of Jesus in the upper room, (chapters 13–16), of the meal being served (13:2) and of Judas receiving bread dipped in Jesus' bowl (13:26).

2. The degree to which John avoids repeating those things which the other Gospels narrate is so remarkable that it can hardly be coincidence. John seems to have gone out of his way to tell us about those things that the other Gospels left out; either on his own human initiative (maybe because he knew of the other Gospels?), or because the Holy Spirit inspired him simply to record the things which he did in order to complete the picture. His comment in 20:30 is again significant: "Jesus did many other miraculous signs in the presence of his disciples, which are not recorded in this book"—but some of them are recorded in the other Gospels.

3. It is worth remembering that every Gospel records some things that others leave out; although John's is the most extreme case of this, it is not absolutely different in this regard. Just over 80 percent of the verses

in John are unique to John; but nearly 45 percent of the verses in Luke are unique to Luke, which is obviously a considerable proportion.

4. And finally, despite the lack of material common to the other Gospels (until we get to the cross and resurrection), the overall picture of Jesus' ministry is essentially the same: it starts with John the Baptist, consists of a ministry of miraculous signs and of teaching, and it ends in Jerusalem with the trial before Caiaphas and Pilate, the cross and the resurrection.

The special themes

The main difference between John and the other three Gospels, and the one which most obviously strikes us, is not in the content so much as in the style. But before we come to that, there are three particular aspects of the *content* of John that are worth noting.

Signs

John stresses Jesus' *signs*. Whilst all four Gospels record many miraculous works, it is John who stresses that these works are "signs"; he uses the word eighteen times, starting in 2:11, when, following the story of Jesus turning water into wine, he adds the comment, "This, the first of his signs,[19] Jesus performed at Cana in Galilee. He thus revealed his glory . . ." The miracles of Jesus are signs pointing to the life that Jesus gives, and to who he is.

It is important that we understand the miracles of Jesus in this way. Miracles are never an end in themselves, and are certainly never intended to produce faith in those who do not have it. They are signs: signs of the nature of Christ (he is the Lord over all creation, the giver of life, the overcomer of evil, etc.) and of the nature of salvation (it means having our eyes opened to the truth to which we are naturally blind; it means being fed with the bread of heaven, the food of eternal life; it means having broken and damaged lives and hearts restored).

Maybe one of the reasons for John's use of "signs" as the word for Jesus' miracles is that it is the word used for the miracles that Moses performed before Pharaoh (Exodus 4:8, 4:17, 4:28, 4:30, 7:3, 8:23, 10:1-2). Many events in Moses' life are referred to in John as pictures or foreshadowings of Jesus: the bronze serpent (3:14), the manna (6:31-33), the water from the rock

---

19. The NIV translates as "miraculous signs"; the Greek simply uses the word "signs."

(7:38); and the revelation that Moses brought is said to be fulfilled in Jesus (1:17, 5:46). Just as Moses' signs were evidence that he was truly sent by God, and were the basis for God's judgment against the Egyptians who refused to respond to God's word despite the signs, so Jesus is a final and greater Moses, and those who refuse to believe in him despite his signs incur the judgment of God.

The Son

The most obvious aspect of the person of Christ in John is that he is presented as the *Son* of God. Whereas in all three synoptics Jesus is frequently called the Son of Man, in John he is supremely the Son of God, or usually just "the Son." John does also use the title "Son of Man" thirteen times; several refer to Jesus being lifted up or glorified on the cross (e.g. 3:14, 8:28, 12:23, 13:31), but more refer to the heavenly Son, the one who has come with the authority of heaven to reveal the Father and to bring salvation (e.g. 1:51, 3:13, 5:27, 6:27, 6:62). But John uses the title "Son of God" (or simply "the Son" as he relates to the Father) twenty-nine times. It is in John above all that we find those sayings that stress the mystery of how the Son is one with the Father, how he has come from the Father, how he is in the Father and the Father is in him, how he does what the Father does and says what the Father has given him to say.

Wisdom

The "Father-Son" language of John is impossible to miss; but there is another aspect of the presentation of Jesus in John's Gospel that is less obvious on the surface, but which against the background of Old Testament and traditional Jewish writing is nonetheless very evident and intentional. In John, Jesus speaks with the voice of *wisdom* in the Old Testament. All the Gospels, including John, see in Jesus the fulfillment of Old Testament prophecy, and he is often portrayed as God's new Moses and the new King in the line of David; but it is in John that we see also that Jesus is the consummation of that distinctive strand of the Old Testament that is called "wisdom."

The meaning of "wisdom" in the Bible is quite separate from any idea of "cleverness" or "education": the person who is "wise" knows in all circumstances what the right thing to do is; wisdom is given by God and is above all else a spiritual awareness of what God wants us to be and do; it is about making right choices and understanding what it means to live a righteous life. In the Old Testament, there are a number of great poems dedicated to wisdom—e.g. Job 28 and Proverbs 1–9—but that tradition was also maintained in a number of other Jewish writings that are not part of the Old Testament, but would be familiar to Jewish people in John's day, such as *Ecclesiasticus* (not to be confused with the Old Testament book "Ecclesiastes"), a major volume of Jewish wisdom dating from some time in the second century BC, and *The Wisdom of Solomon* (or simply *Wisdom*), which is often seen as the greatest example of Jewish wisdom literature: whilst I do not regard these books as part of God's inspired word,[20] I will make some reference to them as they seem to be part of the background to how John writes.

In Jewish "wisdom literature," Wisdom is often personified: in Proverbs, she is depicted as a female voice that calls out to men to avoid the enticing voice of foolishness, which will lure them to their destruction, and instead to follow her and so find life (e.g. Proverbs 1:20–27, 2:13–18, 8:1–21).[21] In John's Gospel, many of the things that are said about Jesus are identical or similar to things that are said of personified Wisdom in the Old Testament and the Jewish tradition of Wisdom-literature. Wisdom existed with God from the beginning, even before there was a created earth (Proverbs 8:22–23); Jesus is the Word who was from the beginning (John 1:1–2). Wisdom is the radiance of the glory of God (Wisdom 7:25), and those who hold fast to her will inherit glory (Ecclesiasticus 4:13); Jesus shared in the glory of the Father before the world was created and reveals God's glory to people (John 1:14, 17:5). Wisdom is said to be a revelation of the eternal light of God (Wisdom 7:26) and lights the path for people to follow (Ecclesiasticus 1:29); Jesus has come from God as the light of the world, and those who follow him will never walk in darkness (John 8:12). Wisdom is said to have come down from heaven to dwell amongst people (Ecclesiasticus 24:8, Wisdom 9:10); Jesus is the Son who has come down

---

20. The two works cited are amongst the collection of Jewish writings from the last couple of centuries BC which are known collectively as "the Apocrypha": the Roman Catholic tradition normally includes them in the Bible and treats them as part of Scripture, but the Protestant tradition has always, in my view rightly, excluded them from the books that are regarded as "canonical," that is, the books that God inspired and gave us to be part of his authoritative Word. The term "apocrypha" is from the Greek for "hidden": it refers to the fact that the "apocryphal" books, as they are not part of God's true Word, are not intended for public reading as Scripture, but that they can be helpful and edifying for private study.

21. The reason why these personified references to "wisdom" are always feminine is very simple: the Hebrew word for "wisdom," *hokmāh*, like its Greek equivalent *sophía*, is grammatically feminine, which makes the personification of Wisdom as a female figure quite logical. Moreover, as was said above, the wisdom of God is the positive counterpart to the personified figure in Proverbs of foolishness, who is depicted as a temptress or harlot, luring men to their destruction.

from heaven to live amongst people (John 1:14). Wisdom shows people the way (Proverbs 2:12-15, 3:17, 4:11); Jesus is the Way (John 14:6). Wisdom calls out to people in the streets and public places (Proverbs 1:20); Jesus similarly "cries out" to people to follow his ways (John 7:28,37). Wisdom trains her disciples so that they can become friends of God (Ecclesiasticus 6:20-26, Wisdom 7:14,27); Jesus instructs his disciples and, in the upper room, tells them that he no longer calls them servants but his friends (John 15:15). Wisdom is often rejected by those who choose the way of foolishness (Proverbs 1:24-25); and Jesus was rejected by many of his own people who refused to listen when Jesus offered them the truth (John 8:46, 10:25-26).[22]

All these allusions to Old Testament wisdom-literature—and those quoted above are far from an exhaustive list—show that, for John, Jesus is the Wisdom of God incarnate. John's uniquely characteristic title for Jesus, the Word, is in fact used only in his prologue, in 1:1 and 1:14; but throughout the whole Gospel Jesus speaks with the very voice of God's Wisdom. There are a few references to Jesus as God's Wisdom in the synoptic Gospels as well: Jesus as a child was filled with wisdom (Luke 2:40); those who heard Jesus' teaching marveled at his wisdom (Matthew 13:54//Mark 6:2); in Luke 21:15 he promises to give his disciples wisdom to enable them to speak; in Luke 11:49 Jesus says "God in his wisdom said, 'I will send them . . .'," and in the parallel saying in Matthew 23:34 it is Jesus himself who says "I am sending you . . ."; in Matthew 12:42//Luke 11:31 Jesus speaks of the wisdom of Solomon, and says that he has come as the one who is greater than Solomon; in the saying in Matthew 11:19//Luke 7:35 about wisdom being justified by her actions, it seems that Jesus himself, whose actions had been criticized by the Jewish people, is the one being referred to as Wisdom personified. Paul also calls Christ our "wisdom from God" in 1 Corinthians 1:30. But it is very particularly John who in his Gospel presents Christ as the one who speaks with the voice of God's Wisdom. The climax of that revelation of Christ as the Wisdom of God is his famous saying in 14:6, "I am the way and the truth and the life": in Jewish Wisdom-literature wisdom points us to the way, speaks the truth of God, and offers life to those who follow her. If it be permitted to paraphrase Scripture (!), in Christ, God's Wisdom became flesh and lived among us.

---

22. The theme of Jesus as God's wisdom is very well treated by Raymond Brown, to whose writings on John I am greatly indebted; see Brown, *Introduction to John*, 259-265.

A different style?

This is the more important issue, for those who feel that John is radically different from the other Gospels. The way in which Jesus speaks in John, it is claimed, is quite different from the Jesus of the "synoptics." It is not just that the content is different; the Jesus of the "synoptics" simply does not talk the same way. Three aspects of John's style are particularly distinctive.

Simple style

One is his *simple language.* He uses very ordinary, everyday words; but he chooses these words with great care. He uses little words that are pregnant with meaning, and which seem quite innocent and ordinary, but which contain, if we have eyes to see it, a wealth of spiritual significance. We cannot possibly look at them all, but let two examples from chapter 1 suffice. In 1:38 Andrew and another disciple ask Jesus, "Rabbi, where are you staying?" On the face of it, that is a simple question; they are asking for Jesus' address. But the word "stay" (or "abide," or "remain") is a key word in John: Jesus tells us to abide in him (6:56, 15:4), to remain in his love (15:9-10), and says that he is the one who remains in the Father's love (15:10). The question therefore has a deeper sense: where is your place of "remaining," where is your real home, where do you belong?—do you belong in this world, or are you from heaven? That is precisely the question that John wants to confront his readers with. And in 1:14 we find the famous words "The Word became flesh and made his dwelling among us." The word translated "made his dwelling" (or "lived for a while") is the word for a tabernacle—the temporary shelter or tent that the Israelites put up on their journey in the wilderness. The Word "tabernacled" among us. That suggests two things. First, Jesus was here on earth for a short time, not permanently; just as the wilderness journey was only a stage on the way to the Promised Land, so Jesus' earthly ministry was a stage in his eternal existence as the Son of God, and in God's plan to bring heavenly life. And second, the tabernacle was the dwelling place of God, a kind of portable temple; and so it is in Jesus that God is now found, and the glory of God is revealed.

As well as John's vocabulary being quite simple, he has a particular love of everyday words with a double meaning. Part of the strangely elusive nature of John's writing arises from the fact that the terms he uses are often multi-faceted; commentators and translators have spent hours debating whether John, by his word A meant it in sense B or C; as near certainly as makes no odds, he invariably intended us to see both senses. His use of words with double meanings is intended to make people think, and is indicative of the fact that the truth of God cannot be neatly "pinned down" in human terms. An early example is found in 1:5, translated in the NIV as "the darkness has not *understood* it"; the Greek verb *katalambánō* can mean "accept," "understand," or "overcome," and there is no need to decide whether John meant that "the darkness" refuses to accept the light, cannot understand the light, or will never succeed in overcoming the light: all three are true. When Jesus speaks to Nicodemus of the need to be born "again" (3:3,7), the word he uses, *ánōthen*, can mean both "again" and "from above." In 3:14 the verb *hupsóō* can mean both "lifted up" (physically, as the snake was on a pole in the desert, and as Jesus would be on the cross), and "exalted": it is by going to the cross that Christ would be most gloriously "exalted." And a classic example of John's use of words with both a "natural" sense and a "spiritual" sense is Jesus' promise to Martha in 11:25–26: "He who believes in me will live, even though he dies; and whoever lives and believes in me will never die." Both "live" and "die" can be used of natural human life *and* of spiritual or eternal life: without spelling out the difference between the two kinds of "life," Jesus' words are deliberately paradoxical, and John leaves us to work out for ourselves how they hold together; they can perhaps be paraphrased as "He who believes in me will live (spiritually), even though he dies (physically); and whoever lives (physically and/or spiritually?) and believes in me will never die (spiritually)."

But the most characteristic aspect of John's simple style is his use of key words that, despite being short and mostly monosyllabic, are recurring theological motifs. John's Gospel, and the teaching of Jesus in it, revolve around a series of little words that are full of spiritual meaning, words like "life," often in the phrase "eternal life," which means the same quality of heavenly, spiritual life that God has (thirty-six times; nearly a quarter of all the references to "life" in the New Testament are in John's Gospel), "love" (nineteen times), "light" (twenty-four times), "glory"[23] (thirty-six times), "believe" (or "faith") (a remarkable ninety-four times). And we mentioned above what is one of the main threads that runs through John, namely the recurring language about "Father" and "Son," and who Jesus is in relationship with the Father.

---

23. What makes this theme of glory all the more remarkable is the fact that, in John, the glory of Jesus is revealed supremely in the cross; the moment when Jesus is glorified is in his death (12:23–28). If people really want to see the glory of God, they should not look to beautiful sunsets, mountain-top panoramas or the majestic night sky. Of course something of God's glory is reflected in the greatness of his creation. But the place where we really and fully encounter the glory of God is, paradoxically, in the least glorious, the most ignominious place of all: in the cross of Jesus.

But perhaps the best-known of John's "little words" are his series of "I am" statements. Many of the long discourses of Jesus in John's Gospel include or revolve around a key "I am" word: "I am the bread of life" (6:35), "I am the light of the world" (8:12), "I am" (8:58), "I am the gate for the sheep" (10:7), "I am the good shepherd" (10:11), "I am the resurrection and the life" (11:25), "I am the way and the truth and the life" (14:6), and "I am the vine" (15:5).

The various images used (bread, light, etc.) obviously speak of the kind of way in which Jesus saves and blesses his people, and what he can be to us. But the key phrase is the "I am." Jesus uses an emphatic phrase in the Greek (*egō eimi*) which was used in the Greek version of the Old Testament to translate the name of God in Exodus 3:14. All Jews were conscious that *egō eimi* had very special significance as the name of God himself. So when Jesus says "I am," he is claiming for himself the name of God; and in particular, when he uses the phrase in an absolute sense in 8:58—that is, without any following phrase: not "I am *this*" or "I am *that*" but simply "I am,"— the Pharisees take up stones to stone him: he is blaspheming, claiming to be God. The "I am" phrase is used in the same way in 8:24, where the Greek reads literally "If you do not believe that I am, you will die in your sins," and in 8:28, where it says "Then you will know that I am";[24] three times in this discourse, Jesus uses the divine name of himself.

Repetitive style

So John's characteristic style is to use simple but deeply significant words. Linked with that is a second feature of his style, namely that it is very *repetitive*. A large part of John consists of long addresses or discourses by Jesus, which are almost impossible to analyze; they have no clear structure. They are not in the typical recommended pattern of an essay (introduction—point one—point two—point three—conclusion); rather, John writes in a way that weaves various recurring ideas and motifs around each other. These discourses are not logical statements of doctrine to be rationally analyzed; they are more like an attempt to convey something of the "flavor" of what eternal life is—and they do it in very simple words, which are repeated over and over again in different ways. The ideas that run through his discourses are like a number of interwoven threads; and whilst it is possible to

---

24. The NIV includes in both these verses the gloss ". . . that I am *the one I claim to be* . . ." This makes a more obviously complete and understandable English sentence than the literal wording ("that I am"), but it slightly obscures the point that Jesus is using the special name of God himself, *egō eimi*, in an absolute way, and is thus making a theologically very challenging and provocative claim.

identify a number of those threads, it is difficult to untangle them from all the others, without losing something of the special "feel" of John: it would be like isolating the different ingredients in a dish—it might help you to understand a recipe, but you would no longer have a meal to taste. John's style gives us a "taste" of all-round eternal life; he speaks more to the soul and the heart than to the intellect.

Metaphorical style

That leads us to the third characteristic of John's style, namely that it is *metaphorical*. John presents Christian faith and life through metaphors.[25] In 10:6 John comments that Jesus spoke using a "figure of speech," and in 16:25 Jesus himself says the same, translated in the NIV as "I have been speaking [to the disciples] figuratively," and the English phrase "figure of speech" is probably the best translation for the Greek word used. All Jesus' "I am" words are metaphorical; Jesus is the bread of life, but he is not "literally" a lump of baked dough. There is a sense in which metaphors are in John what parables are in the other Gospels; they are different ways of illustrating what God's Kingdom and God's salvation are like. There are some who become quite hot under the collar (which is itself another metaphor!) at the suggestion that anything in the Bible is metaphorical. The Bible is *true*, they insist; we can't dismiss it as a mere metaphor. But to say that indicates a misunderstanding about what metaphors are. It is the word "mere" that is misleading: there is nothing "mere" about a metaphor. To say that something is a metaphor is not saying that it is not true, or that it is less than the words used. If anything, it is more. If we say (metaphorically) that someone is "over the moon," we do not mean that he is ever so slightly happy; we mean, assuming that we are using language appropriately, and are not merely exaggerating or being ironic, that he is full of real and overwhelming joy. The phrase "over the moon" is a metaphor; but the joy is a manifest reality.

When Jesus, in John's Gospel, speaks of himself as the bread of life, the light of the world, the gate of the sheep, and so on, he is using metaphors; but the life that he gives, which those metaphors are intended to convey, is

---

25. A metaphor is a figure of speech that is not intended to be understood in a baldly literal way. For example, to describe someone who is desperately sad as "heartbroken" is a metaphor: the physical organ of his heart is not "literally" broken; it is his emotions that are affected. Strictly speaking, a distinction should be drawn between a metaphor and a simile: a simile says that one thing is *like* another ("My love is like a red, red rose"), a metaphor says that one thing *is* another ("You are the apple of my eye"). In this discussion of John's language, I will not always bother to make the distinction, with apologies to strict grammarians.

a wonderful reality. John's particular contribution to our understanding of the Kingdom of God is to convey that reality using the picture-language of metaphors.

John and the "synoptics"

Since John's style is so different from that of the so-called synoptic Gospels, how does its "differentness" affect our view of John as an authentic historical record? A number of points are worth making here, in the light of the widespread assumption that John is less historically accurate than the other Gospels, or that John's language is simply his own, and has nothing to do with the historical Jesus and how he actually spoke.

1. Most of the teaching in John is addressed to the disciples, not to the crowds. We are told in Mark 4:33–34 that Jesus spoke differently in private to his disciples than he did to the general public. What we have here are not the messages about the Kingdom (including the parables) that Jesus preached to the crowds, but the more personal teaching to his disciples about who he is and what he has come to do. It is interesting that the only major discourse in John that is addressed to a wider audience (6:25–59) results in many disciples refusing to follow Jesus any longer, so that he is left with just the twelve (6:60–69).

2. Although the general style is distinctive, John's key words and phrases are also found on the lips of Jesus in the other Gospels. Take the famous "I am"; it is John who gives us the familiar list of "I am" words—bread, light, resurrection and life, etc.—but Jesus uses the characteristic and theologically significant Greek phrase *egō eimi* of himself in the other Gospels as well. In Mark 6:50 Jesus reassures his disciples, who are terrified at having seen him walk on the water, "Take courage! It is I. Don't be afraid"; the middle phrase is literally simply "I am" (*egō eimi*). When Jesus is asked by the Jewish elders if he is the Christ, he replies (Luke 22:70), "You are right in saying I am (= *egō eimi*)." Then there is the word "light"; in John Jesus says that he is the light of the world, and in Matthew he says to his disciples that they are the light of the world (5:14–16). There is no conflict here: it is because Jesus is the light that his followers can reflect his light to the world; and Matthew records Jesus using the same picture of light as a metaphor for spiritual life. Luke uses the word "light" eight times to speak of the new life of Jesus. John's favorite word "life" may be characteristic of him, but it is not unique to him: Matthew uses it to speak of Jesus' gift of eternal life seven times, Mark four times and Luke four times.

3. A number of sayings on the lips of Jesus in the other Gospels are very similar in style to John. A good example is "No one knows the Son except the Father, and no one knows the Father except the Son and those to whom the Son chooses to reveal him" (Matthew 11:27// Luke 10:22). Anyone who was familiar with the different styles of the Gospel-writers but could not remember where precisely that saying comes might well assume that it is likely to be in John: it is so typically how Jesus speaks in John's Gospel. Other examples are "He who listens to you listens to me; he who rejects you rejects me; but he who rejects me rejects him who sent me" (Luke 10:16//Matthew 10:40), or "Whoever welcomes one of these little children in my name welcomes me; and whoever welcomes me does not welcome me but the one who sent me" (Mark 9:37//Luke 9:48). These synoptic sayings show that the Jesus of all four Gospels did speak in the way that we find in John's Gospel: John does not present us with a Jesus whose way of teaching has nothing in common with that in Matthew, Mark and Luke.

4. There is nothing in John which is inconsistent with what is taught in the other Gospels. The style may be different, but the person of Jesus is the same. So, for example, John stresses the Sonship of Jesus—but so does Mark; John stresses the salvation of Jesus—but so does Luke. Though John records (mostly) different miracles from those in the other Gospels, they are the same *kind* of miracles: healings (e.g. 4:46–53, 5:1–13), including that of a blind man (9:1–7), nature miracles of fertility (2:1–11, 6:1–13), miracles showing Jesus' power over nature (6:16–21), miracles of raising the dead (11:1–44). The only kind of miracle that John does not include is the casting out of demons; but there is nothing different about the way in which Jesus works his miracles in John from the other Gospels.

5. Although John does not record any parables as such, there is something parabolic in style about many of his sayings of Jesus. In fact, many of the discourses in John where Jesus uses these extended metaphors have close parallels in the parables found in the synoptic Gospels: Jesus told a parable about yeast leavening a whole batch of dough (Matthew 13:33//Luke 13:20–21), and in John he speaks of himself as the bread of life (John 6:35–51); he told a parable about a shepherd and his lost sheep (Matthew 18:12–13//Luke 15:3–7), and in John he speaks of himself as the Good Shepherd (John 10:11–18); he told parables about God's people as a vineyard (Matthew 21:33–43// Mark 12:1–12//Luke 20:9–18, Luke 13:6–9), and in John he taught that he is himself the true vine (John 15:1–8). That does not mean that the

discourses in John are "John's version" of the parables; but they do at the very least suggest that both the synoptics and John are in their own ways drawing on the same kind of figurative language that Jesus used in his teaching. Certainly, the spiritual lessons of the discourses in John are entirely consistent with the lessons of the parables which use the same or similar metaphors.

6. The most important thing to say, however, is that even if it be true that the Jesus revealed in John's Gospel is a Jesus "filtered" through John's own style and presentation, this does not in any way detract from the validity of this Gospel as part of the inspired and inerrant Word of God. Every writer of Scripture has his personal style: that is part of the human side of the Bible, which goes hand in hand with its divine inspiration. The fact that God inspired the writing of the whole Bible does not mean that it has a uniform style that is devoid of human idiosyncrasies. It is true that John's style is very much his own—but the same is true of Paul's style, or Luke's, or Haggai's, or Isaiah's. John's distinctive style should not cause us to doubt that what he writes is based on what Jesus himself said, and not merely because John himself says so. John's way of presenting what Jesus said does not distort it, but rather sheds a special and distinctive light on it. If we believe that "all Scripture is God-breathed" (2 Timothy 3:16), then we can be confident that the words and the style John used in writing his Gospel were inspired by the Spirit, and that it is the text of John (and Matthew, and Mark, and Luke) as we have it that is the Word of God to us.

Reading John

In Mark, we have the most striking Gospel, in Matthew the most systematic, in Luke the most sympathetic, and in John, the most *spiritual* Gospel; in fact, the early Christian writer Clement of Alexandria (c. 150–215 AD) used that very phrase to describe John: he saw John as conveying the spiritual nature of Jesus and the life he brings, as opposed to the other three Gospels which record more of the "physical" or biographical facts of Jesus' life. John reveals the quality of spiritual life and salvation that Jesus brings; he is the antidote to a secular or purely humanist view of Jesus and of Christian life.

There is a challenge here for those whose approach to reading and thinking is, in the best, not just the worst sense of the word, "academic." Whilst we are certainly called to bring our minds to the study of the Scriptures, and whilst we should seek to understand as much of God's truth as possible, John operates at a level that goes beyond the merely cerebral. We can go only so far in analyzing John. This Gospel presents us with a quality of life that is to be received by faith rather than analyzed by the mind. What John talks about can be experienced—it cannot, or can only in a very limited sense, be explained.

John's distinctive style—his use of simple but spiritually significant words, often with different levels of meaning, his interweaving of repeated key themes, his frequent use of metaphor—means that he can address readers at a level that is different from the other Gospels. Matthew, for example, can in particular teach our understanding; Mark can appeal to our imagination; Luke can touch our hearts and stir our social consciences. But John can—to use another metaphor!—stimulate our "spiritual taste-buds." He can awaken in us an *appetite* for the life of Jesus, which we can receive, not by analyzing it, but by believing in him.

That may, in part, be the reason why John himself says (20:31) that he wrote his Gospel so that those who read it may believe that Jesus is the Christ, the Son of God, and so might have eternal life. This Gospel can act as the appetizer of eternal life. Mark might be a very useful Gospel to give to the person who is quite uninformed about Jesus, and to whom we want to give the most straightforward picture of the person of Christ. John might be the best to give to the person who is, to any degree, hungry for the life that Jesus offers, or who, for whatever reason, might be starting to drift from a focus on Jesus himself as the center of their faith. That is indeed why John says he wrote his Gospel. His words, that he wrote his book "that you may believe that Jesus is the Christ, the Son of God, and that by believing you may have life in his name," might suggest that he wrote to help towards faith those who are not as yet believers—that his Gospel is an evangelistic tract. In fact, there are two tenses of the verb that could equally well be translated as "believe"—one is the so-called "continuous present," which has the sense "that you might *continue to* believe"; the other is the Greek "aorist," which would mean "that you might *come to* believe"—and, as it happens, there are manuscripts of John with both tenses. On the basis of the manuscript evidence, "that you might continue to believe" is probably the more likely to have been what John originally wrote, which would suggest that his Gospel is intended to strengthen the faith of those who were believers, but might have been coming under pressure to back away from their faith-commitment. For all who find themselves in such a situation, and indeed for all of us who have by grace come to know the Jesus of the Gospels, John can both stimulate and satisfy our hunger for the bread of life.

2

The baptism

"I have a baptism to undergo" (Luke 12:50)

The overall story of Jesus in the Gospels starts with his birth; his public ministry, with which we are particularly concerned in this book, begins with his baptism. No one else was ever, or ever will be, born in the same way as Jesus—as the *Apostles' Creed* says, "he was conceived by the power of the Holy Spirit and born of the virgin Mary"—but each one of us can be baptized in the same way as Jesus. But before we come to the baptism itself, we first meet the one who would baptize him. Before the promised Christ was to appear, the Old Testament had said that God would send one who would go ahead of him to prepare the way. So the story of Jesus' ministry starts with his forerunner, John the Baptist.

John the Baptist

All four Gospels speak of John's ministry (Matthew 3:1-12//Mark 1:1-8// Luke 3:1-18, John 1:19-28); Matthew (3:13-17), Mark (1:9-11) and Luke (3:21-22) recount explicitly, and John (1:32-33) alludes to, the baptism of Jesus. John (the Gospel writer) moreover speaks of the importance of John (the Baptist) as a witness to who Jesus is (1:29-34), the Lamb of God who takes away the sin of the world (1:29). In fact John 1 contains three important titles of Jesus, which relate to three essential aspects of his work of salvation. He is (verse 1) the *Word* of God, who reveals the Father; he is (verse 29) the *Lamb* of God, who takes away the sins of the world; and he is (verse 34) the *Son* of God, who baptizes in the Holy Spirit.[1] If we are to be "all-round" Christians, we need Jesus to be all three to us.

John was sent by God in order to prepare the way for Jesus—to get people ready for Jesus to come and bring the Kingdom of God. That is our role too: we are sent into the world to prepare people for the fact that Jesus is coming again, and to help them to be ready for his coming.

The preacher of repentance

John's call to people was to "repent" (Matthew 3:2//Mark 1:4-5//Luke 3:3). To "repent" does not mean, as is often thought, to "say sorry," to "feel sorry," or even to "be sorry." It means to change direction in life, to turn to God, and it involves confessing sins and turning from them. It is not an emotion but a decision. And the challenge to make that decision is always the first step in becoming a Christian. Luke helpfully includes some of John's practical teaching about what "repentance" can and should include (3:7–14), such as a commitment to be generous ("The man with two tunics should share with him who has none, and the one who has food should do the same"), honesty and integrity in all our dealings ("Don't collect any more [tax] than you are required to"), and to avoid using any position we have for self-aggrandizement and for belittling others, but rather being gentle with people ("Don't extort money and don't accuse people falsely"). Luke is not saying that "to repent" simply means to become charitable; but the changed modes of behavior which he mentions would be indicative of the complete change of mind-set and attitude—the moral and mental U-turn—that is repentance; they would be the result of the decision to say, from this day on I will choose to go not my way, but God's way. Or, to put it the other way

---

1. Almost all Bible translations use in verse 34 the title "Son of God"; a few, including later editions of the NIV, and also *The New Living Translation* and the *New English Bible*, follow instead the reading which is found in some manuscripts, "God's Chosen One." As the footnote in the NIV points out, the majority of reliable manuscripts use the title "Son of God," a term that is consistent with John's frequent references to Christ as the "Son" in his Gospel. It is possible that the reading "God's Chosen One" might have been influenced by Isaiah 42:1, which speaks of the servant of the Lord on whom God has placed his Spirit. On balance, I believe "the Son of God" to be the more likely original reading, although whichever of the two titles is preferred, it makes little difference to our understanding of the doctrine of Christ: both "Son of God" and "[God's] Chosen One" are used a number of times elsewhere in the New Testament—e.g. Luke 9:35, Luke 23:35, 1 Corinthians 1:9, Galatians 2:20—and so both are part of our all-round understanding of Christ.

round, the absence of such changes would leave a big question mark over the genuineness of any claim to have "repented."

That raises an important question that is not just a theological issue ("faith and works") but is absolutely central to our understanding of what it means to become a Christian. The Bible is very clear that we are saved by the grace of God alone, not by our own works (Ephesians 2:8-9) nor by fulfilling the demands of the law (Philippians 3:9). Those who stand in the classic reformed tradition of the evangelical church will proclaim that loud and clear; and they are right. Yet the New Testament also expects repentance and faith to be marked by a change of life and by works that demonstrate that change; John here refuses to baptize some who come to him, because they are not as yet showing in their lives any "fruit in keeping with repentance"[2] (Luke 3:8-9), the works that show that people have truly repented.

To understand the relative places of faith and works, of believing and behaving, in becoming a Christian, we need to distinguish two things that are often confused: the question of how we *receive* eternal life, and the question of what eternal life *is*. Evangelical preachers are—if I may indulge in a generalization—often better at telling people how to receive Christian life than at clarifying exactly what Christian life is. How to receive it is clear from Scripture: we cannot, by our own good works or religious ceremonies, ever attain a status of righteousness in God's eyes. We have all sinned, and all our religious and moral works cannot change that fact: if I give to charity, I am a sinner who gives to charity, and if I attend communion, I am a sinner who attends communion. It is the fact that I am a sinner that needs to be addressed if I am to become acceptable to God, not how much I give or how often I attend. I can only be saved from the fact that I am a sinner on the basis of Jesus' death and resurrection. Salvation is achieved by the cross, and it is received through faith in Jesus alone.

But then we come to what salvation actually means, what eternal life is. And one of the things it definitely means, amongst others, is a different quality of life from the one we had before we came to faith, a life lived for God's glory, according to God's Word, and in God's strength. If people do not want that life, then it is simply not God's salvation that they want,

---

2. Both here and in the parallel verse in Matthew 3:8, the phrase is literally "fruit *worthy of* repentance," or "*that befits* repentance." The sense is that real repentance will produce certain changes in our lives; and those changes are the results of and the evidence of the reality of repentance. James said that "faith without works [NIV: 'deeds'] is dead" (James 2:26)—that is, just as fruit growing on a tree is evidence that the tree is alive, so works of Christian service are the evidence that faith is alive, and the absence of such works is a sign that, whatever "faith" people may claim to have, it is not real and living faith in Jesus; and in the same way we might say that repentance without "works"—changes of lifestyle—is dead.

because that salvation will always lead by its very nature to our living what Romans 6:4 calls "a new life." Hence the call to repent. To become a Christian means to turn in a new direction, to set aside the principles and the mind-set that belonged to our past life, and to embrace a different quality of life. We cannot *earn* that life by good works or religious ceremonies, nor can we achieve it by human effort; but we can turn to God's ways in a manner that shows that we want to receive it and live it. If someone applies for a job but, when offered one, never bothers to turn up for work, it is probably safe to assume that he never really wanted to work. And in a similar way, the person who says "yes" to the evangelistic appeal to come to Jesus, but shows no sign of any desire to change the way he is living, is demonstrating just as clearly that what he wants is not Christian *life*, but simply Christian reassurance: that God loves him, that he will get to heaven. The challenge of Christian lifestyle is not "tacked on" to the Gospel message of free salvation; it is not the small print which we only tell people about after they have said "yes" to Jesus. It is what salvation *is*.

The problem is that classic Gospel preaching has not always called people to a new life; it has challenged people to believe in Jesus, but has sometimes left the impression that being a Christian means staying more or less the same as you are, except that you now believe in Jesus and go to church, and when you die you will go to heaven instead of hell.[3] But the biblical Gospel, including the message preached by John the Baptist, was the call to desire a new life, to ask God to cleanse us from the old one, to turn to that new life, and in the power of God's Holy Spirit to start to live it. In a word, to repent.

It is easy to parody the preacher of repentance as a disheveled figure who walks around with a sandwich-board proclaiming "Repent, because the end is near!" But the fact is, with or without the sandwich-board, the end *is* near, and people *do* urgently need to repent. It is not only John the Baptist who said so; Jesus did as well. And the church will never be strong

---

3. Though it is based on a classic hymn, there is a danger of serious misunderstanding in the "Just as I am" kind of evangelistic appeal. In a sense, I *cannot* come to Jesus "just as I am"; I can come only if I am prepared to repent of what "I am," and turn from it. Of course I cannot change myself, and quite certainly I have to abandon the idea that any changes that I attempt to make in my life will earn me God's favor—I will be accepted and blessed by God by grace, on the basis of Jesus' cross, or not at all—and that is what Charlotte Elliott meant when she penned her great hymn ("Just as I am, without one plea, but that thy blood was shed for me . . ."). But even if in that vital sense I can do no other than come "just as I am," it is equally vital to realize also that I can only come to Jesus in a meaningful way if my desire and decision is emphatically *not* to stay "just as I am," but to be radically changed by his grace. To come without that intention is not conversion to Christ; it is at its worst a response to a "cop-out Gospel," which offers me everything good but requires of me nothing morally or spiritually challenging.

unless and until it starts to challenge people to embrace a new life in Christ; until it preaches and practices repentance. Maybe there is a fear in some minds that people who are told they will be required to change their lifestyle when they come to Christ will think twice about coming. But Jesus told us to invite people to count the cost before they make a decision (Luke 14:25–33). He never encouraged his church to rush people into a decision before they really know to what they are committing themselves.

But there are two other common misunderstandings about what repentance means. First, the very word "repentance" can have quite forbidding and finger-wagging connotations; it is often assumed to imply a deeply disapproving and even threatening attitude. That is not the spirit of the biblical call to repentance; whilst it is certainly a challenge to change, it is far better to see the call to repent as God's invitation in Isaiah 45:22 to "turn to me and be saved, all you ends of the earth"; repentance is a positive challenge ("turn from your present life, which can never bring you the fulfillment and blessing that God wants you to know, and turn to God to find in him life in all its fullness!") rather than simply a negative warning ("stop living the way you are, or else . . . !").

Second, and very importantly, repentance is often thought of simply in moral terms. To repent is assumed to mean to stop doing bad things and start doing good things—to turn over a moral new leaf. But although there is a vital moral dimension to repentance, it is not the whole or the essential heart of repentance. It is significant that, when John the Baptist spoke of the moral change of life that he expected to see in those coming for baptism, he defined that change as the "fruit" of repentance. Moral improvement is the fruit, the product, of repentance, not repentance itself.

The New Testament term for "repent" is the Greek *metanoéō*, which means literally "change [your] mind"; repentance is about a change of mindset.[4] "Change your mind" does not mean "change your opinion"; it means to adopt a completely new and different world-view. Paul spells out that change of outlook when he says in 2 Corinthians 5:16, "So from now on we regard no one from a worldly point of view. Though we once regarded Christ in this way, we do so no longer." To repent means to stop thinking as the world thinks, and to start to think about everything—Christ, other people, ourselves, "life, the universe and everything"—from God's perspective. It means to make God the focus of our lives, not ourselves; or, as Paul

---

4. The "*-noéō*" part of the verb *metanoéō* is connected with the Greek noun *noûs*, which means, and in the New Testament is usually translated as, "mind": and modern English still uses the same word "nous" (which in British English can be pronounced to rhyme with "mouse" or like "noose") in the sense of "understanding," "awareness," or "common sense."

says in the previous verse in 2 Corinthians, "He died for all, that those who live should no longer live for themselves but for him who died for them and was raised again." To start to think like that—to begin to live not for ourselves but for Christ—is the essence of repentance. That change of outlook will then in its turn lead to the moral fruit of repentance, to a quality of life that is shaped by Jesus and his principles, not by the world and its values— not even its best values. To try to live a better life, but without that change of essential mindset, is at best a human kind of self-improvement program; but when moral renewal is the fruit of a decision to start to live with God as the center and focus of life, then, John the Baptist would say, that is truly repentance; and Paul would say, in 2 Corinthians 5:17, that that is not the old creation improved, but truly God's "new creation."

The forerunner of Christ

John is seen as fulfilling the promise of Malachi 4:5 that, before the Kingdom of God came, God would send "Elijah" to prepare the way. This promise is reflected in the Gospels in Matthew 11:14, Matthew 17:10–13//Mark 9:11–13, Luke 1:17 and John 1:19–23. John "is the Elijah who was to come" (Matthew 11:14) in the sense that he fulfilled in his own day the same ministry that Elijah had fulfilled in his. Elijah was a prophet who lived in times of great evil, and he called the people back to God (1 Kings 17—2 Kings 2). John comes to do the same; that is why the angel Gabriel says of the future ministry of John that he will go "in the spirit and power of Elijah... to make ready a people prepared for the Lord" (Luke 1:17).

In that case, why does John the Baptist, when he is asked in John 1:19–23 "Are you Elijah?," reply that he is not? The answer is probably that the Jews were literally expecting Elijah himself, the historical prophet, to reappear supernaturally from heaven; the fact that Elijah had ascended to heaven at the end of his earthly life without experiencing death (2 Kings 2:11) merely strengthened that mistaken belief. In that sense, of course John is not Elijah. Or it may be that John is simply too humble to accept such a major role and title for himself, in the same way that Amos said that he was not a prophet, though of course he was (Amos 7:14), and, for that matter, that Jesus was unwilling to be called "good" (though he obviously *is* good) because "good" is the name of the Father (Mark 10:18). Jesus later said that John was indeed the expected "Elijah"-figure; and Matthew 3:4//Mark 1:6 speak of a couple of physical points of similarity between John and Elijah (see 2 Kings 1:8), namely their dress ("clothes... made of camel's hair, and... a leather belt around his waist")—rough clothing, as well as being suitable for a life in the desert, was generally seen as a sign of the prophetic calling—and their diet ("locusts[5] and wild honey," which would be readily available in the desert). That does not mean that John mechanically copied Elijah; rather, his dress and diet epitomized a simple lifestyle which Jesus later commended (Matthew 11:8//Luke 7:25) and which was entirely consistent with John's call to people to turn away from the material values of the world.

In John's Gospel, it is not so much the baptizing in itself that is stressed, but much more John the Baptist's role as a witness to Christ, one who points to Jesus and tells people who he is (1:7-8,29-31,36). John the Baptist is the first of a number of people in John's Gospel who bear witness to Jesus. (Again, remember not to confuse the two Johns, the Gospel writer and the Baptist: they are not the same person!)

John always speaks of Jesus as greater than he, and plays down his own importance. All four Gospels record that John said that he was not worthy even to untie (or carry) Jesus' sandals (Matthew 3:11//Mark 1:7//Luke 3:16//John 1:27). To untie a person's sandals was one of the very lowest and humblest tasks a slave could be asked to do. John is a remarkable example of how we are called to point attention away from ourselves, and to Jesus.

The servant of the Lord

Before we come to the baptism of Jesus, let us summarize the main lessons that we can learn from John, apart from his baptizing.

His role

We start with John's role: to prepare people for the coming of the Lord. He told people to get ready, because the King is coming. Whilst we obviously need to find ways of expressing this message that will be meaningful in today's society, we have the same role, to let people know that there is a different quality of life that belongs to the Kingdom of God, that Jesus has now made it available, and that there are steps that people can take to become part of it, in the sure and certain hope that they will receive it in all its fullness when Jesus comes to consummate his Kingdom.

Luke 3:4-6 includes the whole of Isaiah 40:3-5 as the biblical background to John's role in preparing the way of the Lord; and these words can be taken as metaphorical pictures of three ways in which we can prepare

---

5. However strange it may seem to western taste, such locusts are still part of the staple diet of various Bedouin tribes.

people to encounter Jesus. First, "every valley shall be filled in";[6] those who are socially and spiritually in the depths, who are cast down in themselves and cast aside by society, can be told that God values them, loves them, and is coming to affirm and raise them up. Second, "every mountain and hill [shall be] made low"; those who are proud and feel morally and spiritually self-sufficient need to be challenged to humble themselves in repentance. Third, "the crooked roads shall become straight"; people's warped ideas about God and about life can be straightened out; they can be shown the truth about what God is like and the kind of life he intends for us. Doing any or all of these three things does not save people—that is not our role—but they can help people to be more prepared to respond to Jesus, who *can* save them.

His witness

That brings us to the next thing about John's ministry, which is his witness: he pointed people to Jesus. He did not seek to draw people to himself, but rather to direct them to Christ. Charles Wesley was later to take up John's words and declare, "'Tis all my business here below to cry 'Behold the Lamb!'"[7] That is our business too: no more, no less, nothing different. "We do not preach ourselves, but Jesus Christ as Lord" (2 Corinthians 4:5).

His humility

Following on from that, there is John's humility. He saw himself as a servant, who was not worthy even to carry Jesus' sandals (Matthew 3:11). When John saw that people were turning away from him and to Jesus, he was pleased: that is precisely what he wanted (John 3:25–30). He speaks of himself as a kind of "best man" at a wedding (verse 29), with Jesus as the bridegroom. The best man does not want the bride for himself; he has a role until the wedding has taken place, after which the bride belongs to the bridegroom. The people are "the bride"; they belong to Jesus, the bridegroom. John, as the best man, introduces the bride to the groom—then he steps back. He has done his job. We need the same attitude. There is something disturbingly unbiblical about the Christian preacher who becomes possessive about

---

6. That is the correct translation of the word Luke uses. The original Hebrew phrase in Isaiah 40:4 means literally "lifted up"; hence the traditional translation, "Every valley shall be *exalted*." But the sense is the same: the depths of the valleys will be raised to the heights of the level ground.

7. In the hymn, "Jesus, the name high over all."

"his" converts; the greatest reward for a true leader should be when those whom we lead to and nurture in faith come to see the heart of their faith as focused in Jesus rather than in us. We all need to learn from John, who was perfectly content, indeed privileged, to be the "best man," and to point people away from himself and to the bridegroom.[8] John's humility is all the more poignant when set alongside the later attitude of Jesus' twelve disciples, especially James and John, who argued about which of them was the greatest. And part of John's humility was that he recognized the limitations of his own ministry: he knew that he could baptize people only, so to speak, "on the outside," in water—only Jesus could change them on the inside. We urgently need the same modest awareness of what it is, and is not, in our hands to do.

John clearly had a very effective and widespread ministry: "people went out to him from Jerusalem and all Judea and the whole region of the Jordan" (Matthew 3:5). It has been rightly said that success tests a man even more than failure does; it is important to be able to stomach failure and still continue positively, but it is even more vital, and much harder, to cope with success without becoming proud. The great danger for anyone seeing their ministry having an impact like John's is that they think that they are, as we would say, "on a roll," that they have attained a quality of ministry that elevates them above the also-rans of the Christian church who do *not* see large crowds flocking to hear them speak. There is no trace of that in John: he displays a humility and a servant spirit, and we can safely assume that he would be the same servant whether he were addressing two people or two thousand.

His message

Then there is John's message: he preached *both* the offer of new life—"The Kingdom of heaven is near . . . [Jesus] will baptize you with the Holy Spirit" (Matthew 3:2,11); his baptism was for "the forgiveness of sins" (Mark 1:4)—*and* the challenge of repentance and change. There are some preachers who are forever haranguing their listeners to change, but who seldom if ever tell them about God's wonderful gift of eternal life; there are others who promise people salvation on a plate, but without telling them that they need to repent in order to experience it. John has sometimes been thought of as a mainly negative preacher of judgment, but that does not seem to do justice to what the Bible says: his challenges about the coming judgment

---

8. Jesus uses the same picture of the bridegroom to describe himself in relation to John in Matthew 9:15//Mark 2:19–20.

are particularly addressed to the Pharisees who thought that they did not need to repent. John's message *was* challenging, and *did* leave people in no doubt that they needed to turn to God in repentance; but, as we said earlier, it was not negative ("Repent, or else . . . !"), but positive ("Repent, because God's wonderful Kingdom is coming, and you can turn to him and receive a share in it!").

His priority

That leads to another very important lesson, which we might call John's priority. He was more interested in quality than quantity. He turned away and refused to baptize a number of people in whom he did not see the quality of a changed life. Living as we do in a society (and a church) that can be obsessed with statistics, there is an even greater temptation to measure our ministry by counting heads, rather than by seeking to build characters; the small church that had the encouragement of baptizing three new converts last year can find it somewhat galling to hear that the church on the next street baptized fifteen last Sunday. But John is interested in the quality of changed lives that people are living, not in how many of them there are; for that matter, so is Jesus. A preoccupation with pushing up the numbers of people in our congregations may lead to a statistically large church, but it is less likely to lead to a spiritually effective one; for that, we need to encourage a deeper quality of response to Jesus.

His integrity

Luke tells us, before narrating the baptism of Jesus, what was later to happen to John: because he challenged Herod on the grounds of his adulterous conduct with his brother's wife, Herod had him arrested (Luke 3:19–20). That shows us another vital lesson about John, namely his integrity. He spoke the truth, and did not avoid speaking the truth even though it might cost him, as indeed it did. These days there can be more of a tendency to choose whether or not to speak out depending on whether we feel we are likely to be well received. John did not back away from saying what needed to be said on the grounds that Herod might not like it. As witnesses for Christ, we are responsible for two things: for *what* we say—we are to speak the truth whenever there is an opportunity—and for *how* we say it: our manner needs always to be gracious, not aggressive, even when like John we might need to challenge people. But we are *not* responsible for whether or not people like or accept what we say. Even if we think they might not, John would tell us, provided our manner with people is positive and full of grace, we should speak the truth; and we should never let the fear of any modern-day Herod deter us from saying what God has told us to say.

The baptism of Jesus

Baptism was already known amongst the Jews before John's time. But until John appeared, the only people who were baptized were Gentiles who had decided to turn to the Jewish faith. John was the first person to call on Jews to be baptized; and in fact, Jews would have been—and some were—indignant at the suggestion that they needed to be baptized; surely they were already accepted as God's people?! In Matthew 3:7–10//Luke 3:7–9 John warns Jews who might still think along those lines not to suppose that the fact that they are descendants of Abraham means that they are already acceptable to God, or that they do not need to repent and be baptized. The Pharisees clearly assumed that they had an automatic right to be included in God's Kingdom because they were righteous Jews—they had the "right" religious background. John makes it clear that baptism (as a mark of being ready to enter God's Kingdom) is a personal decision, not a privilege for those from the right background. Response to the Kingdom is a personal choice, not a hereditary birth-right. Moreover, baptism is not, as these Pharisees seemed to think, a formal affirmation of what people already are—members of the family of God's people by birth and background—but the sign of a change, as people recognize that, as they are, their lives are not acceptable to God and so turn to him to become his people. It still is that; having the right religious background is not enough—all people, without exception, need personally to choose to turn to God and to be baptized.[9]

---

9. Those of us who belong to believer-baptizing churches can sometimes be accused of not taking seriously the faith of small children brought up in Christian households, because we regard them as not yet old enough to be baptized. Leaving aside for now the difficult question of "how old is 'old enough'?," what we can say is that the faith of a small child brought up by believing parents can not only be perfectly real, but is commended by Jesus as the model of what our faith as adults should be (Mark 10:15//Luke 18:17); but also that at some point such children will need to make and express the personal decision to base the whole of their life on their faith in the Christ whom they were taught from infancy to believe in, and it is on the basis of that personal decision that they are baptized. My view, for what it is worth, is that it is not reasonable to expect small children to be able to take personal responsibility for decisions that should be binding for the rest of their lives, which is why we normally defer baptism until such time as young believers can make such a responsible decision; but the faith they had as younger children is to be seen as "the real thing," not just as an embryonic form of what we hope will one day turn into the real thing.

In addition to the fact that John offered baptism to Jews, there was another way in which his baptism was different from Jewish "proselyte-baptism," that is, the baptism of Gentiles who wanted to convert to Jewish faith. Proselyte-baptism was always self-administered; but John comes baptizing other people. Although it cannot have the same effect on us today, the repeated use in the Gospels of the verb "baptize" in the passive—"Jesus came . . . *to be baptized by John*" (Matthew 3:13), "confessing their sins, *they were baptized by him*" (Matthew 3:6//Mark 1:5), "Jesus . . . *was baptized by John*" (Mark 1:9), "John said to the crowds coming out *to be baptized by him*" (Luke 3:7), "tax collectors also came *to be baptized*" (Luke 3:12)—would have seemed strange to Jews; and John's formal title "the Baptist," which is used twelve times in the Gospels, was coined precisely because it emphasized the, for the Jews, unusual fact that John came doing for other people what Jewish converts were used to doing for themselves. But John's practice has an obvious and very significant lesson: we are called to allow others to baptize us, rather than baptizing ourselves, as a sign of the fact that we need to call on God to save us, because we cannot save ourselves. Just as we receive salvation from Jesus, so we receive, as a sign of that salvation, baptism in Jesus' name.[10]

In the light of Acts 19:1–7, where Paul, speaking to some in Ephesus who had received baptism from John, but had never received the Holy Spirit, and in which Paul seems to distinguish the baptism of John (verse 4) from Christian baptism, that is, baptism into the name of the Lord Jesus (verse 5), it is worth considering the question, to what degree is the baptism administered by John the same as, and to what degree is it different from, that administered in the church following the ascension of Jesus? Two obvious differences stand out, not least from the story in Acts 19. First, Christian baptism is into the name of Jesus (Acts 19:5, Galatians 3:27). John's baptism was to prepare the way for Jesus; now that he has come, and in particular, now that he has died and is risen, those who turn to him can be baptized into the Christ who has been fully revealed as Savior and Lord. John's baptism was in anticipation of Christ; Christian baptism is into the reality of new life that Jesus has now made possible.

On the question of the name into which we are baptized, there is no need to speak, as some, forever on the lookout for biblical texts that can be twisted into the grounds for controversy, have done of a contradiction

---

10. It might be thought that Peter's appeal on the day of Pentecost—"Save yourselves from this corrupt generation" (Acts 2:40)—contradicts this principle that people cannot save themselves. In fact this is a problem of English grammar and translation, not a theological discrepancy. The Greek verb Peter uses is in fact in the passive, and so means literally "be saved": the sense of his appeal is, "allow God to save you."

between the principle of baptism into Christ and Jesus' words at the end of Matthew's Gospel, that converts are to be baptized "in the name of the Father and of the Son and of the Holy Spirit." All that Jesus does, he does as the representative of the whole Godhead, Father, Son and Spirit, and we must never think of any aspect of Jesus as separate from and independent of the Trinity. The classic example is the cross: it was the Son who died on the cross; but he died because the Father sent him, he died to reconcile us to the Father, and because he died, the Spirit can now be poured out on his believing people. There is no part of life that is "nothing to do with" any member of the Trinity. We baptize people into Christ, but into the Christ who is one with the Father and the giver of the Spirit; baptism is into relationship with God as Father, into commitment to Jesus as Lord, and into the experience of the Spirit as the enabler of our discipleship. Formulae are not the important thing, but I, and many others, prefer to use the form of words in baptismal services that "we baptize you into Jesus Christ in the name of the Father, the Son and the Holy Spirit." Baptism in the name of Jesus and baptism into the Trinitarian name are not different baptisms, or different theologies of baptism: they are complementary aspects of the same thing.

The second difference between John's baptism and Christian baptism is clearly linked with that; one element in Christian baptism is the experience of the Holy Spirit. John said that Jesus is the one who would later baptize in the Holy Spirit; the direct and personal experience of being filled with the Spirit is regarded, from Acts onwards, as one of the normal fruits of repentance and baptism (Acts 2:38).

Having said that, there are clearly a number of ways in which John's baptism—and in particular, the baptism of Jesus by John—is the prototype of Christian baptism. Chief amongst those common elements is repentance. When Paul said in Acts 19:4 that "John's baptism was a baptism of repentance," he did not mean that Christian baptism isn't; he meant that John's baptism was *simply* a baptism of repentance: the fuller reality of new life in the Spirit, which John said that Jesus would bring, was in John's day still in the future. Christian baptism is now into the experience of that which John could only anticipate.

But Christian baptism is still on the basis of repentance, as "Repent and be baptized" (Acts 2:38) makes clear. Without repentance, as Simon the magician was to learn (Acts 8:13-23), baptism is less than real baptism; and certainly it does not automatically convey spiritual blessing. Baptism matters, and is more than merely an outward or symbolic sign. But unless it is received on the basis of repentance towards God and faith in Jesus, it is meaningless.

And that raises the obvious question, why was Jesus baptized? If, as the Gospels make clear, John's baptism was a baptism of repentance, a sign that people had decided to turn away from sin and wanted to make a new start in life, then why did Jesus need it? It is fundamental to our understanding of Jesus that he was always sinless. So why did he need to be baptized? John himself struggled with that apparent anomaly: when Jesus came for baptism, John "tried to deter him," protesting that he needed to be baptized by Jesus, rather than the other way round (Matthew 3:14)—in other words, John is saying to Jesus, I cannot give you anything that you need; rather, I need what you can give me! John is quite right, and it would be good for all Christians to remember that they need Jesus, but that Jesus, though he loves them and wants to offer them his eternal life, does not "need" them: no one is doing Jesus a special favor by offering to enlist in his cause. But, at this time, Jesus knows that the right thing is for him to submit to baptism.

Jesus' baptism took place for three reasons; and all three are significant aspects of the meaning of our own baptism.

Jesus identifies with sinners

By being baptized, Jesus stands alongside sinners. He underwent a baptism of repentance, though he had personally done nothing of which he needed to repent, just as he would later undergo the death of sinners, even though he was not a sinner. Just as the climax of his ministry would be to die in our place, on our behalf, so the initiation of his ministry, in anticipation of that later climax, involved his being baptized as one who, though himself not a sinner, stands in the place of sinners. It is interesting that in Luke 12:50 Jesus speaks of his death as a "baptism." Baptism is a symbolic enacting of death and burial, which is why the biblical form of baptism was always to immerse people in water; it is a picture of burial, as Romans 6:3-4 makes clear: we are "buried with [Christ] through baptism into death."[11] The wages of sin is death; and Jesus underwent the actual death which is the punishment of sin. Because he suffered the reality, we are spared it; we shall not face the judgment of spiritual death for our sins. We go through the symbolic enactment of death, baptism, as a sign that we identify ourselves with the death that Jesus actually died on the cross, that it was for us and for our sins. Just

---

11. The Greek verb *baptízō*, to baptize, means to immerse, submerge, dip into a liquid. It was used in the ancient world, amongst other things, of dying cloth by dipping it in the dye. In John 13:26, which twice speaks of Jesus "dipping" his bread into the bowl, the word translated "dip" is the simple verb which is the root of *baptízō*, namely *báptō*, meaning to "baptize," or in this case, to "dunk."

as Jesus identified himself with me as a sinner in his baptism, so I identify myself with him as the Savior from sin in mine.

Jesus is anointed with the Spirit

In his baptism Jesus was anointed with the power of the Holy Spirit for his public ministry, in fulfillment of Isaiah 42:1 ("Here is my servant, whom I uphold, my chosen one in whom I delight; I will put my Spirit on him . . .") and 61:1 ("The Spirit of the sovereign Lord is on me, because the Lord has anointed me to preach good news to the poor"). Jesus had been conceived by the Holy Spirit; he was no doubt guided by the Spirit all his life, if the incident at the temple at the age of twelve is typical; but he is now anointed with the power of the Spirit in order to be able to begin the public ministry which is his calling. The Spirit is seen resting on him in the physical form of a dove.

If we ask, why in the form of a dove?, the most frequent answer, which is certainly true as far as it goes, is that the dove is seen as a symbol of purity and gentleness; this is the background to Jesus' words in Matthew 10:16 that his followers are to be as "innocent as doves." And since Isaiah 42:1-4, following the promise that the Lord will put his Spirit upon his chosen servant, immediately goes on to speak of that servant's gentle and gracious character, this is probably the main intended association. There may also be an allusion to two other Old Testament passages, which both involve a dove or bird appearing over water, just as here at Jesus' baptism. In Genesis 1:2 the Spirit of God hovers or broods like a mother bird over the primeval waters at the beginning of creation: the baptism of Jesus will be the beginning of a whole new creation. And when Noah was saved from the flood in the ark, he used a dove to ascertain when the waters had gone down, and it was safe to leave the ark (Genesis 8:8-12). Jesus' ministry will rescue people from spiritual judgment, just as the ark rescued Noah from physical judgment. And the dove is associated with the fact that judgment is now over—we are saved from the judgment of God. So the dove is a sign of what Jesus has come to be and do: the *character* of his ministry, the *creation* of a new kingdom, and the *completion* of the rescue from judgment. And in our baptisms, the Spirit seals the same three truths onto our lives, though (usually) without appearing in physical form: we are baptized by the Spirit into a new Christ-like character, we are made part of God's new creation, and we are affirmed as saved from God's coming judgment.

The link between Christian baptism into the name of Christ and the gift of the Holy Spirit has already been mentioned, and is clearly part of the

New Testament understanding of baptism. There have been two issues of dispute, especially over the last century, about the gift of the Holy Spirit; first, about whether the Spirit is given at the very moment of and as an intrinsic part of baptism, or subsequently to baptism in water; and linked with that, the second question as to whether the Spirit is imparted, as it were, subliminally—so that we accept by faith the fact that God has put his Spirit upon us, even though our senses did not have any evidence of this happening—or whether the giving of the Spirit is marked by outwardly observable phenomena. Regarding the second question, the overwhelming evidence of the New Testament is clearly that the giving of the Spirit was invariably marked by signs that were either seen or heard—and often both—by both the person receiving the gift and by others around them. So we have the visible sign (tongues of fire) and the audible sign (tongues) on the day of Pentecost (Acts 2:3–4); in Samaria, Simon "saw that the Spirit was given" as the apostles laid hands on new believers (8:18); in the home of Cornelius, the Spirit fell on Cornelius and his friends, enabling them to speak in tongues and praise God in a way that caused Jewish believers to be "astonished that the gift of the Holy Spirit had been poured out . . . for they heard them . . ." (10:45–46); Paul could ask the Ephesian disciples whether or not they had received the Spirit following their baptism (19:2)—he expected them to be able to say, as a matter of fact, whether or not it had happened. The essential question is not whether or not we are "into" charismatic phenomena, or whether we may have been put off by bad experiences of insensitive and over-enthusiastic Pentecostalists pushing everyone to speak in tongues, whether they wanted to or not—though that is an issue that needs more gracious and, where necessary, penitent handling than it sometimes receives—or whether we understand what speaking in tongues is all about; it is quite simply whether or not we believe that the New Testament is given to us as the normative truth of God that should establish what Christian faith and life are. If we do (and I do) then the model given to us is that the gift of the Spirit is a conscious experience—you know when it is happening to you—with outward evidence. If it be objected that a number of believers in many churches have no experience of that, then we can first point them to Acts 19, where Paul encountered believers who had similarly not experienced it, and immediately took steps to help them enter into the fullness which they were lacking; and second, we can point out (sensitively!) that God wants to raise the level of our experience to that of his Word, not to have us alter our interpretation of his Word so that it matches our experience.

The first question, as to when the gift of the Spirit is given, is already partly answered if we take the New Testament pattern of a conscious experience as normative.¹² The baptism of the Spirit is distinct from, though inter-related with, baptism in water; it is not just another name for the same thing. John clearly intended to teach that water-baptism and spirit-baptism are not the same when he said that he could baptize people in water, whereas Jesus alone would baptize them in the Spirit. Passages like Acts 10:44-47, where Peter sees the people in Cornelius' house receive the Holy Spirit and then says that there is no reason not to go on to baptize them in water—as they have received the one baptism, let's give them the other one as well—confirm this. In the first challenge to baptism in the early church, Acts 2:38, Peter speaks of water-baptism as a command to be obeyed ("Be baptized, every one of you") and of Spirit-baptism as a promise that they can then expect to receive ("and you will receive the gift of the Holy Spirit").[13] Water-baptism is connected with repentance: it cleanses people from their past. Jesus' baptism in the Holy Spirit empowers people for their new future.

Jesus is affirmed by the Father

So Jesus' baptism shows him standing in the place of sinners; being anointed by the Spirit; and also being affirmed by the Father (the voice from heaven) as the Son of God. Those words have an importance that we will come to when we consider the temptation of Jesus; for now, let us simply note that Jesus is publicly affirmed to be the Son of God.[14]

---

12. A "conscious" experience does not necessarily mean an *emotional* experience; in some Pentecostal circles in particular it is often assumed that being baptized in the Holy Spirit is always an emotional experience. That can lead to the frequent misunderstanding that, if someone has not been deeply moved emotionally, it means they have not been filled with the Spirit, and also that getting emotionally "worked up" in worship or prayer will make it more likely that the Spirit will come in power. By a "conscious" experience, I mean rather that the fruit of the baptism of the Spirit will be, amongst other things, that the new believer will be enabled, as a matter of experience, to do things (which may or, in my view, may not include speaking in tongues) that they could not do before: what they "feel" when they are exercising such spiritual gifts is, I believe, fairly irrelevant.

13. This is a distinction that is, I believe, insufficiently noticed. Baptism is commanded; but nowhere are converts told that, as part of Christian initiation, they *have to* receive the Spirit; rather, they are promised that they will. Jesus describes the Spirit as "the *gift* my Father *promised*" (Acts 1:4); there is no biblical justification for pressurizing people to receive the Holy Spirit. Paul's words in Ephesians 5:18, "be filled with the Spirit," are not an evangelistic challenge: they are words addressed to those who are established believers, urging them to continue day by day to "keep in step with the Spirit," as he puts it in Galatians 5:25.

14. There is a view, known as "adoptionism," that in his baptism Jesus *became* the Son of God, or was raised to the status of being Son of God, for the purpose of fulfilling

The baptism of Jesus is one of the "Trinitarian" passages of the Bible; that is, we see all three persons of the Trinity involved together. Jesus, the Son, is baptized; the Father speaks over him from heaven; and the Spirit comes and rests on him. In Matthew 28:19 Jesus says that we are to be baptized "in the name of the Father and of the Son and of the Holy Spirit." This suggests that our own baptisms have the same meaning as Jesus' baptism. By being baptized in Jesus' name, we are identifying ourselves with Jesus, who died for our sins; we are anointed with the power of the Holy Spirit to live a life of Christian service; and God the Father accepts and affirms us as his own children. In his prayer in John 17:24 Jesus said, "Father, I want those you have given me to be with me where I am." That ends in the glory of heaven; but it starts in the water of baptism.

Christian baptism

Because of the variety and indeed confusion that has arisen in the historic church about the mode and meaning of baptism, it is necessary to say at least something about the place of baptism in Christian life and faith. As we have said, John's baptism, whilst it models a number of the essential truths about baptism in the church, was preparatory; the rest of the New Testament gives us a fuller understanding of baptism as practiced by the apostles after Jesus' ascension. And the first thing to say is that baptism in the early church was clearly seen as part of conversion; people were baptized when they came to faith in Jesus. John's baptism was administered to those who confessed their sins (Mark 1:5). Phrases like "believe and be baptized" occur in a number of places in the New Testament, such as Mark 16:16, Acts 2:41, Acts 8:12–13 and Acts 18:8.[15] In the first Christian sermon on the Day of

---

his ministry; in other words, denying that Jesus is in his very nature God's Son. This view might claim support from the full text of Psalm 2:7, from which the words spoken by the Father over Jesus are derived: "You are my Son; *today I have become your Father* [traditionally, have 'begotten you']"; but those words are initially a reference to the human kings in the line of David, and speak of how God will adopt and accept them as his sons: their application to the person of Jesus is at a much deeper level. Many statements in the New Testament affirm Jesus' eternal nature, like Hebrews 1:2 which says that it was through his Son that God created the universe in the beginning.

15. Acts 8:36–37 is often quoted as the classic "proof-text" for baptism on the basis of person faith: "[The Ethiopian eunuch asked] 'Why shouldn't I be baptized?' Philip said, 'If you believe with all your heart, you may.'" In fairness, it should be pointed out that the words from "Philip said . . . ," that is, the whole of verse 37, are almost certainly a later addition to the text of Acts. But the case for believer's baptism does not rest on this verse; it is the norm in the whole story of the early church, and even if verse 37 is a later addition, it is perfectly in keeping with the rest of the New Testament.

Pentecost Peter challenged people to "repent and be baptized" (Acts 2:38). It was a Roman Catholic theologian, Rudolf Schnackenburg, who wrote that "Baptism without faith in Christ is unimaginable for the thinking of the primitive Church."[16]

Linked with that, it is helpful to see baptism alongside the other elements that are mentioned in the New Testament as being constituent parts of Christian initiation. We might compare becoming a Christian to a rope of six strands; so for our Christian faith to keep us securely bound to Jesus and to his eternal life, all need to be in place. The six strands are: *repentance*, the decision to change direction in life, and turn to God and to God's ways; *faith*, the decision to trust in Jesus to save us; *commitment*, the decision to start to follow Jesus and to be his disciples; *baptism* in water; *receiving the Holy Spirit*, the conscious experience of being filled with the power of the Holy Spirit; and *joining the church*, becoming a member of the Body of Christ, and starting to share in the life of God's family.

Those six elements in Christian conversion are seen across a number of passages in the New Testament; but there is no single text which itemizes them all. This highlights the danger of taking our understanding of what people have to do to become Christians from any single passage, but ignoring how that passage fits into the all-round New Testament picture of what it means to become God's people. For example, in Acts 2:38 Peter challenges the crowds to repent and be baptized: he does not specifically mention faith. On the other hand Paul responds to the Philippian jailer's question, "What must I do to be saved?" in the words, "Believe in the Lord Jesus" (Acts 16:30–31) but with no explicit mention of repentance. We must never isolate any one of these aspects of conversion from all the others. Unfortunately there can often be in our church culture what we might call a minimalist approach to faith; the jailer's question, "What must I do?," can for many people today mean "What is the bare minimum that I absolutely *have* to do to be sure of being saved?—because I don't want to do anything that is not essential!" So if baptism or becoming an active member of the church are optional extras, we can forget them. If, say, believing is all that is required, then I'll believe; but I'll leave it at that.

That is quite contrary to the spirit of the New Testament. Faith is always understood as being inextricably bound together with repentance, with a commitment to follow Jesus, with baptism—with embarking in fact on an all-round Christian life in the fellowship of the church. God is looking for people whose desire is for more than merely satisfying minimum conditions; he wants people who aim for the best, who want to strive, in the

---

16. Quoted in Beasley-Murray, *Baptism*, 272, footnote 3.

words Oswald Chambers used as the title of his great devotional classic, for *My Utmost for his Highest*.

The biblical phrase that sums up the essence of baptism is that people are baptized "into Christ" (or "into the name of Christ") (Romans 6:3, Galatians 3:27). Baptism is not into the church, or in the name of any human leader—it is into Jesus Christ. So what does it mean in the New Testament to be baptized "into Christ"?

A step of obedience

We start with the most simple and straightforward thing to say: baptism is a step of obedience. Jesus was himself baptized as our example, and he commissioned baptism in his church (Matthew 28:19, Mark 16:16). Whilst there is far more to it than mere obedience to a command, it remains true that we are baptized because we are told to be. In Acts 10:48 we are told that "[Peter] ordered that they be baptized," which, whilst it may sound more peremptory than we might be comfortable with, leaves us in no doubt that in the New Testament the call to Christian faith included the call to receive Christian baptism.

In fact, the New Testament use of the word translated "ordered" (Greek: *prostássō*) confirms that, far from being simply a command to be obeyed, baptism is a sign of grace offered by God. *Prostássō* is found only seven times in the New Testament. Its first occurrence is in Matthew 1:24, when Joseph, following his encounter with the angel of the Lord, "did what the angel of the Lord had *commanded* him and took Mary home as his wife": Joseph did what God had told him to do, but what God had said was that he should marry the girl he loved—God's command was his invitation to enter into a positive covenant relationship that he had previously feared had become impossible. Three of the remaining occurrences are the parallel verses in Matthew 8:4//Mark 1:44//Luke 5:14; Jesus tells the man he has healed of leprosy to "go, show yourself to the priest and offer the gift Moses *commanded*, as a testimony to them." The law of Moses prescribed sacrifices to be offered when God had healed someone of a serious skin disease; and Jesus tells this man to fulfill that requirement: he has already healed the man by grace, so the offering of the prescribed gift is not a burdensome condition to be fulfilled, but a positive celebration of what the Lord has done, and a "testimony" to his saving power. The same is true of baptism.

A symbol of cleansing

Being put in water is obviously a picture of being washed clean from all our sins; and Paul says in Acts 22:16 that when he was challenged to be baptized, it was in the words, "Get up, be baptized and wash your sins away . . .". John the Baptist proclaimed a baptism of repentance for the forgiveness of sins (Mark 1:4); when people are baptized into Christ, their immersion in water represents outwardly what God does inwardly, forgiving all their sins, and washing their lives clean on the inside.

There are a number of places in the New Testament where the language of "washing" and "cleansing" is used of how Christians have been saved by Jesus: for example, 1 Corinthians 6:11, "you were washed, you were sanctified, you were justified"; Ephesians 5:25–26, "Christ . . . gave himself up for [the church], to make her holy, cleansing her by the washing with water through the word"; Titus 3:5, "[God] saved us through the washing of rebirth and renewal by the Holy Spirit"; Hebrews 10:22, "let us draw near to God . . . in full assurance of faith, having our hearts sprinkled to cleanse us from a guilty conscience and having our bodies washed with pure water." Whilst these should not be seen necessarily as direct references to baptism, they do reflect the fact that a vital element in God's salvation is that we are cleansed from sin, and that that cleansing is powerfully represented in water baptism.

Solidarity with Jesus

We said above that one of the reasons why Jesus was baptized was that he was identifying himself with and standing alongside sinners. In the same way, in our baptism, we identify ourselves with and stand alongside Jesus. The Bible says that baptism unites us to Christ, and specifically to the death and resurrection of Christ; "all of us who were baptized into Christ Jesus were baptized into his death" (Romans 6:3–4), ". . . having been buried with him in baptism and raised with him through your faith in the power of God, who raised him from the dead" (Colossians 2:12). In some way that we may not fully understand, by being baptized into Jesus Christ, God makes us one with Jesus. Just as a kettle needs to be plugged into the electricity supply through a power socket in the wall before it can work, so our lives need to be "plugged into" Jesus, so that his life, his salvation, his power can flow into us. It is in baptism that we are "plugged into Jesus." In baptism, the benefits of his death and resurrection become real for us personally: it is God's seal on our salvation.

We might summarize this by saying that baptism is about both *identification with* Christ—by being baptized we identify ourselves with him as our Lord and Savior—and *incorporation into* Christ: spiritually, we are incorporated by God into the life and work of Christ, so that all that is true of him and all that he achieved for us is now true of us and effectual for us. Identification is our decision: we choose to identify with Christ crucified and risen; incorporation is God's work: he makes us one with Christ.

That element of spiritual incorporation into Christ is reflected in the organic images in the New Testament which describe the relationship between Christ and his people, such as the vine and the branches that are "in" the vine (John 15:5), and the body with its various limbs and organs which form the parts of the body (1 Corinthians 12:27). In baptism, we are grafted into Christ like new branches into the vine, or we are spiritually transplanted into Christ like new organs into a living body.

A statement of commitment

Baptism is a promise and a pledge; and that in two ways. Firstly, *God* promises to all those who are baptized into Christ that he will save them, forgive them, protect them, and be Father to them. That is all summed up in his pronouncement over Jesus at his baptism, "This is my beloved Son," and Paul says that the same is true of every baptized believer: "You are all sons of God through faith in Christ Jesus, for all of you who were baptized into Christ have clothed yourselves with Christ" (Galatians 3:26–27—it is significant that the phrases "through faith in Christ" and "baptized into Christ" are used in parallel as descriptions of becoming Christians). But then, secondly, *we* promise, in being baptized, that we will follow Jesus, obey him, serve him, and allow him to lead us into the new kind of life that he has for us (Romans 6:4). The phrase in Romans 10:9, "Jesus is Lord," is widely assumed to be a basic baptismal confession of faith; those being baptized are affirming, both in a verbal confession and in the very act of being baptized, that they will live henceforth with Jesus as the Lord over their lives.

The start of a new life

Linked with that, baptism marks the beginning of a new life; it is not just that we choose to begin a new chapter in our lives, but that God has actually given us a new life in Christ. Baptism is the end, the burial, of our old life and the start of a new life: see Romans 6:4–14. And note the use of the exodus from Egypt and the crossing of the Red Sea as a picture of baptism in 1 Corinthians 10:1–2; in baptism, we leave behind the old life of slavery to sin and pass into a new life as God's redeemed people.

A sign of the Spirit

We have already spoken of the link between water-baptism and baptism in the Holy Spirit, summed up in the appeal of Peter in Acts 2:38, "Repent and be baptized . . . and you will receive the gift of the Holy Spirit." God promises the gift of the Holy Spirit to those who are baptized into Jesus Christ. Being plunged into water is a sign of the fact that God will plunge us into the life of the Holy Spirit, and into his love and joy and peace. And three things should be remembered if we are to avoid some of the mistakes and misunderstandings that have complicated the whole doctrine of "baptism in the Spirit."

- The Spirit does not come mechanically or automatically, simply because someone has been immersed in water: to think otherwise has more to do with magic or superstition than biblical faith. The Holy Spirit is a *Person*, and he comes to relate to us in a personal way; he fills the lives of those who choose to let him fill their lives: "How much more will your Father in heaven give the Holy Spirit *to those who ask him*" (Luke 11:13). It is normal, and entirely biblical, to pray for people, often with the laying on of hands, that they might be filled with the Spirit; but let us always remember that we are inviting the Person of the Spirit to come, we are not fulfilling religious conditions to "make something happen."

- People receive the Spirit by faith; just as we are saved by faith, and are baptised in water on the basis of faith in Jesus, so we are filled with the Spirit by faith alone. We must at all costs avoid the kind of legalism that lays before people all sorts of conditions that they must fulfill—religious hoops through which they have to jump—before God will give them his Spirit. God *promises* to give his people the gift of the Spirit; faith means trusting that he will do what he has promised.

- The Spirit is given to equip Christians for a life of service. In our very experience-focused culture, it is tempting to stress what people can "feel" at the time the Spirit comes upon them; but the sign of a Spirit-filled life is not immediate feelings but long-term fruit. The Spirit enables us to live as Jesus lived, and to serve as Jesus served.

But it would be wrong to forget that the Spirit does not come only to bless our lives with grace; in saying that he comes to enable us to serve, we do not mean simply that he equips us with the gifts we need—which he certainly does—but also that he strengthens us so that we can face the demands of discipleship. How often do we remind those who are about to be baptized that baptism, whilst it is certainly a joyful celebration of God's salvation, is also the initiation into a challenging lifestyle? That challenge is seen very clearly in what happened to Jesus immediately after his baptism; and to that we now turn.

3

The temptation

"He was in the desert for forty days, being tempted by Satan" (Mark 1:13)

Following his baptism Jesus immediately goes through a time of testing, which is recorded in Matthew 4:1–11//Luke 4:1–13, and briefly alluded to in Mark 1:12–13.

John does not narrate the temptation in the desert; but it is interesting that the three temptations Jesus faced there are also faced in different contexts and at later times in John. In 4:31–32, "his disciples urged him, 'Rabbi, eat something.' But he said to them, 'I have food to eat that you know nothing about.'" The "food" Jesus is referring to is, as he says in verse 34, "to do the will of him who sent me." There is an obvious parallel here with the temptation to turn stones into bread: the devil wants Jesus to use his power as the Son of God to serve his own needs, but Jesus replies that his only purpose is to do what God says; his disciples want Jesus to eat some food, but he says that his priority is to do what God wants. Then in 6:15, the crowd, following the feeding of the five thousand, want to seize Jesus and "make him king by force," a temptation not unlike the devil's showing Jesus all the kingdoms of the world and saying that they can be his. In 7:3–4 his own brothers urge Jesus to go up to Jerusalem at the feast of Tabernacles, and perform miraculous signs there, so that he can "become a public figure"; again, there is clearly a parallel here with the third temptation, to perform (at the temple in Jerusalem!) a remarkable miracle by throwing himself off the top and surviving; that way, Jesus would attract all the crowds he wanted.

It is unnecessary to say that these passages are simply "John's version" of the desert temptations. He is not re-writing history in a revisionist sense. But he is perhaps showing us that Jesus' temptations were not limited to the forty days after his baptism. Though the devil left him at the end of those forty days, he left only, as Luke says, "until an opportune time" (4:13). Those times kept recurring throughout Jesus' ministry; he was constantly tempted. The devil is not mentioned explicitly in the texts in John; but there is no reason to doubt that he was the instigator of any enticement to Jesus to deviate from following the will of his Father. Two things are clear from John's "temptations." First, the devil kept repeating the temptations in the same three key areas; we will come shortly to look at the significance of those areas. And second, he tempted Jesus, not only blatantly, to his face (in the desert), but also through his disciples (4:31–32), the crowds (6:15) and his own family (7:3–4). It is very unlikely that any of these people realized that the devil was using them to tempt Jesus; in the case of the crowds, they were acting out of badly mistaken but no doubt positive intentions, and the disciples were clearly only trying to be helpful. But they were unwittingly the mouthpieces of the Tempter. The kindly-meant words of those nearest and dearest to us can sometimes be the very means exploited by the devil to lead us astray spiritually; which is why we are always to ensure that we are following what God says in his Word.

So John, although he does not narrate the same temptation story as the others, does show Jesus as the one who overcame repeated temptations. We will however concentrate in what follows on the story in Matthew and Luke.

Jesus, the Messiah

Going through and overcoming these temptations is a part of Jesus' calling and ministry, not a distraction from it. Just as sin and evil began with the fall of Satan, who then tempted man into sin, so Jesus' work to undo the effects of the fall begins by his facing the devil in single combat and defeating him, before he can then start to minister to people. Both Matthew and Luke stress that Jesus was specifically led by the Holy Spirit into the desert, in order to be tempted by the devil (Matthew 4:1//Luke 4:1–2). Many people fear that, if they are being tempted, they must be doing something wrong, or they must be in the wrong place. But Jesus was led by the Spirit into this battle with the devil. Being tempted is not in itself wrong. We may sometimes be under intense spiritual pressure precisely because we are in the *right* place and doing the *right* thing.

The Messiah is the perfect representative of God's people; he sums up in himself all that the people were meant to be, but usually failed to be. In the story of Jesus' temptations, we see Jesus re-enacting and fulfilling two important aspects of the history of the Old Testament.

The new Adam

The first is the account of the original temptation in the Garden of Eden. The story of the human race begins with man being tempted by the devil (Genesis 3). The man fell into temptation, and sinned against God. The story of Jesus' ministry begins with his being tempted. But he resists the temptations and remains faithful to God. Jesus is recapitulating the story of humanity, but succeeding where Adam, and all people, have failed; he is making a new start for the human race.

There are a number of comparisons and contrasts between the temptation of Jesus and the original temptation in the Garden of Eden. There, it happened in a beautiful garden; here, in a terrible desert. Jesus lived under much worse conditions, in a spoiled and fallen world: but he still overcame, in a way Adam did not. Second, the devil's temptation to Adam focused on eating a piece of fruit (Genesis 3:1-6). Jesus' first temptation also focused on eating: turning stones into bread. Third, in Genesis 3:6, we see that the woman was originally tempted when she saw "that the fruit of the tree was good for food and pleasing to the eye, and also desirable for gaining wisdom." In other words, she was tempted, as we all are, in three ways: by her *bodily appetites*: here, for food; by *what she saw with her eyes*; and by *what she thought she might become*, namely as wise as God: the devil had tempted her in the words "God knows that when you eat of it . . . you will be like God" (Genesis 3:5). Jesus faced the same three temptations: to pander to his bodily appetites (to turn stones into bread to eat); to see something and want it (the devil showed him all the kingdoms of the world and their glory, and said, all this can be yours); and by what he might become: if he performed a spectacular miracle by throwing himself off the temple and surviving, he would become a sensation—and it would prove that he really was the privileged Son of God. 1 John 2:16 lists the same three principle sources of temptation: "the cravings of sinful man, the lust of his eyes and the boasting of what he has and does," or, literally, "the lust of the flesh and the lust of the eyes and the pride of life." We, like Adam and Eve and like Jesus, are tempted mainly by our appetites ("the lust of the flesh"), by what we see and desire ("the lust of the eyes"), and by what we think or hope we can become ("the pride of life").

The first Adam was tempted and fell. Jesus, the second and greater Adam, faces the same temptations, but overcomes; he wins the victory on behalf of the whole of fallen mankind.

The new Moses

The other important Old Testament background to the account of Jesus' temptation is the story of God's people in their redemption from Egypt in the exodus. Having passed through the waters of the Red Sea (Exodus 14), Israel spent forty years in the desert, which was a time of testing; in Deuteronomy 8:2 God reminds his people "how the Lord your God led you all the way in the desert these forty years, to humble you and to test you in order to know what was in your heart, whether or not you would keep his commands."[1] The Israelites, sadly, failed the tests, by and large: they repeatedly complained about the lack of food and water, rather than trusting that God would provide for them, as he always did; they lacked the faith to go into the Promised Land, and listened to the ten spies who said that the land was well defended, rather than to Joshua and Caleb who said that God would help them to take the land (Numbers 13–14); and they fell into moral sin with Moabite women, sent into the Israelites' camp specifically to tempt them (Numbers 25). Jesus, having passed through the water of baptism, spends forty days in the desert, being tested; but he passes the test. He succeeds fully and completely in being the obedient Son of God, which Israel failed to be.

What is more, the three temptations which Jesus faces all arise from the experience of Moses and Israel in the desert. The first temptation—"Turn these stones into bread"—reminds us of the miraculous gift of the manna which God provided for his people. Jesus is here being tempted to use his

---

1. The wording of this verse and others about God's "testing" us should not be misunderstood, as though it implied that God needs to find out whether or not we are good enough, because he does not know. God knows fully what kind of people we are; the point of his "testing" us is more like what happens when a trainer puts an athlete through what might seem a punishing regime of training: it is to make him fitter and more capable of winning a medal; or when gold is refined in a fire: it is to make it purer and more free of dross. As James 1:3 says, "the testing of your faith develops perseverance": God allows our faith to be tested, not in order to give us "marks out of ten," but to grow our character and give us more moral and spiritual backbone. Living as we do in a sinful and damaged world, all people will face the trials of life; whether they remain simply "trials" to be endured, or become the means under God by which our faith and character are purified, is a choice we can make. We can choose, if we wish, to allow trials to make us bitter, or to make us better, depending on whether we resent them as problems foisted on us or accept them as part of God's training us as disciples.

position and power as the Son of God to meet his own needs rather than trusting in the Father to provide for his needs. On the exodus journey, the Israelites' confidence in God's provision frequently failed them. Although they had been told that God would provide fresh manna every day, so there was no need to store any up, some still decided to try and keep some of the manna overnight, just in case there was no new provision the next day (Exodus 16:19-20); and Christians, even whilst they say they trust in God's provision, can all too often have their own contingency plan in the back of their minds, just in case God doesn't provide in the way they hope. Jesus refused to yield to the temptation: although he was hungry, he remained confident that the Father would give what he needed when the time was right, and he would not make physical bread his first priority, but rather "every word that comes from the mouth of the Lord" (Deuteronomy 8:3).

If the first temptation is based on God's provision of the manna in the desert, the second[2]—"Throw yourself down . . ."—arises from his promise of protection. In Deuteronomy 32:10-11 Moses speaks of God's protection of Jacob in ways that reflect the experience of Israel in the desert: God "shielded him [= Jacob] and cared for him; he guarded him as the apple of his eye, like an eagle that stirs up its nest and hovers over its young, that spreads its wings to catch them and carries them on its pinions." The devil subtly borrows that promise of God's protection and turns it into a temptation to Jesus to throw himself down from the temple simply to see whether or not God will catch him and protect him. That is poles apart from the spirit of God's commitment to care for his people: his promise is "if you get into trouble I will look after you," and the devil turns that into "get yourself deliberately into trouble to see if God will look after you!" Faith that God will protect us is not the same as—indeed, is the very reverse of—putting God on the spot to see whether or not he will live up to his promise to protect us.

If the first temptation relates back to God's provision for Israel, and the second to his protection, the third reminds us of his promise. The devil offers Jesus "all the kingdoms of the world, and their splendor," just as in Deuteronomy 8:7-9 Israel was promised a good, rich and plentiful land in which to settle. Israel however, rather than entering into God's promise on God's terms, was dazzled by the splendor of the surrounding kingdoms and so yielded to the temptation to follow their gods, even though God had

---

2. That is, the second in the order in which Matthew narrates the temptations. Luke puts the devil's offer that he will give Jesus the world's kingdoms if Jesus will worship him second, and the temptation to throw himself down from the temple third. I doubt that the order is of any great significance: it is likely that the same kinds of temptations were repeated regularly, and the lessons we can learn from the story arise from the nature of the temptations, not from the order in which they may have occurred.

already said to them the words that Jesus also quotes to the devil: "Fear the Lord your God, serve him only..." (Deuteronomy 6:13).

So the three temptations reflect three things promised to Israel as the covenant people of God in the Promised Land—provision, protection, and prosperity. Israel failed the tests she faced on her wilderness journey. And all Christians face the constant temptation to want to ensure provision for our own needs, and to see that as a higher priority than heeding "every word than comes from the mouth of God"; to expect God to protect us whether or not we live faithfully in the spirit of his Word; and to desire the blessings and the prosperity of the world without minding too much if those blessings come to be an idolatrous distraction from our single-minded devotion to God alone. We certainly need to learn to withstand those temptations; but the starting point is to grasp that Jesus, our Messiah, when faced with the same tests, won the victory over the devil on our behalf by remaining unflinchingly loyal to the will of the Father, and that it is as we trust in him and so learn to live "in Christ" that we become "more than conquerors through him who loved us" (Romans 8:37); as Campbell Morgan said, "The victory of Jesus over temptation is victory over all the forces of hell; and all men who, abandoned to his Lordship, abide in his will, must share in his triumph."[3] We overcome the Tempter, not primarily by trying to overcome him, but by trusting that Jesus has already triumphed over him.

Jesus, the Servant

"Forty days" is a very significant phrase in the Bible. Often it refers to a period of preparation before something important happens. In the time of the flood, the water fell for forty days (Genesis 7:4). Moses spent forty days with God on the top of Mount Sinai, when he received the Law (Exodus 24:18). Jonah told the people of Nineveh that God would bring judgment on them in forty days (Jonah 3:4). After his resurrection, Jesus spent forty days with his disciples, preparing them for his ascension back to heaven (Acts 1:3). These forty days that Jesus spent in the desert were a time when he was preparing himself for his ministry. As part of that preparation, he was fasting, praying and meditating on God's Word. It is good, before we embark on anything new for God, to spend a similar time in preparation and prayer.

It is significant that the temptation follows immediately after the baptism, when the Father had said over Jesus, "This is my Son, whom I love; with him I am well pleased." Those words in Matthew 3:17//Mark 1:11//Luke 3:22 are the key to what the devil is trying to tempt Jesus to do. They

---

3. Morgan, *Crises of the Christ*, 152.

are a combination of three Old Testament verses: Genesis 22:2, in which God tells Abraham to take Isaac, "your only son, Isaac, *whom you love*," and offer him as a sacrifice on the mountain in Moriah; Psalm 2:7, which is about the Son of God, the victorious King who will rule over the nations with an iron scepter and dash all his enemies to pieces like pottery, and of whom God says *"you are my Son"*; and Isaiah 42:1, which is about the Servant of God, the meek, modest and suffering servant who will by his suffering atone for the sins of God's people, and of whom God says *"with whom I am well pleased"*: the NIV translates as "in whom I delight." Jesus is the all-conquering King, the beloved Son who will be offered as a sacrifice, and the suffering servant of God. In the temptations, the devil is trying to drive a wedge between the Son who is King and the servant who is offered as a sacrifice. Hence the phrase (Matthew 4:3,6//Luke 4:3,9) "If you are the Son of God . . ."—if you are the Son, forget about being the servant, forget about going the way of sacrifice. It is often assumed that when the devil says *"If* you are the Son . . . ," he is trying to sow the seed of doubt into Jesus' mind about whether he really is the Son of God. Maybe; but it is more likely that he is saying, "Since you are the Son, then act like the Son!" Use your power as Son to feed your own needs (turn these stones into bread), to perform spectacular miracles to attract attention (cast yourself down from the temple), receive the kingdoms of this world as a gift from me. But Jesus will have nothing to do with this. He is the Son, but he is also the Servant. He will bring the Kingdom, not through sheer power and domination, not by spiritual "strong-arm tactics," but through self-sacrifice, patient service, and total submission to God alone.

We need to have the same balance in our own lives. We are sons of God by faith, and we are one with the risen, victorious Christ. But we are also humble servants of God. The church can often tend towards one or other of the two sides of our calling. There have been many great examples of those whose lives are given in humble service, who have washed the feet of the poor, and no one would want to disparage their remarkable and exemplary work. But such service can sometimes seem to be quite secular in character, scarcely any different from the work of the social services. When that is the case, it may be legitimate to ask, in the midst of all this patient and sacrificial ministry, where is the resurrection power of Jesus?, where is the Gospel of redemption that has the potential to transform lives?, where is the evidence of being "more than conquerors"? On the other hand—and for the modern evangelical church, this is by far the greater danger—there is a form of Gospel triumphalism which is only too willing to affirm repeatedly that we are more than conquerors, that regards any hardship or struggle as the sign of inadequate faith, that claims to be completely free from what Hamlet described as "the thousand natural shocks that flesh is heir to," that revels in signs and wonders; but where, we might ask, is the servant-spirit, where is the reflection of Jesus the suffering servant?

In the wonderful *Sacred Diary of Adrian Plass*, a speaker at Adrian's church refers in his sermon to Mother Teresa of Calcutta. "Afterwards, Richard Cook whispered to us, 'Ah, yes, but is she saved?' Gerald whispered back, 'Ah, yes, but how many filthy beggars have you washed this week, Richard?'"[4] Actually both questions can be legitimate; the problem is that the first can too often be asked as a snub, or even paraded as a badge of spiritual superiority: maybe others feed the hungry, but *I'm* born again! But the confident evangelical who would ask the first question would do well to start by asking the second of himself, and remembering that we follow Jesus the Servant.

Lessons from the temptation story

There are a few more lessons we can learn from the temptation narrative.

The essence of temptation

We tend to think of "temptation" in simple moral terms. The devil tries to "tempt" us to do wrong things—to commit moral sins. Of course he does that. But these temptations of Jesus are not simply enticements to moral wrong-doing. Jesus was no doubt tempted morally; Hebrews 4:15 says that Jesus was "tempted in every way, just as we are." But these temptations are not about moral rights and wrongs, but about how Jesus was going to fulfill his life's ministry for God: was he going to follow the devil's temptation to assert his rights as the Son of God, or was he going to follow the path of the humble and suffering servant? That is the most important question, for Jesus and for us. The devil will be quite pleased if he can get us to lie, or cheat, or lose our temper, or whatever. But what he really wants to do is to side-track us from fulfilling the ministry that God has prepared for us. The tragedy is that we can sometimes be confident that we are on the right track because we have successfully resisted the temptation to lapse into lying, cheating or losing our temper; but we might nonetheless be missing, or even avoiding, God's call to service in our lives. Temptation is not just about the devil wanting to stop us being good people, but to prevent us from becoming fruitful servants of the Kingdom.

---

4. Plass, *Sacred Diary*, 8. Warmly recommended.

The Victor over temptation

Going through temptation is what qualifies Jesus to represent us before God. Hebrews 4:15 says that Jesus is able be our Great High Priest, and can stand on our behalf before God, because he has been through all the trials and temptations that we go through. Therefore, he can also sympathize with our weaknesses—he has been through them himself. Whenever we are tempted, we can find the strength to overcome, not primarily by gritting our teeth, but by looking to Jesus, who overcame temptation for us. As the hymn[5] puts it, "When Satan tempts me to despair, and tells me of the guilt within, upward I look, and see him there who made an end of all my sin."

The answer to temptation

Following on from that, we can learn from the way in which Jesus responded to each of the devil's three temptations. He quoted the Bible. When faced with the devil's suggestions, he always said "It is written . . ." The better we know the Bible, the better we will be able to resist the devil's suggestions, and indeed to recognize them as temptations in the first place. Someone once said, "when the devil tries to tempt you, don't argue—quote!"

The three Scripture texts which Jesus quotes to reject the devil's temptations are all from Deuteronomy (8:3, 6:16, 6:13). The book of Deuteronomy is Moses' re-statement of the law of God to the people, as they are about to enter the Promised Land. They have been wandering in the desert; they are about to settle in a new country. They have been living in tents; they are about to start taking and populating cities. They are, in other words, about to embark on a new and different life. To prepare them for that challenge, Moses repeats the law of God, and reminds them of the essential principles of what it will mean for them to continue to be God's faithful people. In a similar way, Jesus is about to embark on a new and vital phase of his life. He has been living and growing up as the "son" of a carpenter in Nazareth; he is about to start his public ministry of teaching and doing the works of God's Kingdom. It seems that, to prepare himself for that role, Jesus had been meditating on Deuteronomy, which may be why those texts, that protected him from temptation, were in the forefront of his mind.

There are two things we can learn from this. One is that, whenever we are about to embark on a new phase in our lives, or a new sphere of service and ministry, we could do a lot worse than to prepare ourselves by reading carefully through Deuteronomy. Jesus did; and it helped him get his

---

5. "Before the throne of God above" by Charitie Lees Bancroft (1841–1923).

ministry off to a good start, rather than, humanly speaking, risking falling at the first hurdle. But more generally, it was because he took his understanding of what his life and ministry were to be from the Scriptures that he was able to resist the temptations. Being steeped in the Bible will not prevent us from being tempted. But it will help us to recognize suggestions of "other ways"—more attractive ways, ways that are more in tune with our high-tech and high-flying world—of pursuing our lives as disciples and servants of God as temptations to be resisted rather than as opportunities to be considered; and to have seen that they are temptations is already half the battle.

The greatest temptation

Finally, the end of these forty days was not the end of Jesus' temptations. We have listed some occasions in John's Gospel when he was tempted in ways similar to these original three temptations. But the most frequent and potentially dangerous temptation he faced was to avoid going to the cross. That temptation, the idea that the way of cross could, perhaps, be set aside for another way, came to him from his own disciples (Matthew 16:21–23// Mark 8:31–33), and, in his intense trial in the Garden of Gethsemane, from his natural human tendency to shrink from the ordeal (Matthew 26:36–39// Mark 14:32–36//Luke 22:40–44). And whilst on the cross, he was tempted by the crowd to come down and save his own life (Matthew 27:39–40//Mark 15:29–32). But in all these temptations, he remained totally faithful to God's will. We too will repeatedly be tempted to make the center of our life and faith something—anything!—other than the cross, to walk any road except the way of the cross, to face any challenge except that of taking up our own cross to follow Jesus. It is not a weakness or a failure to find that challenge daunting; Jesus did, as the agony in the Garden of Gethsemane shows only too clearly. But Jesus neither dodged nor yielded to those temptations, a fact to be remembered when we respond, albeit with some trepidation, to his call to "Follow me."

4

Going public

"... that he might be revealed to Israel" (John 1:31)

Following the baptism and temptation, Jesus' public ministry begins. There are two series of events that are recorded; and, as so often, John gives us the account of one, and the three so-called synoptic Gospels give the other. If the question be raised about the order in which these events occurred, it appears that John's story precedes the synoptics' account of Jesus' proclamation of the Kingdom in Capernaum. The reason for saying this is that John's story (1:35—4:54) includes the comment in passing that (3:24) "this was before John was put in prison"; the synoptics say that it was when John was arrested that Jesus began his ministry in Capernaum by announcing the imminent arrival of the Kingdom of God (Matthew 4:12//Mark 1:14.) So it seems likely that it is the events recounted in John 1-4 that come next; chapter 4 ends with Jesus in Galilee, and near Capernaum (verses 43-47); the three synoptics then pick up the story with the announcement in Capernaum that "the kingdom of heaven is near" (Matthew 4:12-17). Having said that, the order is of very little importance. There are things we can learn from both parts of the story, and those lessons are not affected by which part came first.

But we start with John, who tells us that, before settling in Capernaum, and beginning his ministry of preaching and teaching, Jesus began by travelling round the whole of the Palestinian area, beginning at Bethany[1] (1:28), and then moving out into Galilee (1:43).

First Disciples

Following the witness of John the Baptist, the rest of chapter 1 (from verse 35) tells us of Jesus' first contact with five men who would later become his disciples. John does not include the story of how Jesus eventually chose his twelve apostles. But it is typical of John that he gives us some of the details that the other Gospels leave out. John's account of these preliminary meetings with, amongst others, Peter and Andrew, means that Jesus' later call to them to follow him, to which they responded by leaving everything behind, was not "out of the blue," and their decision was not impulsive. They had already had some contact with Jesus, and had had time to start to understand something of what following him would be like; a point that is worth remembering, especially if in our zeal as preachers or witnesses we tend to push people to make "snap decisions."

From these verses in chapter 1, four things stand out.

Witness to Jesus

One is the fact that those who have met Jesus then tell others about him and bring others to him. Andrew, having heard of Jesus from John the Baptist, goes with Jesus and spends a day with him; then "the first thing Andrew did was to find his brother Simon" (verses 40–42), and bring him to Jesus. Later, Jesus invites Philip to follow him, upon which Philip finds Nathaniel, tells him about Jesus, and, when Nathaniel seems somewhat skeptical about the possibility that Jesus (from Nazareth!) might actually be the promised Messiah, Philip, rather than launching into a long argument, wisely says to him simply "Come and see" (verses 45–46). Without laboring the point, John is reminding us that it is quite normal for those who have met Jesus to lead others to meet him. The modern church, that can tend to over-complicate evangelism and witness with all sorts of "methods" and "programs," needs to remember that anyone who has had a real encounter with the Lord Jesus is likely to have a spontaneous urge to tell others what they have discovered;

---

1. This "Bethany" is said to be by or beyond the Jordan; it is clearly not the same place as the better known "Bethany," the home of Lazarus, Mary and Martha, which was near Jerusalem. That two places have the same name need not concern us; after all, there are in England eleven Prestons, six Longfords and sixteen Uptons; for that matter, there are over twenty Bethanys in the USA.

that urge should be encouraged. And if the best they can say in answer to the cynical questions of their friends is "Come and see," we should let them simply say it. It worked for Nathaniel.

Titles of Jesus

There are also the names and titles that people use of Jesus. At first he is called simply "Rabbi," meaning "teacher" (verse 38). Andrew, having spent a day with him, tells his brother that Jesus is "the Messiah"[2] (verse 41). Then Philip repeats the same thing when he says that Jesus is "the one Moses wrote about in the Law, and about whom the prophets also wrote" (verse 45)—that is, the King promised in the Old Testament. Finally, Nathaniel says that Jesus is "the Son of God" (verse 49). John's Gospel is all about who Jesus is; and here, people start to realize who Jesus is, not by being told by others, but by meeting with him personally. Moreover, their awareness of who Jesus is increases. We need never be too distressed when people regard Jesus at first as a teacher; that is how Andrew and his unnamed friend saw him. People will come to know Jesus as Son of God and Lord when they genuinely want to get to know about him, even if they start by thinking of him as teacher and example; and if they do not want to get to know him, they will not be convinced by our insisting that they have to accept him as the Son of God. As we over a period of time tell people more about Jesus, we need to pray and trust that the Spirit of God will reveal to their hearts more of who he is.

The knowledge of Jesus

We also see here the fact that *Jesus knows all about people*. Jesus, on his first meeting with Simon, looks at him (verse 42) and says that he will be called Peter[3]—a sign that Jesus already knows what Peter's future character and role will be. The name Peter means "rock." There are two great encouragements for us in Jesus' prophecy here. One is that he knows from the beginning what our future place in his Kingdom will be. From the moment Jesus

---

2. "Messiah" is a Hebrew word meaning "the anointed one"; it was a title for the promised King whom God would send to save his people. The Greek translation of "the Messiah" is "the Christ."

3. John actually gives the Aramaic name *Cephas*, and then translates it with the Greek name "Peter"; both words mean "the rock." Peter is referred to as *Cephas* eight times by Paul in his letters, but this is the only occurrence of the Aramaic version of his name in the Gospels.

draws anyone to himself, he knows precisely in which ways he will call them to serve him, even if they themselves do not discover their vocation until years later. The other great encouragement is that our capacity to fulfill that vocation has nothing to do with what kind of people we are at the time when Jesus calls us. Jesus sees us, not just as we are, but in terms of what we can become, and what he can make of us. There is not much that is "rock-like" about Peter as we see him in the Gospels: the Peter who has the faith to step out of the boat and walk on water, then within seconds is panicking, sinking and crying to Jesus to rescue him; the Peter who, within a few hours of swearing that he would never deny Jesus did so three times. Yet this is also the Peter who, when he had been filled with the Holy Spirit, preached the first Christian sermon and, humanly speaking, founded the church in Jerusalem. When Jesus looks at us, he sees what he can make of us. Christians can be quite dismissive of suggestions that they could actually accomplish significant things for God; but whilst modesty is very necessary, and we are rightly suspicious of the self-appointed and self-promoting "leader" who is quite convinced that he is more than equal to any challenge that might come his way, we need nevertheless to trust that Jesus can make of our lives "immeasurably more than all we ask or imagine" (Ephesians 3:20). It has been said that faith means that every time we look at an acorn we see an oak-tree. What kind of tree does Jesus see, as he looks at the fragile seed of our present character? Those who insist that they are destined to remain seeds for life are not being "humble"; they are denying that Jesus has the ability to grow anything in them.

After Peter, there is Nathaniel, whom Jesus describes, when he sees him coming towards him, as a man without deception in his character[4] (verse 47). He then adds that he saw Nathaniel "under the fig tree" (verse 48). This seems to be a phrase that was used to mean a place of private prayer, devotion and meditation. Jesus discerns that Nathaniel is a man with a deep personal spiritual life. Clearly, Jesus knows what people are like "on the inside," even before they come to him.

---

4. What Jesus actually said ("Here is a true Israelite, in whom there is nothing false") involves a play on words that arises from the name of Abraham's grandson; he was originally called Jacob, but God later changed his name to Israel, after which the whole nation descended from him was named. "Jacob" means literally "grasps the heel," referring to how, at birth, Jacob, the second of the twins to be born, emerged from the womb clutching the heel of his older twin brother Esau; the phrase "to grasp the heel" meant, figuratively, to deceive. And indeed, Jacob frequently lived up to the metaphorical meaning of his name: he tricked his brother out of his birth-right (Genesis 25:29–34) and his father out of his blessing (27:1–36). So when Jesus says of Nathaniel, "Here is a true Israelite, in whom there is nothing false" (literally, "in whom there is no deceit"), he is saying, in effect, "Here is an Israel in whom there is no Jacob!"

It is interesting, incidentally, that Nathaniel, the disciple-to-be whose spiritual devotion Jesus commends in such positive terms, is also the one who is initially the most dismissive of Jesus, on the grounds that he comes from such an unimpressive place as Nazareth. The man of deep spirituality is also the man who at first is skeptical about Jesus. Admittedly, he is quickly convinced that Jesus is "the Son of God . . . the king of Israel"; but he is convinced not by what Philip told him, but by meeting Jesus himself. We can often be disappointed when our witness to Jesus is greeted with negative or dismissive comments; but under the surface (where Jesus can see, but we cannot), people might, for all we know, be searching for something that is spiritually real, as Nathaniel was. Rather than merely taking their unpromising responses as a sign that they will never come to Christ, we can instead pray that the Lord Jesus will find the ways to reveal himself to them, as he did to Nathaniel, as the one who can answer their questions and be the end of their searching.

The revelation of Jesus

There is finally Jesus' own claim about who he is. His words in verse 51 ("You shall see heaven open, and the angels of God ascending and descending on the Son of Man") are another reference back to the story of Jacob, namely to the incident in Genesis 28:10–17 in which Jacob, whilst on the run from his brother Esau, dreams of a ladder connecting heaven and earth, with angels ascending and descending on it. Jesus is again comparing Nathaniel to Jacob, but this time to a more positive aspect of Jacob's life; he was a man who had many remarkable visions of and encounters with God, one of which was his dream at Bethel. Nathaniel is going to discover in Jesus something even more wonderful than what Jacob saw: that Jesus himself is the real connection between heaven and earth, the one who can bring the blessings of heaven down to us ("angels descending"), and raise us up to be part of God's heaven ("angels ascending").

New Creation, New Israel

As we come to the series of events in John chapters 2–4, there are two lessons about Jesus embedded in them. The first arises from the way that John carefully notes the passage of time through chapter 1, culminating in the story of Jesus turning the water into wine at Cana in chapter 2. The time between the beginning of John's testimony (1:19) and the wedding in Cana (2:1) covers seven days. On day one (1:19–28) John is questioned by some representatives of the priests and by a group of Pharisees about who he is; on day two (1:29, "The next day . . .") John points to Jesus as the Lamb of God, and baptizes him; on day three (1:35, "The next day . . .") Jesus makes his first contact with Simon and Peter; on day four (1:43, "The next day . . .") he meets Philip and Nathaniel; then finally (2:1) "on the third day" (that is, three days after that) there is the wedding at Cana. Jesus' first miracle takes place on the seventh day of the week in which he is for the first time seen in public as the Christ. John's time references seem to be hinting that the beginning of Jesus' ministry is the beginning of a new act of creation, in seven days. John has already drawn an obvious parallel between the original creation in Genesis 1 and the coming of Jesus, by starting his Gospel with the words from the opening of Genesis ("In the beginning . . ."); here he is doing the same thing again. Jesus brings the start of God's new creation.

But then we come to the series of events and encounters in chapters 2–4; and here there is another strand that runs through them all. We have the miracle of the water turned into wine at Cana (2:1–11); then, in Jerusalem, the cleansing of the temple[5] (2:12–25), which took place at the Passover (verse 23); then, still in Jerusalem, the discussion with Nicodemus about being born again (3:1–21); in Judea, a discussion of baptism by John and Jesus, and John's final testimony to Jesus (3:22–36); and finally, in Samaria, the discussion with the woman at the well about the water of life, and the ensuing revival in Samaria (4:1–42).

John has recorded these incidents to show how Jesus challenges and supersedes various aspects of Judaism.

- *Jewish ceremonies* (2:1–11). John emphasizes that the jars used for the water at Cana were those normally used for ritual washing ceremonies (verse 6). Jesus brings the spiritual reality which all the Jewish ceremonial rituals merely symbolized; he replaces those ceremonies and symbols with the real "new wine" of the life of God's Kingdom.

- The *Jewish temple* (2:12–25). Jesus' body is the new temple (2:19,23); he brings the real and personal presence of God, which the old building merely represented.

---

5. This purging of the temple is sometimes thought to be the same event as the one which the other three Gospels record following the ride into Jerusalem on Palm Sunday, in other words, very near the end of Jesus' ministry. This is quite possible: John seems to have arranged his Gospel thematically rather than chronologically. The other possibility is that there were two such "purgings," this one at the beginning of Jesus' ministry, and another at the end. It seems to me that the significance and the lessons of these stories are not affected one way or the other, whether or not there were two such occasions, or just one; and it is the lessons of Jesus' ministry that matter, not the details of its timetable.

- *Jewish lifestyle* (3:1–21). Nicodemus is introduced (verse 1) as a Pharisee, one who was devoted to scrupulously obeying the law in every area of day-to-day life; he represents Jewish Pharisaic leadership at its best, yet even he needs to be "born again" through faith in Jesus in order to have the real quality of life that God wants for his people.
- *Jewish prophecy* (3:22–36). John the Baptist is the greatest pinnacle of the prophetic tradition, yet his words in verse 30 ("He must become greater; I must become less") show his own awareness of what Jesus was later to say of him, that even the least in God's new Kingdom is greater than he (Matthew 11:11//Luke 7:28).
- *Jewish parties* (4:1–42). The Samaritans were a people that had, culturally, politically and spiritually, branched off from mainstream Judaism. But the coming of Jesus brings an end to the long-standing theoretical disputes between Jews and Samaritans; he brings instead a new quality of life in relationship with God, which both Jews and Samaritans can share equally (4:19–24). And this record of how a whole town in Samaria responds positively to Jesus, and declares him to be "the Savior of the world" (verse 42), contrasts with how he will later be rejected by his fellow-Jews.

So Jesus is here presented as the absolute fulfillment of all that the Jewish tradition represents. In fact, this theme of Jesus as the fulfillment of Old Testament Judaism continues through the rest of John's Gospel. In the long section from chapters 5–10, Jesus is presented as the spiritual fulfillment of the main Jewish festivals.

- In chapter 5, Jesus heals a man on the *Sabbath* (verse 9); this is the day on which people are not allowed to work, but, as Jesus points out, the Father is always doing his work, including on the Sabbath (verse 17), and so the Son too brings life and blessing on the Sabbath.
- In chapter 6 Jesus compares himself to the manna from heaven: manna was particularly associated with *Passover*, and Jesus here stresses that he, not the manna, is the true bread from heaven (verse 32).
- Chapters 7 and 8 take place at the Feast of *Tabernacles*, which was popularly celebrated as a festival of water and light; and Jesus speaks of himself as the source of the true water of life (7:37–38) and the light of God (8:12).
- In chapter 10 we find Jesus at the festival of *Dedication* (or *Hanukkah*): this was not one of the religious festivals prescribed in the law of Moses, but had been established as a commemoration of the

re-consecration of the temple by Judas Maccabbaeus in 165 BC, after it had been desecrated by the Greek king Antiochus Epiphanes. Jesus here speaks of himself as the one whom the Father has consecrated as his very own (verse 36).

One of John's consistent themes is that Jesus brings the reality of spiritual life which all the Jewish traditions and institutions could merely symbolize.

And in a wider sense, he is seen as fulfilling all the religious traditions and aspirations of the whole world. The five strands of Judaism listed above represent five important strands in all religion and faith, including the historical Christian church. There is the *ceremonial*—every religious tradition has its ceremonies and rituals. But Jesus brings the reality which ceremonies in themselves cannot bring, not even church ceremonies. There is the *institutional*—every religious tradition has its structures and organizations (and buildings!); but Jesus brings the life which institutions do not in themselves bring. There is the *moral* and *lifestyle* side of every religion, just as the Pharisees represented the strict tradition of keeping the Jewish law. Jesus gives a quality of life which is not based on keeping rules, but which the Holy Spirit grows in Jesus' people, when they are born again through the Spirit. There is the *teaching* aspect of every religion—a body of truth which is taught, just as the prophets in Israel taught the people. Jesus is the one who brings the reality which teachers can talk about only in theory. And there are in every religion different *groups* and *parties*, just as the Jews had become divided, and the Samaritans represented a sub-group of God's people who were despised by the rest. It is in Jesus that we find life—not in belonging to this or that group or party.

So John is stressing that Jesus is the fulfillment of all these religious strands, and that, apart from him, they are at best less than, and at worst an empty substitute for, "the real thing." Jesus himself is "the real thing."

This highlights an ever-present danger for the church. The essence of Christian life is always a personal relationship with God through Jesus; Paul said of his own faith that "to me, to live is Christ" (Philippians 1:21), and the same should be true of every part of our own life and faith: it is all about Jesus, who he is and what he has done. But there is always a tendency for the various aspects of church life, like the five strands of Judaism listed here, to cease to be means to the end of drawing closer to Jesus, and to become ends in themselves. There are those whose "religion" is focused in rituals and ceremonies, but who have never tasted the real new wine of life in relationship with Christ. There are those who are part of and devoted to the institutional church, with its structures, traditions and hierarchies, but who have never experienced what it means to know Jesus, the living temple. There are those for whom being a Christian is all about living a good life, but who like Nicodemus have no idea what we are talking about if we point out that they need to be born again. There are those who immerse themselves in the writings and teachings of Christianity—who know the Bible from cover to cover—but who are like those of whom Jesus was later to say that all those writings were intended to point people to him, so that they can come to him to find eternal life (John 5:39–40); they know the Scriptures of the Lord, but they have never come to know the Lord of the Scriptures. And there are those whose awareness of what "religion" means to them is primarily partisan or denominational ("I'm a good Catholic!," "I've always been Methodist!"), just as the woman at the well in Sychar was quick to raise the (to her) important distinction between "we Samaritans" and "you Jews"; but they have never tasted the living water of Jesus, and may not even know that it is available.

In the face of all such religious means that can become ends, John presents Jesus, whom to know is eternal life; Jesus who is the fulfillment of all forms of religion. These chapters raise two challenges for us. The first is to examine ourselves, regularly and often, and to be on the look-out lest any aspect of church life, however good and worthy in itself, is starting to become more of a focus for our faith than Jesus himself. The second challenge calls for some sensitivity. Keen evangelicals can occasionally be somewhat scathing about those in whom they see, perhaps rightly, a lot of religious tradition and practice, but no evidence of spiritual life; the question, "Are you born again?" can sometimes be asked in a way that is intimidating rather than helpful. But the question is valid, and might sometimes need to be asked. We should note that Jesus is entirely positive and constructive in his dealings with Nicodemus and the Samaritan woman. He invites them to receive and experience the inner reality, rather than condemning or belittling them for having only the outer formality. We can only challenge formal religion if we do it in the same spirit.

"Born Again"

The best-known saying of Jesus in these chapters is his word to Nicodemus, "you must be born again" (John 3:3,7). This word, with its key phrase "born again," is essential: Jesus says you *must* be born again. But it is also terribly misunderstood; it has become in many people's eyes a catch-phrase rather than a spiritual reality. So it merits some attention. It occurs in the first of the long "discourses" that are a major feature of John's Gospel, and which covers 3:1–21 (though it is possible that Jesus' own words end at verse 15 and that verses 16–21 are John's comments, added as a summary of some of Jesus' teaching). This first discourse contains a number of the familiar themes of John's Gospel: in particular, the fact that Jesus is the one who came down from heaven (verse 13); that he was sent by God into the world (verses 16–17); and the very important subject of faith, which leads to life (verses 16,18). These themes are recurring *leitmotivs* in John's Gospel. Another regular theme in John is also found here: the fact that there are some who believe in Jesus and others who do not (verses 18–21). This has already been mentioned in John's prologue (1:10–12), and it will keep recurring. John stresses that Jesus faces us with a clear choice: we either believe in him, which brings life, or we reject him, which leads to death and judgment.

It is in that context that Jesus says that all people need to be "born again." That means that they need to receive a completely new kind of life. To be born is to receive life. People have been "born of the flesh"—that is, they have been physically born with ordinary human life, which they get from their parents ("flesh gives birth to flesh," verse 6). But that ordinary human life will not bring them into God's Kingdom (verse 3). They need to have a different kind of life "birthed" in them, which in the Gospels is usually called "eternal life." "Eternal" is, in its most basic sense, the opposite of "passing" or "transient," as 2 Corinthians 4:18 ("For what is seen is temporary, but what is unseen is eternal") shows. But it also has the sense of belonging to the spiritual world of God, as opposed to this passing natural world. The word translated "eternal" (*aiōnios*) is used of God (Romans 16:26) and of the Holy Spirit (Hebrews 9:14), and of things pertaining to God, such as his glory (1 Peter 5:10) and power (1 Timothy 6:16, where "honor and might forever" is literally "honor and eternal might"). So "eternal life" means "God's kind of life" as opposed to ordinary human life—the life we have by nature.

The Spirit of God reproduces that kind of life in those who believe in Jesus ("the Spirit gives birth to spirit," verse 6—in other words, God's Spirit reproduces in us the spiritual life that God has). It is possible to have religious practice and moral principle—all the things covered in the five strands of religious formality found in these chapters in John—as part of our ordinary human lives; religious practice is not in itself the same as or evidence of being born again.

The phrase "born again" in verses 3 and 7 would more accurately be translated "begotten from above." The verb can be used of what a mother does (giving birth), but is far more often used of what a father does. The old-fashioned word "to beget" is the best way of translating this in one word. It means to become the father of, to "father." God reproduces his own kind of life in those who believe in Jesus.

And the adverb that goes with "begotten" can certainly be used in the sense of "again," but its basic meaning is "from above." It is the word used for how, when Jesus died, the veil in the temple was torn in two "*from top* to bottom" (Matthew 27:51). It is the word Jesus uses (John 3:31) to describe himself as "the one who comes *from above*," that is, from heaven. This "new birth" is not something that we can ever bring about ourselves. It is not a human achievement. It comes from above, from God himself.

The phrase "born of water and the Spirit" (verse 5) may reflect a number of ideas; it may for example include a hint about the place baptism plays in becoming a Christian, as the Bible refers to both baptism in water and baptism in the Spirit. But the most likely basic meaning of "water" is that it is a euphemism for male sperm. The two words "water and spirit" are probably to be understood as a single idea, namely "spiritual seed"[6]—you need to be born, not just with "natural seed" from a human father, but of "spiritual seed" from God's Spirit. In John's Gospel, Jesus often uses the symbol of water to refer to the life of the Kingdom of God. He does so in the very next chapter, for instance (4:10–14). The point is that it is the Spirit of God who "plants" the life of God in us.

This is not the only place in the Bible where this language about being "born again" is used: it is found also in John 1:13, 1 Peter 1:3, 1:23, 1 John 2:29, 3:9, 4:7, 5:1. But in addition, all the phrases in the Bible about our being "God's children," and about God being our Father, are based on the same idea that we are "born again" when God reproduces his spiritual life in us.

Two other places in the New Testament, as well as this passage in John 3, speak of where the new birth comes from. Here in John 3:5 Jesus says that it is the work of the *Spirit* of God: it is the Holy Spirit who imparts the new life of God. In 1 Peter 1:3 we read that Christians are born again "through the *resurrection* of Jesus Christ from the dead": when Jesus rose from the dead, he did not merely return to the ordinary human life he had had for thirty-three years; he rose with a glorified heavenly life. It is that new kind of life that the Spirit shares with us, which will be ours perfectly in heaven. To be born again means to receive a share in Jesus' resurrection life. And later in the same chapter, Peter says (verse 23) that "you have been born again . . . through the living and enduring *Word* of God": it is through hearing

---

6. The technical grammatical term for this kind of construction is "hendiadys" (pronounced "hen-dire-diss"), which is defined as the expression of a single idea using two terms as though they were separate elements, usually linked by "and." This was frequently used in Greek (the language of the New Testament) and Latin; it is less common in English, but an example would be the phrase "nice and warm," which is not saying two things—that something is (a) nice, and also (b) warm—but one thing, namely "nicely warm"; this is very similar to "water and spirit" = "spiritual water."

and responding to the Word of the Gospel that people come to faith and are born again.

Faith

How do people respond to the Word, and so receive this new birth? The context of the "born again" saying, in this section of John 2–4, makes it very clear that it is not through formal religious means, through rituals or ceremonies. Jesus has come to bring a life that supersedes all such outward practices. The answer is stated in the famous verse 16, as well as many times in John: it is through faith in Jesus.

The word "faith" (which, in the language of the Bible, is the same as the verb "believe") can be used in a number of different senses in the Bible. Very occasionally, it is used in the sense of "the faith," the body of doctrine and truth that Christians believe.[7] This is not the most usual sense of the word; however, there is a doctrinal content to the faith. But it is mostly used in the sense of "an attitude of personal trust" in Jesus; to have faith means to trust Jesus to do for us what we cannot do for ourselves.

There are a number of aspects of faith that we need to be aware of, in order to avoid being misled by thinking simply in normal secular terms of what it means to "believe things."

Faith is a gift from God

In Philippians 1:29 Paul writes that "it has been granted to you . . ."—that is, given to you by God—". . . not only to believe on him, but also to suffer for him"; and in Acts 16:14, we read of Lydia (the first convert in Philippi) that "the Lord opened her heart to respond to Paul's message"—in other words, God enabled her to believe. Faith is not a feature of human personality, or an ability some people have but others haven't. People will often say "I wish I had your faith!," and the Christian can quite properly reply, "You can have it—it's a gift!" And because faith is not a feature of our human personality, we cannot "do" things to try to stimulate faith in ourselves or others; we can however pray for ourselves and for others to be given the gift of faith.

---

7. For example, in Acts 14:22, Galatians 1:23, Philippians 1:27, Colossians 2:7, 1 Timothy 2:7, 3:9, 4:1,6, 5:8, 6:10,21, Jude 3.

Faith is focused in Jesus

To believe always means to believe in Jesus. Many will say they believe in God, but, as James points out, even demons, in a sense, "believe in" God (James 2:19). People may say that they believe in prayer, or that they believe in the church, or that they believe in the Bible, or that they believe in Christianity; but unless all those things are expressions of the fact that they believe in Jesus, what they have is not the faith of which the New Testament speaks.

Faith is faith in Jesus alone

There is a very widespread religious mindset in the western world which might be called "Jesus *plus*": yes, I have faith in Jesus, but I also hope that other things—the fact that I attend church regularly, or was baptized, or pray a lot—will carry at least some weight in God's eyes and earn me a bit of extra spiritual credit. In fact, as has been rightly said, "Jesus *plus*" always means "Jesus *minus*": to put any part of our faith in anything else, in addition to Jesus, is in effect to say that Jesus on his own is less than sufficient; maybe Jesus will get me part of the way to heaven, but I have to supplement the saving work of Jesus with something else of my own to be sure of actually arriving there.[8] The Bible clearly affirms that Jesus alone is our all-sufficient Savior, and that to believe that something else is required will in fact detract from our assurance of salvation: if anything of my own is required to "top up" the grace of Jesus, how can I ever be sure that my contribution will be good enough? Biblical faith can be full of assurance precisely because it rests on the absolute sufficiency of Jesus to save us, and he certainly *is* "good enough": as Colossians 2:10 says, it is "in Christ" that we have been given "fullness." The nineteenth-century pastor Edward Mote (1797–1874) wrote a classic hymn which begins with the lines, "My hope is built on nothing less than Jesus' blood and righteousness"; and when he says "on nothing *less*" he also means that his confidence is in nothing *more* than—that is, in nothing else in addition to—Jesus and his death on the cross. That is New Testament faith.

---

8. The Roman Catholic doctrine of purgatory, the idea that serious sins committed in this life, although they are forgiven, still require us to undergo a period of purification after death before we can be admitted to heaven, is in effect precisely such a denial of the absolute efficacy of the saving work of Jesus on the cross. It is the blood of Christ that purifies us from *all* sin (1 John 1:7); to say that the redeemed are still not adequately purified until they have completed a term in purgatory is to say that it doesn't.

Faith is trust

We can use the phrase "believe in" in at least two different ways in English. Sometimes to "believe in" means to be of the opinion that something exists; in that sense people may say they believe (or don't believe) in fairies, in Father Christmas, in UFOs, in the Loch Ness monster. But we can also say that we "believe in" someone in the sense of trusting them. If I say that "I believe in my doctor," I do not mean that I am of the opinion that my doctor exists. Doubtless I am; but what I mean is that I trust him, I have confidence in him. I am ready and willing to entrust my medical needs into his hands.

Many people might say that they "believe in God"; but they will often mean it in the first sense: they believe that there is a God, they are not atheists. But faith in the New Testament is very seldom thought of in what we might describe as a "credal" sense—believing things about Jesus, believing that certain things are true—and almost never in the sense of believing in the existence of God. In fact, James 2:19 is the only place in the New Testament where "believe" has that specific sense of believing that God exists,[9] and James' reason for using that phrase is precisely to stress that such belief is not "faith" in the Christian sense. Biblical faith always has at its heart a personal decision to trust Jesus for our spiritual welfare, in the same way as we put our trust in a doctor for our medical welfare.

Faith looks to Christ crucified and risen

The faith that brings us into eternal life is not just faith in God in general, and not even faith in Jesus in general. It is the faith that believes and trusts that Jesus died on the cross for our sins and rose again from the dead. The great passages about justification by faith, like Romans 3:21–26, are speaking specifically of the fact that Jesus died on the cross for our sins; the famous verse in John 3:16 about those who "believe in [Jesus]" having eternal life is preceded by verses 14–15 which speak of how Jesus will be "lifted up" (on the cross) to become the one to whom people can look to find life; and Romans 10:9 says explicitly that the faith that justifies us is the faith in Jesus as Lord that believes "that God raised him from the dead." Faith that leads to new birth and new life is cross-shaped.

---

9. Hebrews 11:6, speaking of the importance of faith, says that anyone who comes to God "must believe that he exists." But the same verse also speaks of faith as "earnestly seeking him," which already implies a level of personal engagement with God that goes way beyond a belief in his existence. And the whole of Hebrews 11 is about the fact that true faith is never passive: it always involves people committing themselves to an active lifestyle that arises from their faith.

Faith looks for help and salvation

Following on from that, faith is not simply believing things about Jesus, but looking to Jesus for salvation and mercy. If faith is simply theoretical, and does not arise out of sense of personal need, it is not biblical faith. Real faith is not a creed, but a cry; it says not merely "I believe," but "Lord, have mercy on me, a sinner!"; it is the faith that trusts Jesus to save us, and is confident that he will.

Faith is a commitment

Faith that leads to new life means entrusting ourselves to Jesus. John 3:16, that famous verse which says that God loved the world so much that he gave his one and only Son, "that whoever believes in him shall not perish but have eternal life," indicates this in a small but very important way: the phrase translated "believes in him" is, in the Greek, literally "believes *into* him." Faith is not static but dynamic. I can stand on a station platform and believe in the train in front of me; but it is if I get *into* the train that I will actually get where I need to go. Faith does not mean believing "in" Jesus, but getting on board with Jesus—believing "into" him, handing our lives over to him.

Faith is a choice and a decision

Just as faith is not merely a belief in our heads, so it is not merely a feeling in our emotions. The Bible uses phrases about believing "in our hearts" or "with all our hearts" (e.g. Proverbs 3:5, Acts 16:14, Romans 10:9–10); but whenever we use such language, we need to remember that the metaphorical use of the "heart" in the Bible is not the same as its use in the tradition of western lyrical poetry. In that western tradition, the heart is understood as the seat of the emotions; hence, for example, William Wordsworth's poem which begins "My heart leaps up when I behold a rainbow in the sky," or phrases like "I love you with all my heart." But in the Bible the heart is understood as the seat of the *will*. It is with the heart that we make choices and decisions; it is like the bridge of a ship, where the course is set that the ship should follow. To trust in Jesus with our hearts does not mean to make an emotional response to him; it means to make a conscious choice that we will trust him and start to follow him.

Faith is made evident in works

The famous passage in James 2:14–26 about faith and works is *not* saying that we are saved by works rather than by faith; rather, it is saying that the faith that saves us will always lead to works. If someone says they have faith, but their lives are showing no fruit in works of Christ-like service, devotion and mission, then we have grounds to doubt whether they have real faith at all. The same point is made in the famous roll-call of the saints of the Old Testament in Hebrews 11—all had faith, but all *did* things because of their faith. So the challenge for us is that faith must make some real difference to our lives in terms of moral lifestyle and Christian service. In principle, to ascertain whether or not a person has faith, we should not need to ask him what he believes, but simply to look at how he is living. In our desire (rightly!) to stress that people are saved by faith in Christ alone, we must never drive a wedge between faith and devoted lifestyle: the one must inevitably lead to the other.

Jesus points this out in his conversation with Nicodemus. In verse 8, immediately after having repeated, "You must be born again," he continues: "The wind[10] blows wherever it pleases. You hear its sound, but you cannot tell where it comes from or where it is going. So it is with everyone born of the Spirit." Jesus is saying two things of great importance here. The first is that we cannot control the wind; it blows "wherever it pleases." In the same way, we cannot regulate where, when and how the Spirit works; he is sovereign, and he comes at the Father's good pleasure. Like every aspect of spiritual life, the new birth is ours to receive; it is not ours to control. But the second thing is that we cannot see the wind; we can however see its effects—trees swaying, leaves rustling. In the same way, we cannot "see" ourselves or anyone else being born again of the Spirit. We can however see the results that will follow; we can and should expect to see the fruit of the Spirit, the changed lives ("works") that the Spirit will produce in us. Fruit growing on a tree is evidence that the tree is alive; and spiritual fruit growing in our lives is evidence that our faith is alive.

---

10. The Greek word for "Spirit" is the same as the word for "wind" (*pneûma*, from which we get our English word "pneumatic," meaning filled with and powered by air), which is no doubt part of the reason why Jesus speaks of the wind as an illustration of how the Spirit works.

Faith leads to a relationship with Jesus

Finally, we do not simply "have" faith; we are called to "live in" faith. Faith that is real is something that affects the way we live our whole lives. Many people can "believe things," such as many of the facts they learned at school; but they are in effect simply items of information—of "general knowledge"—stored up in their heads, which do not make any real difference to how they live their lives from day to day. We need, sensitively and without being or sounding judgmental, to understand, and to help others to understand, that a theoretical faith in their heads that does not impact their lives is not real saving faith in Jesus. Faith brings us into a relationship with Jesus, which is real to us now and in eternity. And that is the faith on the basis of which we are born again.

5

Announcing the Kingdom

"Jesus went into Galilee, proclaiming the good news" (Mark 1:14)

The main ministry of Jesus can broadly speaking be divided into two halves; the first is his ministry in Galilee, the second is his wider ministry, as he travels around other areas, culminating in his arrival in Jerusalem for the last week before going to the cross. The ministry in Galilee starts in and around Capernaum, in fulfillment, as Matthew 4:14–16 points out, of Isaiah 9:1–2, "Land of Zebulun and land of Naphtali, the way to the sea, along the Jordan, Galilee of the Gentiles[1]—the people living in darkness have seen a great light; on those living in the land of the shadow of death, a light has dawned." This first stage of his ministry begins with his announcement of the arrival of the Kingdom of God.

The King

The event that marks the time for Jesus' ministry to begin is the arrest of John the Baptist (Matthew 4:12//Mark 1:14, Luke 3:19–20). Following this arrest, and before his ministry in Capernaum, Jesus does two other things. John

---

1. The northern area of Galilee had for some time been a very cosmopolitan region, with a mixed Jewish-Gentile population, unlike the area around Jerusalem in the south, which was much more strongly nationalistic. It is a sign of the grace of God and the nature of Christ's ministry that he comes first to this mixed-race area of "Galilee of the Gentiles."

tells the story of his healing of the official's son (4:46–54); and Luke gives us the account of how Jesus preaches and is rejected at Nazareth (4:14–30).

There are two key lessons in this second story. The first is that Jesus is the one in whom the prophecy of Isaiah 61, which Jesus reads in the synagogue, is fulfilled. Jesus is the promised anointed one. The people in the synagogue seem to have no problem with that ("The eyes of everyone in the synagogue were fastened on him . . . all spoke well of him," verses 20–22). But then Jesus starts to say that the Kingdom will not just be for Jews, but for others outside Israel; and he illustrates God's concern for the Gentiles from the Old Testament stories of Elijah and Elisha (verses 23–27). This is too much for the people of Nazareth, whose response is to try to kill Jesus (verse 29).

Some people will at various times be offended at who Jesus claims he is: the Son of God, the King. But others, as here, are offended when they see that Jesus comes for "the wrong people," and spends time with those whom they regard as unworthy. That opposition, which will grow throughout the Galilean ministry, starts here in Jesus' home town. And it has not been completely eradicated from the church of Jesus. It is easy to parody the popular "middle-class" and "respectable" image of the church; unfortunately the image can sometimes be uncomfortably close to the reality. If the socially acceptable, the established and the prosperous feel more at home in our churches than the socially marginalized, the less-than-acceptable, the "outsiders," then we should perhaps be asking ourselves some searching questions about whether we might have more in common with the synagogue at Nazareth than with the Jesus who preached there.

Jesus then moves to Capernaum, and announces that the Kingdom of God is at hand (Matthew 4:13–17//Mark 1:15, Luke 4:31). He calls four fishermen, Andrew and Peter, James and John, as his first disciples (Matthew 4:18–22//Mark 1:16–20//Luke 5:1–11). It is perhaps significant that Jesus calls Peter and Andrew to "be fishers of men"—that is, to bring people into God's Kingdom. Both Peter and Andrew are often seen in the Bible to be bringing people to Jesus. James and John were "preparing" their nets when Jesus called them. The word translated "preparing" is the same one that Paul uses in Ephesians 4:12 for "preparing" or building up the church so that it is better able to serve God in the world. James and John both seem to have ministries that were primarily to build the church. In the two aspects of these men's jobs as fishermen, we see a symbolic picture of the two key ministries of pastor—preparing the church for works of service just as a fisherman prepares his net for the work of fishing—and evangelist—proclaiming the Gospel in the world in order to invite people into the new life of God's Kingdom, just as a fisherman throws out the net in order to catch many fish.

We will come in a later chapter to look in more detail at Jesus' training of his twelve apostles. But these four fishermen are not only the first of Jesus' future apostles; they are also amongst the first of that wider group of those who were his disciples. The word "disciples" is used only in the Gospels and Acts,[2] where it occurs 264 times as the most common word for the community of Jesus' followers. The word at its simplest means one who learns; the Greek word for "disciple," *mathētēs*, is derived from the verb *manthanō*, meaning "to learn"; it is used in a quite everyday sense in, for example, Acts 23:27, where the Roman commander writes to Governor Felix about Paul that "I had *learned* that he is a Roman citizen." It was the normal Jewish word for the pupil of a Rabbi. We might summarize what it means to be a disciple as follows.

1. A disciple is a follower. As we see in Matthew 4:19//Mark 1:17, Jesus, in his own ministry, always called on people to "Follow me." The very word "follow" implies an ongoing process; and it calls for obedience to Jesus, and a quality of consistency—people can't be real disciples in fits and starts. *Jesus is the Master whom we follow.*

2. A disciple is a learner; as we said, it is the standard term for the pupil of a Rabbi. To be Jesus' disciples means to be learning more and more of what it means to be one of Jesus' people, and how to live for him. This calls for submission, and a quality of teachability, which many adults, it should be said, do not have by nature; but we can pray to be given it by grace. *Jesus is the Teacher from whom we learn.*

3. A disciple is a trainee or apprentice. In the Jewish world of Jesus' day, a person was the disciple of a Rabbi in the hope that, one day, he might become a Rabbi himself. Being a disciple is the preparation for becoming a fully-qualified servant of God, able to do what Jesus and the apostles in the New Testament did, having come through a period (in the case of the twelve disciples of Jesus, a period of three years) of apprenticeship. *Jesus is the Model whom we imitate.*

Of course, there is more to discipleship than simply trying to copy what Jesus did; it is only as the Holy Spirit works to reproduce in us supernaturally the character-qualities of Jesus and the Kingdom ministry-gifts of Jesus that we can in any sense become like him. But there is nonetheless a

---

2. In the letters, by far the most common word for believers is "the saints," meaning those whom God has called and set apart for his own holy purposes. But there is no need to see a major distinction between "disciples" and "saints": they are both words for Christian believers. It might perhaps be said that the word "saints" emphasizes the fact of God's holy call on our lives, and "disciples" speaks more of our decision by faith to respond to that call; but those are simply the two sides of the coin of Christian life.

real call in the New Testament, as we rely solely on the Spirit to change us, to do what Jesus did. Paul tells the Corinthians, "Follow my example, as I follow the example of Christ" (1 Corinthians 11:1). Part of the call to faith is the call to become disciples of Jesus: to learn from him, follow him, and start to do the works of the Kingdom in the ways he did.

The call of these first disciples is followed by a series of miracle-stories: a man in the synagogue is set free from a demon (Mark 1:21-28//Luke 4:31-37); Peter's mother-in-law is healed of a fever (Matthew 8:14-15//Mark 1:29-31//Luke 4:38-39); and there is further general ministry to large numbers of people (Matthew 8:16-17//Mark 1:32-38//Luke 4:40-43). In these three paragraphs, we see a summary of the different spheres in which Jesus—and we—can do the works of God's Kingdom that can change people's lives: in church (the demonized man in the synagogue), in the home (Peter's mother-in-law), and in the community ("the whole town gathered . . . ," Mark 1:33): the Lordship and grace of Christ are not to be contained within the walls of the church.

The Kingdom

The heart of Jesus' ministry in Capernaum is the fact that he announces the coming of God's Kingdom. The Kingdom of God is the great theme of all Jesus' teaching. He begins his public preaching by announcing that "the Kingdom of God is near" (Mark 1:15). The theme of "the Kingdom of God" will dominate most of the ministry of Jesus, certainly its first half. So here is a simple overview of what the Bible means by "the Kingdom."

The fact of God's Kingdom

The first thing to say is the simplest and most essential: the Kingdom of God means *the fact that God is King*. God's Kingdom means his "Kingship," as affirmed in those psalms that start with the statement that "the Lord reigns!" (93:1, 97:1, 99:1). The Kingdom is not primarily a territory but a fact: God reigns as King.

It is however fatally easy to think of "King" as a kind of courtesy title that we conventionally use to refer to God. The Bible speaks of God's Kingship much more positively, in two ways in particular. There is first the fact of God's *actual government*. God, who created all things, maintains the whole created order in being from moment to moment; nothing exists or continues to exist independently of God's government. Hebrews 1:3 speaks of God, through his Son, the Lord Jesus, "sustaining all things by his powerful word"; and the verb translated "sustaining" is the Greek *phérō*, which means "carry" or "bear along"—it is often used in the New Testament to mean "to carry or convey something from one place to another for a specific purpose," such as when four men "carried" their paralyzed friend to Jesus on a stretcher, or when the servants at the wedding feast in Cana "brought" the water that Jesus had turned into wine to the steward for him to taste. So the thought is not that God simply "sustains" things in being, but that he is actively and purposefully carrying all created things along to their proper end, and the fulfillment of his own perfect will. Ephesians 1:11 speaks of how Christ saved us "according to the plan of him who works out everything in conformity with the purpose of his will." In the film *The King's Speech*, King George VI, brilliantly played by Colin Firth, talks of the frustration of being a constitutional monarch who has no actual executive power: "If I'm a king, where's my power? Can I form a government? Can I levy a tax? Declare a war? No!" By contrast, God is not a constitutional monarch; he is the "hands-on" governing King of creation.

Second, the fact that God is King speaks of his *awesome glory*, his majesty, his splendor and magnificence. "The Lord reigns, he is robed in majesty; the Lord is robed in majesty and is armed with strength . . ." (Psalm 93:1); "O Lord my God, you are very great; you are clothed with splendor and majesty. He wraps himself in light as with a garment; he stretches out the heavens like a tent . . ." (Psalm 104:1–2).

The rejection of God's Kingdom

However, all people have rebelled against God's Kingship. That is the essence of sin. All people have rejected God as King over them, and chosen to live their lives independently of God's reign; like the men in Jesus' parable (Luke 19:14), we have said, individually and collectively, "We don't want this [God] to be our King." We do not necessarily mind having God as God, so to speak; we are often quite content to believe in God. But what we object to is the idea that God should actually be the King who governs our lives.

As we said above, we are familiar in the UK with the principle of a constitutional monarchy. We have a monarch, who fulfills significant constitutional and ceremonial roles; the Queen is in many ways the figure-head of the nation. But she does not decide the country's policies. Decisions about how we are governed as a nation are made by Parliament, and specifically by the Prime Minister. And many people are only too happy to use the title "King" for God, so long as it is clearly understood that God is King for the formal religious ceremonies; as far as the day-to-day government of my life is concerned, God is a constitutional monarch. I have no objection to joining in singing "Rejoice, the Lord is King!"; but when it comes to who makes decisions about where my life is going, *I* am Prime Minister. I decide the policy; I set the agenda.

That is precisely what the Bible calls sin. And as a result of our rejection of God as King, we do not experience the blessings of God's reign.

The promise of God's Kingdom

There are promises and prophecies throughout the Old Testament of a future time when *God will re-establish his reign on earth*. God will send a special King who will bring the reign of God back into human history. Then there will once again be an age of justice, peace, joy, and, as the fountain from which all these other blessings of God's reign flow, the knowledge of God.[3]

The arrival of God's Kingdom

The Gospels affirm that *Jesus is that King*. He has come to re-establish God's reign on earth. When he reads in the synagogue at Nazareth from one typical prophecy of the coming King, Jesus adds the momentous comment, "Today this Scripture is fulfilled in your hearing" (Luke 4:21); in other words, "I am the one this prophecy and all the others like it are speaking of."

The signs of God's Kingdom

The works of Jesus are signs that the Kingdom has come. Jesus' miracles are signposts directing people to God's Kingdom which is now among them; as he says in Luke 11:20, "If I drive out demons by the finger of God, then the kingdom of God has come to you." John, in his Gospel, always calls the miracles "signs"—they are pointers to the fact that God's reign is impacting the human world. They are signs that God reigns as King and of what life under God's kingly rule is like. When John the Baptist sent messengers from prison to ask Jesus "Are you the one who was to come, or should we expect someone else?," Jesus replied, "Go back and report to John what you hear and see: The blind receive sight, the lame walk, those who have leprosy are cured, the deaf hear, the dead are raised, and the good news is preached to the poor" (Matthew 11:2-5). Those things are the signs that the Kingdom

---

3. Typical such prophecies include Isaiah 9:6-7, 11:1-9, 35:1-10, 40:4-5, 51:3,11, 55:12-13, 60:18-22, Jeremiah 23:5-6, 33:15-16, Amos 9:11-15, Micah 4:1-5, 5:2-5.

truly has come in Jesus; that the benefits and blessings that come when God reigns as King are starting to be experienced in a new way by people in this world.

The increase of God's Kingdom

Jesus' parables explain that the Kingdom is growing. Many of the parables begin "the Kingdom of God is like . . ." Just as the works (miracles) are *signs* of the Kingdom, so the parables are *illustrations* of the Kingdom. And the parables explain one thing that is different from what the Jews in Jesus' day were expecting. They expected the Kingdom to arrive all at once, "with a bang," and the whole world to be changed, more or less literally, overnight. Jesus' parables of the sower sowing the seed (Matthew 13:3–9//Mark 4:3–9), the growing seed (Mark 4:26–29), and many other parables of growth explain that the Kingdom comes in ways that are more subtle than that. It comes, in fact, in three stages. First, there is a stage of *sowing*. Jesus sows the seed of the Kingdom into this present world. Second, there is a stage of *growing*: the Kingdom grows and develops—we are still in that second stage of growth, as the Kingdom is spreading more and more over the world, sometimes, it is true, in remarkable "growth spurts," but often gradually and sometimes barely perceptibly. And third, there is the stage of *reaping*. At the end of history, Jesus will return, and his angels will gather his redeemed people into his heavenly Kingdom (Mark 4:26–29). Then the Kingdom will come fully and finally.

Submission to God's Kingdom

To become a Christian means to acknowledge God as King. It means to agree to live under his kingly rule, and to accept the quality of life that belongs to his Kingdom. For the overwhelming majority of people, to become a Christian does *not* mean to move from not believing in God to believing in him; it means to move from believing in God to submitting their lives to God as King: that is what "repent" means. Jesus says "repent, for the kingdom of heaven is near" (Matthew 4:17); in other words, God's reign is at hand, so people need to make a personal conscious choice to turn to it and to live under it. To repent means to stop living our lives independently of God's reign, and to submit instead to God as King. It should be a contradiction in terms to want to have Jesus as our Savior without as a result having God as our King. Becoming a Christian is not simply about changing our beliefs or our lifestyle: it means choosing to come under a different spiritual jurisdiction, and starting to live as a citizen of God's Kingdom.

The salvation of God's Kingdom

When people become Christians, they are transferred from the dominion of sin and death to the kingdom of Christ. Colossians 1:13 says that "[God] has rescued us from the dominion of darkness and brought us into the kingdom of the Son he loves." This present world is under the dominion of the devil, whom Jesus calls "the prince of this world" (John 12:31). When we become Christians, we are spiritually translated from one sphere of reality to another. We no longer belong to the present order of the world—we belong to God's Kingdom. This is the theological principle that lies behind the fact that Christian lifestyle is far more radical than is conventionally assumed. Christians are not people who live as part of the same world as everyone else, but just have (or are supposed to have) different beliefs and better morals than others; rather, they belong to a different sphere of reality. The ordinary life of the fallen world and the new life of God's Kingdom co-exist in the same space, but they are totally different realms; and when someone becomes a Christian, he or she becomes part of that new Kingdom; as Paul says, "our citizenship is in heaven" (Philippians 3:20). Like a plant unearthed from one patch of soil and re-rooted in another place, we have been transferred from the sinful soil of this present world-order, and replanted in the spiritually healthy soil of God's Kingdom. It is from Christ that we now derive all our life, not from this world. British subjects living in another country are of course bound to respect the culture and obey the laws of the country in which they live, but they are not subjects or citizens of it; in the same way Christians are bound to do all they can to play a positive and constructive role in the human society in which we live, but we are not part of it: we are "ex-pats of heaven."

The experience of God's Kingdom

The Holy Spirit gives us a foretaste of the future Kingdom. Jesus has planted the life of the Kingdom in this world. But the Kingdom has not yet come in all its fullness. That is still in the future. However the Holy Spirit gives us now a foretaste of the life of God's heaven. On three occasions Paul uses a word for the Holy Spirit which means "deposit," "down payment," or "first instalment" (2 Corinthians 1:22, 5:5, Ephesians 1:14). Through the Spirit, we can taste *now* a measure of the holiness, joy and peace of heaven. But it is not just this much holiness, joy and peace now—it also carries with it the guarantee that we shall know perfect and unlimited holiness, joy and peace in the future.

The mission of God's Kingdom

The church is to bring more of God's Kingdom to more of this world. The church and the Kingdom are not the same thing. The Kingdom is the reign of God and the quality of life that we can start to know when we live under his reign. The church is the fellowship of people who are the citizens of the Kingdom.

The church, certainly in its institutional form, is not simply the same thing as the Kingdom; but there is obviously a connection between the two. The simplest and most helpful definition of the relationship between the church and the Kingdom that I have ever heard was given by Lesslie Newbigin in a talk at a pastors' conference in 1989: "the church is sent into the world as sign, instrument and foretaste of the Kingdom." The church is, first, a *sign* of the Kingdom. It points people to the Kingdom, to the fact that God is King, and that there is a different quality of life that can be lived under his reign. Second, the church is an *instrument* of the Kingdom. Through our work and witness, we can by the grace of God bring more of the justice, the healing, the peace, the joy of God's Kingdom to people now. And third, the church is a *foretaste* of the Kingdom. The Christian church is not (or should not be) merely a place where we talk about the Kingdom, or campaign for the Kingdom, or look forward to the Kingdom; rather, in the fellowship of God's believing people, we can know and share with others *now* a foretaste of the holiness, joy and peace of heaven, which one day we will know in its fullness and perfection.

The fulfillment of God's Kingdom

Finally, Jesus is coming again to consummate the Kingdom. When Jesus returns, we will see the eternal perfection and complete fulfillment of the Kingdom. That which we can now know in part, we will then see face to face; that which we taste now in part will then be a glorious banquet spread before us.

That is the biblical understanding of God's Kingdom, which provides the background to Jesus' announcement in Capernaum that "the Kingdom of God is near." The word translated "is near" is literally the verb "has drawn near"; the same word is used, for example, in Luke 18:40, which tells how, as Jesus was passing by, a blind beggar started calling out to him for mercy. "Jesus stopped and ordered the man to be brought to him. When he *came near*, Jesus asked him . . ." The blind man was no longer shouting to Jesus from a distance, but had come close enough to be able to talk with him and interact with him. That is the sense in which Jesus says that the Kingdom has now "drawn near": it is no longer something that exists in some other "spiritual dimension"—up in heaven, separately from this world of human history and human life—or that will come at some unknown time in the future. It is right here, right now; it is confronting people. The Kingdom is here, among us, because the King is here, among us.[4]

Proclaiming the Kingdom today

At least some of that understanding of God's Kingdom would have been familiar to Jesus' first hearers in Capernaum, though many aspects of it would need to be clarified and filled out during his ministry. But when Jesus says "The Kingdom of God is at hand," it is reasonable to suppose that he expected those who heard him to have at least some idea of what he was talking about. Clearly, the same is not true in our own western culture. The term "the Kingdom of God" will either be completely unknown to most people, or will connote all sorts of misleading and unhelpful ideas, such as the crusades. Worse still, the phrase "until kingdom come" is used in a quite secular and negative way to refer to death or the end of the world, usually with the implication that until then things will remain unchanged here and now.

In the light of that, what does it mean for us today to preach the Kingdom? It will not do simply to stand on a street corner and declare "the Kingdom of God is at hand!"; what we preach needs to be meaningful and helpful as well as true. On the other hand, the church has paid a heavy price

---

4. That is the meaning of Jesus' words in Luke 17:21, which are often translated as "the Kingdom of God is *within* you." The Greek word *entós* can indeed mean "in," "within," or "on the inside"; but when followed by a word in the plural (as it is here—the "you" is plural) it often means "amongst" or "in the midst of." That is far more in keeping with the New Testament understanding of the Kingdom. Nowhere is the Kingdom thought of as being an internal part of people's lives. Moreover, the people to whom Jesus addresses this phrase are not his disciples, but Pharisees (verse 20), so he is hardly likely to be saying that they have the life of God's Kingdom inside them—he is much more likely to be challenging them that the Kingdom has come *among* them, and so they need urgently to make up their minds how they are going to respond to the King. In other words, Jesus is saying what he had said in Capernaum: that the Kingdom of God is present amongst people in this world, because the King is now living amongst people in this world.

for engaging in forms of evangelism that ignore the essential message of the Kingdom; the result can often be that people will respond (quite genuinely) to Jesus as the one who will forgive them and become their friend, but with no idea at all, because no one has ever told them, that coming to Christ will transform their lives into the character and enlist their lives in the service of God's Kingdom.

Clearly, the importance of teaching Kingdom truth and Kingdom principles to Christians cannot be overstated; and, as we said in the first chapter, Matthew in particular is a great resource here. In terms of evangelism, and the essence of the message that we present to the world, whilst we may not always use the straightforward Kingdom language that Jesus could use in Capernaum, there are a number of themes, touched on above, that need to be more central to how we call people to Christian faith.

Submission to the Kingdom

It is important that we remember that the invitation to become Christians has at its heart the urgent call to submit to God as the King who has authority over our lives. Too often God can be the means to an end; if the social services, or my doctor, or my family, or my local MP cannot give me the kind of help in life that I want, then maybe God can. And of course, he can. But to come to God in the hope that he will be able to do for me what others cannot, that he will solve my problems on my terms, that he will give me the kind of life that *I* want, is poles apart from Christian conversion. Kingdom life has to mean that we want God for God's sake. To repent does not mean to improve my life, or to hope that God will improve it for me; it means to renounce a life that is lived on *my* terms, even if those terms include a lot that is positive and wholesome, and accept a new life which will be lived on *God's* terms.

Service for the Kingdom

In calling people to conversion, we are calling them, not only to (in the favorite evangelical phrase) "a personal relationship with God," but also to a life lived in the service of God. Jesus did not call his first disciples in Capernaum by saying simply "Come follow me"; he said "Come, follow me, *and I will make you fishers of men*" (Matthew 4:19//Mark 1:17). He called them to give their lives in the service of God's Kingdom; he gave them work to do.[5]

---

5. There may be a point here that is often missed. It has frequently been said that,

To call people to the experience of personal salvation, without at the same time telling them that this goes hand in hand with giving our lives to God in his service, is at best an over-simplified Gospel, and at worst dishonest, like the salesman who hopes his client will not read what is in the small print until the deal has been finalized. But living to serve God's Kingdom is not the "small print" of salvation: it is what salvation *is*.

Signs of the Kingdom

We need to rediscover the vital place of the signs of the Kingdom in the church's life and mission. Sadly, it can so often seem that the whole church is divided into one of two forms of error: on the one hand those who do not believe in or expect to see signs and wonders these days; and on the other the extremists who seem to believe that anyone who does not see six miracles a day before breakfast, or who ever has a problem that is not instantly healed, does not have "real" faith. Whilst rejecting such nonsense, we can nonetheless believe, as I do, that the signs of the Kingdom should be as normal in the ministry of the church as the preaching of the Kingdom. We urgently need to become a church that lives the quality of life of the Kingdom, so that the works of the Kingdom can be done among us. And that has to be the key. We will never see the signs of God's Kingdom by reading more books and attending more seminars on "how to do signs and wonders." God will do Jesus' works through those who are living Jesus' way, who are learning to be holy, to grow as disciples, to be obedient to his Word.

And yet the signs are vital. People are more likely to listen to the message of God's Kingdom when they see the signs of the Kingdom; certainly, that was the norm in both the Gospels and the book of Acts. The people of modern Britain are not waiting to hear the Gospel; they are waiting to see it.

Seeking the Kingdom

Very importantly, we need to reinstate the future dimension of the Kingdom as an essential element in our proclamation of the Gospel. Jesus is coming

---

by and large, women find their fulfillment primarily in relationships, whereas men find their fulfillment primarily in work; this is of course a generalization, but there is perhaps a measure of truth in it. Is the fact that there are far more women than men in the western church, and the fact that women constitute a higher percentage of converts than men, in any way connected to the fact that the classic way in which western churches have preached the Gospel is as a call to a relationship with Jesus? Does that kind of language perhaps appeal more to the female psyche than to the male? When Jesus called men, he called them to a challenging task for the Kingdom.

again, and when he comes, he will consummate his Kingdom. Preaching the second coming of Jesus has dropped out of fashion,[6] and many people are afraid, I suspect, that if they even hint at it, people will laugh at them. I cannot help remembering that they laughed at Jesus; indeed they did a lot worse than merely laugh. The fact is, Jesus *is* coming again; and our task as witnesses for the Lord is to tell people that there is a future that they can inherit which goes beyond anything this world can offer. When Jesus read from the scroll of the prophet Isaiah, in the synagogue in Nazareth, he read from the beginning of chapter 61: "The Spirit of the Lord is on me, because he has anointed me to preach good news to the poor." But of course those words follow immediately from the last words in chapter 60: "The sun will no more be your light by day, nor will the brightness of the moon shine on you, for the Lord will be your everlasting light, and your God will be your glory. Your sun will never set again, and your moon will wane no more; the Lord will be your everlasting light, and your days of sorrow will end." Those words are taken up at the end of the book of Revelation; they are a description of heaven. That is the "good news" that was to be preached to the poor; there is a future glorious Kingdom, and, because of Jesus, you are invited to be part of it. Many people will dismiss teaching about heaven as "pie in the sky"; but there are a lot of hungry people in our world, for whom a slice of heavenly pie is just what they need. Who gave us the right to withhold from them the fact that it is real, and that Jesus freely offers it to them?

---

6. As a student, I once preached in a church on the coming again of the Lord; an elderly lady came up to me after the meeting, and, as well as thanking me for the word, said that she had been attending (evangelical) churches for about forty years, and that it was only the second time she had heard a sermon on the second coming. Heaven help us.

6

Teaching the Kingdom

"The crowds were amazed at his teaching, because he taught as one who had authority" (Matthew 7:28–29)

Having publicly announced that the Kingdom of God is at hand, Jesus embarks on his Galilean ministry proper. He begins by teaching about the Kingdom in words, and demonstrating the Kingdom in works. There is a general summary statement, that Jesus moved around Galilee teaching and healing (Matthew 4:23–25//Mark 1:39//Luke 4:44), followed by more details about Jesus' preaching and his miracles. This gives rise to a number of controversial discussions with the Pharisees, who become increasingly hostile to Jesus. And he selects, trains, and commissions his twelve disciples to work with him, so that, after his ascension, they can continue to work for him. But we come first to Jesus' teaching ministry around Galilee.

Clearly the content of Jesus' teaching about the Kingdom of God is of the utmost importance, and it is on that that this chapter will primarily focus. But it is worth mentioning what it was that first struck his immediate hearers as most distinctive about Jesus' teaching, namely his *authority*. "The crowds were amazed at his teaching, because he taught as one who had authority, and not as their teachers of the law" (Matthew 7:28–29). What made the greatest impression was not primarily *what* Jesus taught, but *how* he taught. Jewish teachers of the law (traditionally: "scribes") normally taught by referring to previous writers and commentators; they did not speak for themselves, but cited earlier authorities to back up their words ("As Rabbi so-and-so said . . ."). Jesus was not like that; when he taught, he spoke as one who needed no authority to validate his words other than the fact that he himself was speaking them. Even the Old Testament prophets did not talk like that: the classic introduction to a prophetic message was, "Thus says the Lord" (usually translated in the NIV as "This is what the Lord says . . ."); prophets spoke as messengers from God and in the name of God. Jesus spoke with the authoritative voice of God himself. This distinction between the style of the Jewish scribes' teaching and that of Jesus is seen most starkly in the famous "six antitheses" in the Sermon on the Mount, to which we will come shortly: six times Jesus says, "You have heard that it was said by the people long ago . . . But *I* tell you . . ." (Matthew 5:21–22; also in 27–28, 31–32, 33–34, 38–39, 43–44). "It was said by the people long ago . . ." is almost certainly a reference to the tradition of teaching by Rabbis and scribes over the years; it is true that Jesus' words could be equally well translated as "It was said *by* the people of long ago" or "It was said *to* the people of long ago," and in fact the NIV reads "to the people." If "to the people" is the correct sense, it probably refers to how God gave his law through Moses to the Israelites at Mount Sinai; if we understand it as "by the people," it is reflecting the way in which past generations of Rabbis expounded the law. My main reasons for preferring the sense "by the people" are that, first, Jesus has just said (verse 17) that he has not come to abolish the law but to fulfill it: but if in the six antitheses he is opposing his own authoritative teaching to the law as originally given to the people, he would indeed appear to be abolishing the latter; and second, Jesus seems in most of the six antitheses to be opposing, not the laws in themselves, but various rabbinical ideas about their application which, Jesus says, have distorted their true meaning. In saying "But I say to you . . . ," he is not speaking as a typical Rabbi, who might offer an interpretation of a particular Old Testament text which differed from that of other Rabbis, and would make his case by citing authorities who agreed with his own view, but rather he is speaking with the authoritative voice of the God who gave the original laws in the first place, and establishing what they really mean.

In contrast to that teaching which relies on the authority of tradition, Jesus speaks in his own voice: "*I* say to you." In chapter 1 we discussed the (alleged) radical difference between the Jesus of John's Gospel and the Jesus we find in the synoptics. In John, Jesus teaches primarily about himself as the one who has come down from heaven and brings the spiritual life of heaven. Much of the content of his teaching in the synoptics is different; but we see in the *way* Jesus taught the same awareness that he is the one who alone can speak in his own right as the one to whom the Father has given "all authority in heaven and on earth" (Matthew 28:18). And that surely has to have profound implications for how, as Jesus' disciples, we are to respond to his teaching. If Jesus indeed speaks with the authority of God himself, it is not our place to decide whether or not we agree with him; Jesus does not propose ideas for debate and discussion: he says "I say to you . . . ," and calls on all who would be his people to follow in faith and obedience.

The Sermon on the Mount

The Galilean phase of Jesus' ministry begins with the "Sermon on the Mount" (Matthew 5–7);[1] it has at its heart the "Sermon on the Plain" (Luke 6:17-49); and it ends with the parables teaching about the coming and growth of the Kingdom (Matthew 13:1-52//Mark 4:1-34//Luke 8:4-15, 13:18-21).

The Sermon on the Mount is Jesus' teaching about what it means to live as his disciples. It is not to be seen as simply a set of rules or laws to be obeyed. And it is certainly not a description of what we have to do to become acceptable and pleasing to God. God saves us by his free grace, through faith in Jesus. This sermon is a description of the life of the Kingdom of God, the kind of life into which God wants to lead us; it is not about "how to get saved," but what it means to live as people whom God *has* saved. It is a manual of Christian discipleship.

What I offer here is not a detailed exposition of the text of the Sermon; I want rather to give a general outline of its main sections and, in particular, to highlight the central theme or thread that runs through the whole Sermon, which is that the values of the Kingdom of God are the opposite of those normally held in the secular world. The Sermon on the Mount does not affirm what is best in the world's values; rather, it turns them on their head—if anything, this Sermon is even more of a challenge to respectable and decent people than it is to the manifestly wayward and morally corrupt. The disciple, as Paul was later to say (Romans 12:2), is not to conform to the lifestyle of the society around him, but is rather to be transformed, to live by Kingdom principles that are completely different from and often the reverse of the norms of the unbelieving world.

---

1. I will treat the Sermon as a single address. Most commentators assume that the Sermon is a compilation of different bits of Jesus' teaching given at various times, which Matthew has brought together and presented as one sermon. That is quite possible—Matthew, perhaps more than any of the other Gospel writers, seems to have arranged his work thematically rather than chronologically—and it does not greatly matter so far as understanding the content of the Gospel is concerned. But the text of the Sermon as we have it in Matthew 5–7 is presented as one extended discourse; so that is how we will handle it.

The disciple's character

The Sermon starts with a description of the character-qualities of Jesus, which his Spirit wants to grow in us (5:3–12). They are the opposite of what the world regards as normal or desirable. But they are the qualities which bring us God's blessing; or, more correctly, they are the qualities that God will grow in the lives of those who have made the choice to live their lives under his reign and his blessing. The very first of the "beatitudes"[2] sets the tone: our world would regard one of the keys to success as being self-sufficient, able to stand on your own two feet and make your own way in life; Jesus says that, on the contrary, true blessing from God depends on our being "poor in spirit," that is, recognizing how spiritually needy we are, and depending on God for everything. To be happy and successful on this world's terms is not the same as, and can be the opposite of, being blessed on Kingdom terms. The word translated "blessed" (Greek: *makários*) means quite simply "happy," "in the best or most fortunate circumstances": Jesus is saying that the key to true happiness is not to seek for what would normally be understood to be the pre-conditions for happiness on this world's terms. So when some versions of the Bible translate *makários* as "happy"—e.g. the *Good News Bible*, "Happy are those who . . ."—they are not in fact watering down the more "religious-sounding" word "blessed," but are saying exactly what Matthew wrote.

The disciple's influence

Our character—what we are in ourselves—will necessarily determine what kind of effect we have on those around us; and so Jesus turns next to the fact that his disciples are called to be a good influence in the world, like salt and light (5:13–16). In Jesus' day, and for many centuries after it, salt was used primarily as a preservative; it prevented meat from going off too quickly. Christians, by their presence in the world, can preserve a better and cleaner quality of life.[3] Light speaks of truth and goodness shining in the midst of error and evil. Again, the key to having a positive influence in the world is

---

2. This is the conventional word for Jesus' "Blessed are . . ." statements; the term comes from the Latin for "blessed."

3. That leads to a disturbing thought. Christians will often be the first to bemoan the decline in standards in our society, to lament that the country is morally and spiritually going to the dogs; if that is true, and if Jesus says that it is Christians who are to be the moral and spiritual preservatives in society, who is to blame?—the country or the church? But the fact that it is a disturbing thought does not mean that we should not think it.

that, in their nature and character, Christians are different from the world; the more indistinguishable we are from the secular world around us, the less we will be effective as salt and light. We are called, not to reflect the best aspects of the world—to improve morally according to the world's scale of values—but to shine the light of God's Kingdom in the midst of the darkness of this world. And we must never forget the lesson contained in the fact that Jesus' "salt and light" sayings follow immediately after his description of Christian character in the beatitudes: it is only as we allow the Holy Spirit to reproduce in us more of Jesus' character (verses 3–12) that we will be effective as salt and light in the world.

The disciple's righteousness

The rest of chapter 5 is about the disciple's righteousness (5:17–48); and this, Jesus stresses, has to be very different from merely obeying rules. In his list of six contrasts with traditional Jewish teaching ("You have heard that it was said . . . But I tell you . . .") Jesus is not setting the Old Testament law aside, but is rather expounding its true meaning, as opposed to the sometimes limited or distorted view of the law in the Jewish scribal tradition. He says that he has come to fulfill it in a deeper way (verse 17). He is not contradicting the laws of the Old Testament; in the case of the first two subjects, he is reaffirming the law, but then taking it further, and applying it not only to outward acts but to inward motivations. So the law against *murder* still applies, but not only to the outward physical act, but also to the attitude of hatred in the heart (5:21–22); the law against *adultery* still applies, but not just to the physical act, but also to the wrong and lustful desire of the heart (5:27–28). Our world believes that moral rules apply only to what we actually do to other people; Jesus says that in God's Kingdom what matters is not just the goodness of our actions but the purity of our hearts.

In the next four cases he is saying that the way in which some Jewish teachers had applied the law was wrong, and he is correcting their misunderstandings. The *divorce* law (5:31–32) was given as a concession to human need, not as permission to regard divorce as normal and marriage as non-binding, as some had assumed. Jesus' prohibition of *oaths* (5:33–37) is not saying that oaths in themselves are wrong—after all, God himself is said in Hebrews 6:13–17 to have confirmed his promise to Abraham with an oath—but rather is a rejection of the kind of hypocrisy which was quite widespread amongst the Jews of his day, to the effect that a promise made with an oath in God's name had to be kept, but if someone made a simple promise (without an oath), he was not bound by his word. The citizens of

God's Kingdom, Jesus insists, should always say what they mean and mean what they say; they don't have to shore up every promise with an oath in order to be assumed to be telling the truth.[4] Jesus' words in 5:38–42 about *non-retaliation* have given rise to the frequent accusation that there is a contradiction between the Old Testament and the New; the Old says "an eye for an eye," and here in the New Jesus says we should forgive people and "turn the other cheek." But there is no contradiction. The Old Testament "eye for eye" saying established the legal principle that the severity of the penalty imposed by a magistrate for a crime should be proportionate to the seriousness of the offense committed: the punishment must fit the crime. The law was given precisely to discourage private vengeance; the wronged person should allow the court to settle the matter objectively. But some amongst the Pharisees had taken the "eye for eye" principle to be giving people permission to retaliate, to give like for like ("he hit me, so I can hit him!"), in other words to be condoning the very thing that the original law had intended to prohibit. In God's Kingdom, we do not take private vengeance. If someone has actually committed a crime against us, it may well be right and necessary for them to go to court and be tried for it. But our personal attitude must always be one of forgiveness. And finally, the command *"love your neighbor"*—which, to a Jew, meant "fellow-Jew"—did *not* mean "hate your enemy," i.e., the Gentiles (5:43–44): Jesus' followers are to love their enemies too (5:43–48). Christian ethics are to go way beyond what the world would regard as normal standards of good behavior. To love one's friends and not love one's enemies would, as Jesus points out (verses 46–47), be regarded in the world as normal: but the citizens of God's Kingdom are not to take as their standard the world's norm, or even the world's best, but rather God's perfection.

The disciple's devotion

Chapter 6 brings us to the disciple's devotion (6:1–18). Jesus speaks of giving to the needy, prayer, and fasting. The point he stresses in all three is: do it for God only, not in order to be seen and admired by people—to "look righteous." He addresses the confusion, which has so frequently been found

---

4. Some Christians who have been required to give evidence in court have had qualms about swearing the formal oath, on the grounds that Jesus here says that his people should not swear. In my judgment Jesus' words in the Sermon on the Mount are nothing to do with court oaths, which are a formal legal commitment to tell the truth when giving evidence. Christians who appear as witnesses in court can quite properly swear the oath: Jesus' point is that everything else that they say when they are not "on oath" should be just as true and trustworthy.

in our own culture, with its church-going and "Sunday best" traditions, between being devoted and looking respectable. And there is a new form of "looking righteous" which can be found in our more charismatic churches, namely the encouragement of outward physical expressions of worship (dance, raising hands, clapping) and prayer (intense and impassioned tones of voice, arms earnestly raised to heaven). Some may say that these outward signs of prayer and praise can be an expression of the genuine devotion of the heart. Of course they can, and when they are, they are entirely right and pleasing to God. But Jesus' words about praying in our own room with the door closed[5] give us the criterion by which to assess our own motivation: do we pray in the same way and with the same passion when we are on our own with the Lord, or only when there are other people around to see? If the latter, Jesus' words should prompt us to ask some serious questions about those outward expressions of devotion. What are they actually expressing?—our desire to worship God with all our hearts, or our hope that other people around us will be impressed by how super-spiritual we are?

In this section of the Sermon, Jesus mentions "rewards" many times (verses 1,2,4,5,6,16,18). Those who parade their piety in order to be seen and admired by other people have already "received their reward in full": what they wanted was to be admired by men, and they have been admired by men—they have achieved their goal, and they can expect no further reward from God. But the true disciples of God's Kingdom, those who seek only to worship and please the Father, will be rewarded by God. It hardly needs to be said—but I will say it anyway—that when Jesus speaks of "rewards" he does not mean the word in a materialistic sense: prayer is never to be understood as a means of acquiring "things" for ourselves. As C. S. Lewis put it in *The Problem of Pain*, "heaven offers nothing that a mercenary soul can desire."[6] The rewards of true devotion are spiritual: a closer walk with God, a deeper experience of God's peace and joy, a renewed filling with the Spirit by whom we cry, "*Abba*', Father." "The rewards of prayer" does not simply mean that we will always get what we ask for; but if the heart of all our devotion is "your Kingdom come," then our true reward is to see more

---

5. These words of Jesus about going into your own room and praying in secret to your Father are not saying that corporate prayer is wrong. In the Bible prayer was frequently, even usually, prayer *together*. Jesus is opposing, not the practice of praying together with others, but the attitude that sees praying in front of others as an opportunity to parade one's own greater spirituality. In the New Testament church Christians regularly prayed together: e.g. Acts 1:14, 1:24, 4:24. The best and most effective prayer in our church today would be that which combines the attitude commended in Matthew 6 with the practice recorded in Acts.

6. Lewis, *Problem of Pain*, 133.

of God's Kingdom coming, whether or not it comes in precisely the ways for which we had prayed.

The disciple's priorities

The rest of chapter 6 is all about the disciple's priorities (6:19–34). We need to focus on the things of God's Kingdom, not the things of this world, because God will always ensure that we have the essentials we need. Again, we see how different the life of Jesus' Kingdom is to the life of the world: the normal assumption in our society is that providing for our practical and financial security is and should be the first priority; Jesus says, if we live a life of righteousness, and give ourselves to the service of God's Kingdom, God will take care of our practical needs.

There are some who would insist that this teaching of Jesus precludes Christians from having anything to do with those things that provide any form of financial security, such as pension plans, insurance policies, even bank accounts. And it is all too easy to dismiss such social non-conformity by saying, "Of course, Jesus didn't mean we shouldn't take care to provide for our futures," thereby neatly side-stepping the uncomfortable fact that Jesus really *is* calling us to a lifestyle that is the opposite of our materialistic and market-driven world. But the thread that runs through this section of the sermon is that of "worry"; Jesus does not say that we should not *work* for a living—indeed, the New Testament insists that we should (2 Thessalonians 3:6–12)—but that we should not *worry* about whether we will be able to get by. If we give ourselves to the service of God's Kingdom, we need never be concerned that we will lack what Baloo called the "bare necessities of life"; we may not be financially prosperous, but when a need arises, God will ensure that it is met. But that is never to be taken as an excuse for laziness or irresponsibility; the promise is made to those who are prepared to work harder at serving the Kingdom than the secular world ever works at providing financial security. That is the paradox of the famous and much-quoted verse 33, about seeking first the Kingdom of God in the confidence that all the other necessities of life will be provided: it is as we stop seeking the things of this world that God will ensure that we have as many of the things of this world as we need.

The disciple's relationships

Chapter 7 starts by speaking of the disciple's attitude towards his fellow-disciples: do not judge one another (7:1–6). In the fellowship of the church, we must never be quick to point out others' failings, but rather take responsibility for correcting our own. Unlike the secular world, the church should be noted for its absence of rivalry and competitiveness.

Having said that, some discrimination is also needed: verse 6, the strange saying about throwing pearls to pigs, warns us to be wise about how we handle important spiritual truth. We are not to treat holy truth and holy things ("what is sacred") lightly. There are some people who show themselves to be consistently dismissive of spiritual truth and Kingdom principles; and whilst we are right to give some time to seeking to urge them to come to Christ and to embrace Christian discipleship, the point can be reached when wisdom suggests that we are, humanly speaking, wasting our time. Jesus was later to say the same thing when he told his apostles, when they went out preaching, that if a town did not receive them, they were to shake the dust off their feet as they left. So verses 1–5 cannot be taken to mean that there is no place, where necessary, for appropriate pastoral discipline in the church; but Jesus does very strongly rebuke superior or critical personal attitudes to our fellow-Christians.

The disciple's faith

From our relationships with each other, Jesus now turns to our relationship with God, and to the disciple's faith; and specifically, faith in the sense of confidence that God will give us the right things that we need (7:7–12). The invitation to "ask . . . seek . . . knock" is *not* saying that God will give us anything we happen to fancy and pray for; God is not a vending machine. The invitation to ask for things has to be seen in the context of the principle in 6:33, that we seek first the Kingdom of God and his righteousness. It is as we make that our priority that God promises that he will supply all we need to live effectively for him, and to be able to bring more of his Kingdom to more of this world. In a similar way, the promise "knock and the door will be opened" recalls ways in which the New Testament uses the image of a door to speak of missionary opportunities ("a great door for effective work has opened to me," 1 Corinthians 16:9) or spiritual potential ("I have placed before you an open door that no one can shut," Revelation 3:8).

Given that proviso, that Jesus' invitation to "ask . . . seek . . . knock" is not offering an easy solution to all life's problems, but is a promise to those who are steadfastly seeking and committedly serving his Kingdom, his words nonetheless stress that his disciples do not need to perform lots of religious duties in order to secure blessings from God. The more ritualistic branches of the historical church have sometimes used elaborate systems of ceremonial and sacramental hoops through which those hoping to receive anything from God have to jump: this number of penitential prayers, that number of "Hail Marys," so many masses, fasts or pilgrimages. Nor is the contemporary evangelical-charismatic church always free from similar legalism: I have known Christians who have been given lists of Scripture verses that they were told to learn by heart and repeat daily, so that they might be sure of God's blessing. All such mechanical religion has far more in common with the Pharisees, who, as Jesus says, would "tie up heavy loads and put them on men's shoulders" (Matthew 23:4) than it has with Jesus' Kingdom, in which God gives good gifts "to those who ask him" (7:11). Here is another contrast with the norms of the secular world: God's blessings are freely given, they are not earned. Our world would say, in a sense rightly, that we need to work hard to provide for ourselves; Jesus says we need to avoid carrying that mind-set over into how we understand spiritual life. In God's Kingdom the only basis for life and growth is not "work, and you will earn," but "ask, and you will receive."

The disciple's challenges

The sermon ends with three warnings about things that can either mislead us or make us ineffective in our discipleship (7:13–27), against which we are urged to be on our guard. One is *following the crowd* (verses 13–14)—doing what most people do. Belonging to Christ will always make us a minority that will stand out, not only from those who are obviously wicked, but also from the "moral majority."[7] Another is *being misled by persuasive people* (verses 15–20). False prophets can seem very attractive, and can pull a crowd. But if they are not preaching Jesus, and following him themselves, avoid them! The third is *agreeing with Jesus in theory, but not following him in practice* (verses 21–27). Saying we are believers—or using lots of impressively devotional language ("Lord! Lord!")—is meaningless if we don't do what Jesus says.

The famous parable about the men who built their houses on the sand and the rock, which concludes the sermon, is often misrepresented as though it were an evangelistic appeal to unbelievers. Many a preacher has exhorted people along the following lines: if you build your life on anything

---

7. Verse 14—"only a few find [the road that leads to life]"—must not be taken to mean that not many people will be saved, or that only a tiny minority will be in heaven. It is not thinking in terms of eternal life in heaven; and it is certainly not giving us a mathematical hint as to the proportion of the human race that will be there. It is saying that, within this life, following Jesus will always make us stand out from the norms of the world's culture, which many follow unthinkingly.

else—on wealth, on achievement, on popularity—your life will come crashing down around you; but if you build your life on Jesus as your Savior, you will stand.

This is all true, and it a good challenge to present before people. But it has little, if anything, to do with what Jesus means in the story of the two house-builders. To begin with, this whole sermon is addressed to those who, as 5:1–2 tell us, are already his disciples. And the "moral of the story," as illustrated by the difference between the two builders, is not that one was a believer and the other was not; it is that one heard the words of Jesus, whereas the other heard his words and then obeyed them. Jesus is not comparing Christians with non-Christians; he is comparing obedient Christians with disobedient (or semi-obedient) ones. The storms of life and of discipleship will surely come, just as the winds battered against both houses; the one who will come through those storms with his faith intact, just as the wise man came through the storms with his house intact, is the believer who is practicing what Jesus preaches, who is living in a way that is different from the norms of even the best in the world, rather than thinking that faith simply means adding religious belief to the world's idea of moral goodness.

The Sermon on the Plain

At the heart of Jesus' Galilean teaching is the Sermon on the Plain (Luke 6:17–49). There are obvious similarities in content between this Sermon on the Plain and the more famous Sermon on the Mount. But they appear to be two separate occasions. First, Matthew clearly tells us that the Sermon on the Mount was preached after Jesus went up a mountain (Matthew 5:1); Luke tells us that the Sermon on the Plain was preached after Jesus came down from a mountain, and was on a level place (Luke 6:12,17). Second, there are different emphases in the two sermons, which are particularly noticeable in Matthew's and Luke's versions of the beatitudes (Matthew 5:3–12, Luke 6:20–26). There is nothing abnormal about this; all preachers will preach similar messages in different places, slightly adapting them to suit the different occasions, or to emphasize different aspects of the truth at different times. Third, Luke tells us that Jesus preached this sermon directly after choosing the twelve disciples, which places it some considerable way into Jesus' ministry.

Luke has a great concern for the theme of social and moral justice. That is why he uses a version of Jesus' beatitudes which is much more to do with real social poverty. Luke's first beatitude omits Matthew's "in spirit," and says simply "Blessed are you who are poor"; and Luke adds to his "Blessed are . . ." sayings the opposite "woes" (Luke 6:24–26)—a word of judgment against the rich, the prosperous, the socially privileged.[8] And whilst Matthew's beatitudes are mostly in the third person, making general statements *about* people ("Blessed are the poor . . . , the meek . . . , the merciful . . . , for theirs is the Kingdom . . ."), Luke's are addressed *to* people ("Blessed are you who are poor . . . blessed are you who hunger now . . . woe to you who are rich . . . woe to you who are well fed . . ."); he shows Jesus directly comforting the poor and challenging the rich. Matthew's Sermon on the Mount is more about the spiritual life of the Kingdom; Luke's Sermon on the Plain is more about social responsibility. Both matter.

Another way of putting it would be to say that Matthew's Sermon on the Mount shows that Jesus' Kingdom is different from the norms of religious and respectable society, and Luke's Sermon on the Plain shows that it is different from the norms of established and prosperous society. There is a long-standing tradition of "the church" being seen as one of the props of the *status quo*, part of the settled ethos of the middle and upper classes. The fact that the ironic description of the Church of England as "the Tory party at prayer"[9] is less than wholly accurate has not prevented it from being used to this day, and its premise—that the church is one of the pillars of the establishment—is often taken for granted; and for a long time the church was regarded as one of "the professions" into which the gentry and the rising upper-middle classes would send their sons, alongside the law, politics and the army. The very fact of having an "established" church in which a number of bishops are entitled to sit in the House of Lords, and that the formal mode of address for an Anglican bishop is "my Lord," does little to counter the widespread assumption that the church is the religious face of the ruling classes; and that perception of the comfortable religious establishment is found both in popular culture and in many works of literature: John Betjeman wrote a delightfully ironic poem entitled *In Westminster Abbey*, which

---

8. In the week in which I started writing this chapter, an editorial appeared in *The Times* under the sub-heading "Wealthy individuals in Britain could do a lot more with their fortunes"; it pointed out that despite the recession, the number of extremely rich people in the country has greatly increased—Britain at the time had fifty-three billionaires and over 284,000 millionaires: those numbers have risen since—but that there is not in this country the same strong tradition as is found in the USA of the rich using their wealth for philanthropic purposes: "charitable giving does not permeate Britain's wealthy as it should."

9. The phrase seems to have been coined by Maude Royden (1876–1956), a religious writer and suffragette, who said in a speech in the Queen's Hall, London in 1917 that "The Church should go forward along the path of progress and be no longer satisfied only to represent the Conservative Party at prayer." (Quoted in Partington, *Oxford Dictionary of Quotations*, 549.)

is the prayer of a clearly very respectable and well-heeled lady that God will preserve English society as it is and safeguard her own prosperity and position; and in Jane Austen's *Pride and Prejudice* the sycophantic clergyman, Mr Collins, seems to regard the main purpose of his life and vocation as being to ensure that he remains in the favor of his patroness, Lady Catherine de Bourgh—one can hardly imagine Mr Collins preaching on a text from Luke's Sermon on the Plain such as "Blessed are you who are poor . . . woe to you who are rich." It is probably true to say that, in proportion as the church becomes part of established society, it loses its ability properly to fulfill Jesus' mission *to* society. Commenting on the story in Acts 3:1–10 of Peter healing the lame man at the temple, Ajith Fernando tells how the medieval priest and theologian Thomas Aquinas (1225–74), on arriving for an audience with the Pope, found him surrounded by piles of money. "The Pope remarked, 'You see, Thomas, the Church can no longer say, "Silver and gold have I none."' Aquinas replied, 'True, holy father; but neither can she now say, "Rise up and walk."'"[10]

The Parables of the Kingdom

This phase of Jesus' Galilean ministry concludes with the parables of the Kingdom (Matthew 13:1–52//Mark 4:1–34//Luke 8:4–15 and 13:18–21). A parable is a practical story to illustrate a spiritual point.[11] Jesus uses familiar events in the world of nature (like sowing seed), or in human experience (like finding treasure in a field), to illustrate truths about the spiritual Kingdom of God. Jesus always used parables when talking to larger crowds

---

10. Fernando, *Acts*, 149.

11. That is the most common sense of "parable" in the New Testament, and the normal understanding of what a parable is. In fact the Greek word *parabolē* was used to cover a wider range of sayings than the well-known parable-stories. It could refer to a proverb or aphorism—the saying quoted by Jesus in Luke 4:23, "Physician, heal yourself!," is called a "parable," translated in the NIV as "proverb"—or to a short verbal illustration or analogy, such as Jesus' words about the *parabolē* (NIV, "lesson") that can be learned from a ripe fig-tree (Matthew 24:32//Mark 13:28). Some of Jesus' short pithy sayings, such as that about how "a kingdom divided against itself cannot stand," and "tying up the strong man" (Mark 3:23–27) are called "parables." And even historical characters and events can be described as "parables," that is, types or illustrations, of spiritual truth: in Hebrews 9:9 the temple furniture and priestly service of the Old Testament are called a *parabolē* (NIV, "illustration") of how Jesus is our Great High Priest, and in Hebrews 11:19 Abraham's faith, as seen in the story of how Isaac was at the last minute spared from death, is said to be a "parable" of faith in the resurrection: the phrase translated in the NIV as "figuratively speaking" is literally "in a parable." So a "parable" can be any form of figurative, illustrative or proverbial language, as well as a story with a spiritual meaning.

(Matthew 13:34//Mark 4:34). To his disciples, he explained things in more detail.

Why did Jesus use parables? Partly, as Matthew characteristically informs us, in fulfillment of the Scripture (Matthew 13:35). But there are three particular reasons for Jesus' use of parables. First, as *illustrations*. They make spiritual and abstract ideas concrete; Jesus' parables are the prototype of the familiar anecdotal sermon illustration. Second, *to challenge people to think*. Jesus doesn't simply "spoon-feed" spiritual truth to people. He gives them teaching in a way that requires them to reflect on what it means.

So far, so good; those purposes are fairly clear and uncontroversial. It is the third reason for Jesus' use of parables that is more complicated. The words in Matthew 13:10–15 (which are given in a more succinct form in Mark 4:10–12//Luke 8:9–10) should not be misunderstood.

> "This is why I speak to them in parables: 'Though seeing, they do not see; though hearing, they do not hear or understand.' In them is fulfilled the prophecy of Isaiah: 'You will be ever hearing but never understanding; you will be ever seeing but never perceiving. For this people's heart has become calloused; they hardly hear with their ears, and they have closed their eyes. Otherwise they might see with their eyes, hear with their ears, understand with their hearts and turn, and I would heal them.'"

It might be possible to take these words to be suggesting that Jesus used parables deliberately so that people would not understand him. That is obviously not what is meant; parables are not intended to obscure the truth, but to illumine it. But parables give people *the opportunity to grasp the truth or not*. If people have a heart and mind that is to any degree seeking God and his truth, the parables can lead them to understanding. But if people are really not interested in seeking God—if, like those of whom Isaiah spoke, they have calloused hearts—the parables will remain just stories; they won't see the point. They will hear the stories with their ears, but their hearts will not receive the truth those stories are intended to convey. The words about "though hearing, they do not hear" are not saying that God does not *want* them to hear—they are saying that some people do not want to hear the truth. Sherlock Holmes said to Dr Watson, "You see, but you do not observe"; and Jesus says to his disciples that some hear the stories but do not grasp the meaning, although, unlike Dr Watson, that is not because of any lack of skill or practice, but because of the moral and spiritual predisposition of their hearts. Teaching in parables means that the people who grasp the truth are the people who are actually seeking it; the essential truths about God's Kingdom are conveyed, not in intellectual propositions calling for the assent of the mind, but in illustrations by which God can reveal spiritual truth to the hearts of those who are open to receive it.

We mentioned earlier, in the summary about the Kingdom of God, that one of the most important aspects of the teaching of the parables was to correct the simplistic idea that the Kingdom of God would arrive all at once, and the whole world would be changed overnight. Jesus' parables of the sower sowing the seed, and the growing seed, and many other parables of growth explain that it is not quite like that. Many of the parables of the Kingdom are drawn from the world of agriculture; and the point that they have in common is that the Kingdom grows gradually, sometimes barely perceptibly. That no doubt seems less dynamic and dramatic than the popular expectation that the Kingdom should come all at once, with a cataclysmic bang; but they also make the point that the Kingdom is organic: seed may look small and unimpressive, but it has *life* in it; and Jesus' Kingdom is about life that is planted, grows, and eventually reaches the time of maturity and final fulfillment. And the parables set his hearers' present lives and embryonic faith in the context of God's wider purposes through history and into eternity. What begins with a group of people listening to Jesus in Galilee, and starting to grasp some of the key truths about God's Kingdom, will grow until it reaches God's grand finale, when he sends his angels out to gather his chosen people from across the globe, and ushers them into his heavenly Kingdom, which Jesus depicts as a great harvest celebration. One of the things that Jesus' parables tell us is that we are part of something that is far bigger than we can fully imagine; and yet he conveys that truth through the most homely and accessible of stories.

The sower

The first great story in Matthew 13 and Mark 4 is the parable of the sower (Matthew 13:3-9,18-23//Mark 4:3-8,13-20; it is also in Luke 8:1-15). This focuses on the "sowing stage" of the Kingdom. Jesus sows the life of the Kingdom—the Gospel—into people. Whether it grows, and how well, depends on how they receive it—on the quality of their hearts and minds ("the soil"). There will be those who, like the hard paths, do not receive the Word at all; there will be others who do receive it, at least at first, but, either because, like the thorny soil, they want to have the life of God's Kingdom, but without weeding out of their lives all the worldly behavior that will sooner or later choke the life out of their faith, or because, like the shallow soil, they find the challenges of the Kingdom too demanding, they do not stay the course. But there will also be those (the good soil) who not only receive the Word, but grow in it, and allow it to bear fruit in their lives.

This parable, whilst challenging every believer about the quality of his or her own response to Jesus' Word, also reassures the Christian preacher and witness. Our responsibility is to scatter the seed of God's Word; we are not responsible for whether or how people respond to it. Whether or not the seed produces a harvest does not depend on the quality of the seed—Gospel seed is Gospel seed—nor on the quality of the sower; it depends on the disposition of the hearts into which it is sown. And that is not the preacher's responsibility. Once the doctor has diagnosed the illness and prescribed the cure, it is down to the patient to take the prescribed medicine every day: the doctor cannot take it for him. Fortunately, the preacher can also pray that God will do what we cannot do and improve the quality of the soil in people's hearts, so that, as we sow the seed, it can put down roots into better ground.

One thing is distinctive about the parable of the sower in particular: of all Jesus' parables, this is the only one that comes close to being an allegory.[12] It is usually a mistake to try and read Jesus' parables as allegories, in which everything and everyone is assumed to symbolize something about spiritual life. The parable which has often been portrayed as an allegory of spiritual salvation is the story of the Good Samaritan in Luke 10:30–37. R. C. Trench offers an ingenious and fascinating summary of how the parable can be seen as a picture of the story of mankind's fall into sin and redemption by Jesus; for example, he even suggests that the fact that the robbers left their victim "half dead" is an indication of the fact that the human race is physically alive but spiritually dead.[13] But, although everything he says is true, it has little, if anything, to do with Jesus' purpose in telling the parable: the context makes it clear that Jesus told the story to illustrate what it means to love one's neighbor, and to answer the question "who is my neighbor?" Even H. W. Fowler, who says that "allegory" and "parable" mean more or less the same thing, recognizes that, in modern usage, a parable is an "illustrative story designed to answer a single question or suggest a single principle."[14] Jesus' explanation of the significance of the parable of the sower certainly suggests

---

12. An allegory is a story that is specially constructed so that everything in it corresponds to, symbolizes and represents something else. The most famous allegory is probably Bunyan's *Pilgrim's Progress*, in which every proper name (the Giant Despair, the "beautiful damsel named Discretion" and her sisters Prudence, Piety and Charity, etc.) clearly points to the characteristic or attitude that the character represents: in other words, the characters are not in fact "characters," but simply symbols or personifications.

13. Trench, *Notes on the Parables*, 112–113.

14. Fowler, *Modern English Usage*, 558.

that he saw the four kinds of soil as pictures of four different kinds of human heart and attitude. That should not however encourage us to see the other parables as allegories, and to try and pin down a specific spiritual reference in every detail: each parable has essentially one central point or lesson, and it is on those key lessons that we need to focus, not on the secondary detail which is often simply filling in the story to make it more realistic and recognizably set in our day-to-day human world.

The wheat and the weeds

The parable of the wheat and the weeds (Matthew 13:24–30,36–43) focuses on the "growing stage" of the Kingdom. As the life of the Kingdom of God grows in people and in the world, there are also the "weeds," the evil things that are still in the world, sown by the devil. God does not immediately root them out, as people seem to think he should—how often have we heard the complaint, "Why doesn't God come and *do something* about all the evil in the world?!" That is precisely what the servants in the parable suggested (verse 28). God is wiser than that; he knows that a "quick-fix" solution will not in fact fix anything. But one day he will act in judgment. The lesson of the parable is that we must be neither simple optimists, people who see only the wheat ("everything's getting better and better!"), nor simple pessimists, people who see only the weeds ("everything's going from bad to worse!"). We recognize that the Kingdom of God is growing; but that evil is also increasing.

Interpreters of this parable tend to be divided into two camps. There are those who understand the wheat to refer to the church and the weeds to the secular world, so that the parable is saying that the evil in the world continues to thrive even as the Kingdom of God is growing; in that sense, the parable answers the question, why does God not act immediately to eradicate all evil from the world?, why does the bad world keep getting worse, even though the life and mission of the church is also growing? Others see the whole parable as referring to the church: there are in the visible church the true people of God (sons of the Kingdom); but there are also within the historical church those deviant traditions and heretical theologies, and people who are not born-again believers. The parable therefore answers the question, why is there still corruption in the church? Jesus' answer is, there always will be, because of the corruption of the human heart; whilst the true life of the Kingdom grows, heresy will also thrive, nominalism will increase, deviant and corrupt elements will always threaten to bring the church into disrepute. In a sense, we do not need to choose between the two views.

Jesus, in his interpretation of the parable in verse 38, says that "the field is the world"; in that sense the first view, that the weeds represent the evil in the world, is true. But of course the evil in the world has an alarming tendency to keep infiltrating and corrupting the church; in that sense the second view is also true, which is why in verse 41 Jesus speaks of the angels at the end weeding "out of his Kingdom" everything that causes sin, in other words, any impurities that have tarnished the church through its living in proximity to the weeds of the world.

The growing seed

This parable in Mark 4:26–29 also focuses on the "growing stage" of the Kingdom. Like the parable of the yeast, this stresses that growth happens slowly, over a period of time. We are looking for long-term growth in God's Kingdom. In our society, and sometimes in the modern church, we tend to look for immediate results, rather than thinking in the long term; this parable is a much-needed corrective to that. And it provides the truth which must always be kept in balance with that of the parable of the sower. There the emphasis was on the importance of our response to the seed of the Gospel. Here is the equal but opposite truth: that God's Kingdom will come, regardless of human help or hindrance. Once the Kingdom has been sown, it will continue to grow and to move towards its final glorious harvest, "whether [the farmer] sleeps or gets up." The church can sometimes seem to be asleep; but God's Kingdom will come, with or without us. That is not an excuse for spiritual sleepiness; but it is a reassurance that the final harvest does not depend on us. We can be part of the coming of the Kingdom by our service, but we cannot prevent the Kingdom coming by our non-involvement.

The mustard-seed

The parable of the mustard-seed (Matthew 13:31–32//Mark 4:30–32; it is also in Luke 13:18–19) stresses that the Kingdom of God seems to have very small and insignificant beginnings. It all begins with Jesus, the cross, and a small group of followers. But it will grow to an enormous final harvest. The same principle is true of each individual believer; there is a first small, probably hesitant, response to the good news; but what Jesus can grow from that over a lifetime is full of potential for fruitful service.

The yeast

The parable of the yeast (Matthew 13:33; it is also in Luke 13:20-21) speaks of the slow process by which the Kingdom of God permeates and transforms the world. Just as yeast gradually works through dough, so the life of God's Kingdom slowly works through the life of this world, changing it. God does not want to scrap this world, but to transform it. This is very similar to Jesus' saying that his disciples are the salt of the earth (Matthew 5:13). Again, the emphasis is on the ongoing process of Kingdom growth. Many today want what we might call "microwave Christianity"; one prayer, and we get the answer, one sermon, and we will have converts galore, one series of nurture groups, and we are guaranteed a church of mature disciples. Most of us know from experience what Jesus tells us in this parable—that it doesn't work like that. The Kingdom of God is not a microwave oven, but more like a slow-cooker. It is the *process* that produces lasting results for the Kingdom.

The hidden treasure and the hidden pearl

These two parables about "treasure-hunting" (Matthew 13:44-46) both stress the supreme value of the Kingdom of God. We must not misunderstand Jesus' words, that the men in the parables "bought" the field in which they had found treasure, and "bought" the pearl. No one can "buy" the life of the Kingdom of God. Salvation is always a free gift from God that we receive by faith. The language about selling what you have in order to buy the field or the pearl is part of the human story that Jesus is using as an illustration. The point of the parables is not that we can "buy" the life of God's Kingdom, but that that life is of such enormous and incomparable value that it is worth giving up everything else—all the worldly values, projects, hopes and dreams on which we might previously have set our hearts—in order to embrace the new life of God's salvation. The American missionary Jim Elliot, who with four others was killed in 1956 in Ecuador, wrote in his diary, doubtless in the light of the comments of those who were puzzled as to why he had given up a settled and potentially successful life in order to go to such a remote and dangerous place, "He is no fool who gives what he cannot keep to gain what he cannot lose."[15] That is exactly what Jesus is saying in these parables.

---

15. Quoted in Blanchard, *Gathered Gold*, 271.

The fishing net

Finally, the parable of the fishermen sorting the fish they have caught (Matthew 13:47–50) is similar to the story of the wheat and the weeds. It focuses on the final "harvesting" stage of the Kingdom. Jesus will separate out those who are his, and bring them into his heaven. In this world, we are intermingled with people who do not follow Jesus, just as all the fish are caught up together in the net. But on the last day, Jesus will separate his people from those who are not his people.

The challenge of Jesus' teaching

The teaching ministry of Jesus, as well as containing many specific challenges which the church needs to hear, also has a number of general lessons for us: I will highlight two.

The call to be radical

Perhaps the most obvious and yet also the most challenging thing about Jesus' teaching is the radical quality of life that he is looking for in his disciples, as seen in the Sermons on the Mount and on the Plain. Any bland idea that Jesus' message can be summed up, as Douglas Adams put it in *The Hitch-Hiker's Guide to the Galaxy*, as "how great it would be to be nice to people for a change" is ruled out when we read and take seriously the kind of lifestyle to which Jesus calls his disciples. What we find here is a way of living that turns the normal standards of the world—and, very importantly, not just the wicked and sinful world, but also the very respectable, decent and well-behaved world—on their heads. To be a disciple means to abandon the widespread assumption that we have a right to stand up for ourselves or that it is important to act in ways that will commend us to others and make us popular. It means accepting that morality is as much about what we think as about what we do, and that that radical holiness is not just for monks and hermits, but for factory-workers, businessmen and shopkeepers. Above all, Jesus abolishes the belief that we can have a place for God in our lives ("the religious bit"), but manage the rest ourselves. The former Prime Minister Viscount Melbourne, who was one of Queen Victoria's chief political advisers, once complained that "things have come to a pretty pass when religion is allowed to invade the sphere of private life."[16] Being a respectable church-

---

16. Quoted in Partington, *Oxford Dictionary of Quotations*, 456; the entry notes that Lord Melbourne made the comment "on hearing an evangelical sermon." No doubt

goer is one thing; but perish the thought that being a Christian should actually make a difference to how we live our day-to-day lives! Jesus insists, not only that it does, but that the difference will make us the opposite of what the respectable religious establishment regards as normal.

The great danger for the western church is comfortableness, the successful attempt to hold the assurance of Christian faith and salvation in one hand, and the benefits of a prosperous and respectable place in society in the other. I say, the "successful" attempt; in fact, the widespread assumption that Jesus probably did not mean it literally when he said that we cannot serve both God and mammon,[17] or, if he did, that "serving mammon" refers to a level of materialism far deeper than we ourselves have sunk, has enabled many believers to be very successful in worldly terms; but it has certainly not led to the church in our nation being notably successful in manifesting the life of the Kingdom of God to the world, or being effective as salt and light in society. Watchman Nee began his classic book *The Normal Christian Life* by pointing out that even a brief reading of the Sermon on the Mount is enough to demonstrate that the "normal" Christian life is a very different thing from the life of the average Christian;[18] but that does not mean that it should be.

One of the greatest needs for the church is a return to taking the teaching of Jesus about radical Kingdom lifestyle at face value. When it is normal for all our converts and church members to be deeply rooted in the Sermon on the Mount, and to see Jesus' teaching as a manual for daily living rather than the statement of an admirable (but unrealistic) ideal; when our understanding of a biblical lifestyle stops being watered down and re-packaged as what Alfred Doolittle in *Pygmalion* called "middle-class morality"; when Christians' righteousness really does surpass that of the Pharisees and the teachers of the law; when "be perfect, as your heavenly Father is perfect" is seen, not as hyperbole, as a deliberately exaggerated way of saying "be as good as you can," but as the literal standard of Kingdom life—then perhaps we might find a higher proportion of professing believers amongst the good seed that, having taken root, bears fruit thirty-, sixty-, or one hundred-fold.

---

some who heard the original Sermon on the Plain may have reacted in a similar way.

17. *Mammon* is an Aramaic word that simply means "wealth" or "profit"; it is used in the New Testament only in Matthew 6:24 and Luke 16:9,11,13. Christ clearly regards *mammon* as not merely the neutral fact of having wealth, but the potential ensnaring power of wealth: the things that a man owns can so easily come to own him. In that spirit, Paul says in Colossians 3:5 that greed "is idolatry."

18. Nee, *Normal Christian Life*, 9.

Personal lifestyle and Kingdom vision

Another general lesson arises from a consideration of passages like the Sermon on the Mount alongside Jesus' parables of the Kingdom. Clearly, he regarded both forms of teaching as vital. The Sermon describes Christian lifestyle; the parables set that lifestyle in the context of God's larger purposes for the coming of his Kingdom in the world. To be effective as Christians, we need *both* to practice Christian lifestyle, to be salt and light, *and* to have some understanding of the fact that our lives are part of God's larger plan. There are those who only ever think in cosmic Kingdom terms, who are always looking forward to and speaking about the return of the Lord in glory, who delight in the hidden treasure and fine pearl of the Kingdom, and yet at the same time find loving their neighbors somewhat irksome and the call to give to the needy an inconvenience, and whose idea of goodness is to be as pure-ish in heart as they can reasonably manage without cramping their style too much; such people, unfortunately, are unlikely to be worthwhile servants of the very Kingdom for whose consummation they are longing. On the other hand, without the vision of the growing Kingdom, and the assurance that the day is coming when the Lord will reap his full and final harvest, it is all too easy to lose heart, as we struggle to remain peacemakers amongst people who do not want peace, when loving our enemies doesn't stop them from being our enemies, or in those moments when we are more conscious of the narrowness and roughness of the road than of the life to which it leads. The promise of the final victory of the Kingdom in the parables should always be the encouragement and the stimulus to pursue the lifestyle of radical discipleship to which the sermons call us, and they remind us that that future consummation is what makes the present challenge infinitely worthwhile. And conversely, it is as we work out our discipleship in the spirit of the sermons that we will be playing our part, as Peter says (2 Peter 3:12), in not only waiting for the day of the Lord, but also speeding its coming.

John's Gospel

Before we leave the teaching ministry of Jesus we should say a word about the teaching in John's Gospel. John, as we have said, does not include the details of Jesus' Galilean ministry, although he does refer a number of times to the fact that Jesus spent time in and around Galilee, and these references all come in the first half of John;[19] from 7:10 onwards Jesus is based around

---

19. John 1:43, 2:12, 4:3–4, 4:43, 6:1, 7:1.

Jerusalem. But since most of John consists of the words of Jesus to his disciples, we need, if we are to have all-round picture of his teaching ministry, to set these discourses alongside the Galilean sermons and parables, and not to worry too much about exactly where the recorded ministry in John fits into the synoptic history of Jesus' ministry.

The most striking thing about Jesus' teaching in John is that it focuses entirely on himself: who he is, his relationship with the Father, and what he has come into the world to do. Until we come to the upper room discourse (chapters 13–16) nothing Jesus says in John contains any instruction to his disciples, except the repeated invitation to believe in him; in fact, when Jesus was asked by the crowds by the Galilean lake what they needed to do in order to do the works God requires, Jesus replied (6:28–29), "The work of God is this: to believe in the one he has sent."

It would be quite wrong to infer from this that John thought that Christian discipleship was passive, that following Jesus does not actually involve us in doing anything except believing. But he does remind us of an essential truth: that Christian discipleship can only be real if it is first and foremost focused in Jesus, who he is and how he brings new life. Mere Christian activism—doing things for the Kingdom—is not discipleship unless it all arises out of a deep awareness and appreciation of who Jesus is. To learn how to serve God's Kingdom is not simply a matter of deciding to live according to the Sermon on the Mount; it will happen as we allow ourselves increasingly to be drawn into Jesus' heavenly life, so that, just as he said that he only ever did what he saw the Father doing (5:19), we too can experience Jesus continuing the Father's work in and through us.

There are those who will not find this comfortable; like the crowds by the lakeside, they would prefer Jesus to give them instructions about things they can just get on and do. But there is a reason why our New Testaments include John's Gospel. The heart of Christian life is not what we do but who he is. That needs saying, in a church culture that is increasingly program-driven—churches these days are expected to have programs of training, of mission, of youth work, of social ministry—and in which leaders are increasingly seen (and increasingly see themselves) less as pastors and preachers and more as project-managers.[20] Christian life is never a program; it is always about growing in the kind of faith that receives life from Jesus (John 5:21), feeds on Jesus (6:35, 53–56), walks in the light of Jesus (8:12), hears and follows the voice of Jesus (10:4); the kind of faith that, by dwelling

---

20. It may be significant, and it is perhaps troubling, that some younger pastors refer to the room from which they work not, as was traditionally the case, as their "study," but often as their "office"; what does that imply about how they see their primary role?

on how Jesus speaks of himself and his spiritual life, seeks the grace to be increasingly incorporated into that life.

But John is not an alternative to Matthew and Luke; for just as there are those who prefer straightforward instructions to the more metaphorical, even mystical language of John, so there are others who are only too happy to immerse themselves in John's simple yet strangely elusive phraseology, so long as they never actually have to get out of their chairs and do anything. That is why God has left us with four Gospels, not just one. It is as we feed on the spiritual life that John conveys, as we are increasingly drawn into the life of the Jesus who says "I am," that we will be enabled to start to live out the Sermon on the Mount. In one of the great classics of the medieval monastic tradition, *The Ladder of Perfection*, Walter Hilton begins by quoting Saint Gregory's statement that there are two different ways of life for the Christian, which he calls the active life and the contemplative life. "The active life consists in love and charity shown outwardly in good works, in obedience to God's commandments . . . The contemplative life consists in perfect love and charity inwardly experienced through the spiritual virtues, and in a true knowledge and perception of God and spiritual things."[21] Presumptuous though it may seem to take issue with such great authorities, I doubt very much that the New Testament would have us regard the life of active service and that of inner contemplation as alternatives between which we are to choose; they are rather the two sides of the same Christian coin. Feeding spiritually on Jesus' revelation of himself in John's Gospel—which we might call a form of "contemplative life"—should then issue in living more fruitfully for the Jesus who in Matthew and Luke taught us how to live as citizens of God's Kingdom.

To use a slightly over-simplified analogy: if discipleship is like a car, we might describe John as the fuel that drives the motor, and the synoptics as the steering column that guides the car where it should go. Without the fuel of Jesus' own heavenly life, we can turn the steering wheel of Christian projects as much as we want, but we will not actually move anywhere. On the other hand, the fuel is there for a purpose, and that purpose is not to leave the car stationary with its engine idling; it is to go somewhere. If the Galilean teaching tells us where to go, it is only by being regularly re-fueled by Jesus' teaching about his own life in John that we will stand any chance of getting there.

---

21. Hilton, *Ladder of Perfection*, 2–3.

7

Demonstrating the Kingdom

"People were overwhelmed with amazement. 'He has done everything well,' they said." (Mark 7:37)

Throughout Jesus' Galilean ministry passages of teaching alternate with narratives of mighty works, especially of healing, which are signs of the Kingdom. There is no need to comment on each individual miracle story, or even to list them all; but some stories have particular points of interest.

Miracles in the Gospels

"Pronouncement stories"

Some accounts of miracles incorporate a particularly significant short saying of Jesus, of which the miracle is an illustration. These narratives are often called "pronouncement stories"; that is, stories which are told in order to provide the context for those important and pithy words of Jesus, which need to be remembered alongside the more substantial blocks of teaching that we have been considering, like the Sermon on the Mount, as characteristic of Jesus' preaching ministry. Typical pronouncement stories, with their key sayings, are the healing of the paralytic at Capernaum (Matthew 9:1-8//Mark 2:1-12//Luke 5:17-26)—"The Son of Man has authority on earth to forgive sins"; the healing of the woman with the severe bleeding (Matthew 9:20-22//Mark 5:25-34//Luke 8:43-48)—"Your faith has healed you"; and the healing of the man with the shriveled hand (Matthew 12:9-13//Mark 3:1-5//Luke 6:6-10)—"It is lawful to do good on the Sabbath."[1]

The sovereignty of Christ

Matthew, Mark and Luke all include one particular sequence of four miracles: the calming of the storm (Matthew 8:23-27//Mark 4:35-41//Luke 8:22-25), the healing of the man with a legion of demons (Matthew 8:28-34//Mark 5:1-20//Luke 8:26-39), the healing of the woman with severe bleeding (Matthew 9:20-22//Mark 5:25-34//Luke 8:43-48), and the raising of Jairus' daughter to life (Matthew 9:18-26//Mark 5:21-43//Luke 8:40-56). These four miracles all demonstrate Jesus' power over the whole of life (nature, demons, sickness, and death). And they all show Jesus dealing with an extreme case, in which all human help has proved useless. The men in the boat with Jesus were professional fishermen, yet all their skill could not save them—they had to call to Jesus in panic that they were drowning (Mark 4:38). The only thing that people could do with the man with the legion of demons was to try and chain him up, to contain the problem—and even that had not worked (Mark 5:4). The woman had spent all her money on doctors, but had only got worse (Mark 5:26). And when Jairus' daughter died, all that people could do was to provide a party of official mourners to weep and wail at the house (Mark 5:38). In all these cases of extreme need, where all human help has been seen to fail, Jesus can bring life and rescue people from danger, from demons, from disease and from death.

Christians' patience and Christ's power

Remaining with that series of four miracles, Mark's version of them shows us a third lesson. In Mark's arrangement of his Gospel, those four miracles immediately follow the series of four parables in 4:1-34. As was said in the last chapter on the teaching of Jesus, one of the main themes in those parables is the slow, gradual process of the growth of God's Kingdom, which starts as a tiny seed, and over a period of time, in ways that are sometimes barely perceptible, develops and increases until the day of the final harvest. Those parables are then followed by four miracles which show Jesus intervening dramatically to transform apparently hopeless situations.

---

1. There are a number of other "pronouncement stories" which do not involve miracles, but which are similarly built around an important pithy saying; for example, the feast at the home of Matthew (Mark 2:15-17)—"It is not the healthy who need a doctor, but the sick. I have not come to call the righteous, but sinners."

The juxtaposition of parables of gradual growth and miracles of dramatic intervention shows us a vital truth about the life of God's Kingdom: that Jesus can and does work sudden and unexpected miracles—but that Kingdom life is also a process. Some people want only one or the other. There are those for whom the whole of Christian life is the gradual, step-by-step process of daily life—of plodding on in faith—but with no expectation that God will ever actually "do" anything, and certainly nothing in any way dramatic or dynamic. And of course there are also those who only ever thirst for the dramatic and the miraculous, but who have no time at all for the idea of patiently growing in faith and discipleship. Jesus' teaching and miracles tell us clearly that both are equally vital aspects of the life of the disciple in God's Kingdom. The person who has been suddenly and dramatically transformed by an encounter with Jesus as life-changing as that of the man possessed by a legion of demons—and I have known some of whom that has been true—still needs to commit himself to the patient and ongoing process of learning to be a disciple. And the faithful believer whose motto for Christian life is "keep on keeping on" needs to develop a greater expectation that, as we indeed continue to follow him one step at a time, there will also be those occasions when our Lord intervenes and demonstrates that he is still the Savior who sets captives free in remarkable ways.

Miracles and costly discipleship

Matthew 8–9 are structured in a deliberately significant way: three groups of three miracles alternate with short sayings or incidents which present the challenges of discipleship. The first three miracles, the healing of the man with leprosy (8:1–4), of the centurion's servant (8:5–13) and of Peter's mother-in-law and various other people in Capernaum (8:14–17), are followed by Jesus' responses to two would-be-disciples, in which he speaks of the *personal challenge* of following him: it can mean a hard life (verse 20) and one that may often need to take priority over personal and family commitments (verse 22). Then the second triad of miracles—the calming of the storm (8:23–27), the healing of two demon-possessed men (8:28–34)[2] and

---

2. This is clearly the same incident as is recorded in Mark 5 and Luke 8, which speak only of one man. This need not be seen as contradictory. First, it would be normal for people with the kind of condition from which this man suffered to stay together in groups of two, three, or more. Second, Matthew frequently mentions that two people were present at or involved in an incident where the other Gospels mention only one—another example is the blind man/men in 20:29–34. This is probably because of his Jewish mind-set: it is a principle of the Old Testament law that a fact is established on the testimony of two witnesses, so Matthew mentions that two people witnessed Jesus'

of the paralytic let down through the roof (9:1-8)—is followed by the story of the call of Matthew and his subsequent dinner party, which demonstrates the *social challenge* of following Jesus: the Pharisees object strongly to the fact that Jesus spends time with "tax collectors and sinners." After the third group of three miracles—the raising of the ruler's dead daughter,[3] the healing of the woman with severe hemorrhaging (9:18-26) and the healing of blind and mute people (9:27-34)—Jesus speaks of the *spiritual challenge* of following him in a world where we will find ourselves surrounded by vast crowds of "harassed and helpless" people.

By so ordering his Gospel, Matthew seems to want to stress that the fact that we may be given power and authority to work miracles in Jesus' name does not mean that discipleship and ministry will be easy. God's miracle-working power does not make our service less costly, less challenging or less emotionally draining. Lesslie Newbigin gets the balance very well:

> "Jesus consistently attacked the power of evil. In no recorded case did he ever advise the handicapped and the sick to accept their lot; his unfailing response to their presence was to put forth his power to heal. He sent out his disciples with a commission to do the same. And yet he also told them that they must of necessity suffer, just as he would have to suffer. This paradox is at the very heart of the Gospel. 'He saved others; himself he cannot save.' It belongs to the mission of the church to the end. The power given to the church to meet the power of evil is just the power to follow Jesus on the road that leads through suffering, through total surrender to the Father . . ."[4]

Jesus and the demonic

One particular kind of miracle calls for some comment, namely Jesus' casting out of demons. Most people will be aware that there are in the modern

---

works to underline the reliability of his account. Third, the reason the other writers mention only one is probably that only one of the pair took a sufficiently leading part in what happened for them to think it necessary to mention that a second was also present.

3. From Mark and Luke we know that the "ruler" was called Jairus, and that he was a leader of the local synagogue. Incidentally, the same is probably true of the rich young man who asked Jesus what he had to do to gain eternal life, and who is described in Luke 18:18 as a "ruler"; this probably means he was a religious leader, rather than a political or aristocratic leader, which makes his finding that the demands of discipleship were too much for him all the more poignant.

4. Newbigin, *Open Secret*, 121.

church two opposite extremes. On the one hand, there are those who dismiss the idea that demons really exist; centuries ago, they might say, people used to believe in evil spirits, but these days, we know that what in the Gospels is described as being "demonized" is simply what we now understand to be mental illness. Belief in real demonic spirits seems to many to have no place in the modern, sophisticated, scientific world. At the opposite extreme, there are a number of groups who have made a great deal of the ministry of casting out demons, sometimes unfortunately with the kind of over-dramatized hype that reflects very little credit on the cause of Christ. And there are are some who seem to attribute every human weakness or failing to demonic influence and insist that what people need is deliverance; so for example, when seeking to help someone with a persistent habit of, say, telling lies, whilst most Christians will suggest ways in which he can develop the disciplined practice of speaking the truth, some will immediately conclude that he needs to be delivered of "a lying spirit," and start shouting at the demons to come out of him.

Both extremes are to be avoided. If we take Scripture seriously as God's Word of truth—and I do—we cannot dismiss its teachings about Satan and the demonic as the primitive superstitions of a pre-scientific age. Jesus clearly believed in the reality of evil spirits; and it takes a quite special kind of arrogance to think that we understand more about the world of spiritual reality than he did. But equally, we have to take an over-fascination with and an over-emphasis on the demonic with, at best, a pinch of salt, not least because one of the dangers of attributing everything that is wrong in our lives to demonic powers is that it lets us off the hook rather too easily. If my problems are (mostly) due to my mistakes, I need to learn to make better and wiser decisions about how I live my life; but if everything is the devil's fault, I need someone else to take the responsibility to minister deliverance to me. Blaming everything on the devil and shouting at demons is far easier, and, dare I say, far more fun, than learning to make godly choices and to live godly lives.

But we still take at face value the biblical accounts of Jesus confronting the powers of evil. Four things should be said about this aspect of Jesus' ministry.

- There is no doubt that a major aspect of Jesus' ministry is that of overcoming the powers of evil. The first thing Jesus did following his baptism was to face the devil in single combat and overcome his temptations. He spoke about his tying up the strong man (= the devil) so that he could release those whom Satan had held captive (Matthew 12:29//Mark 3:27//Luke 11:21–22); indeed, in the same context, he said that the fact that he was freeing people from demonic powers was the definitive sign that in his ministry the Kingdom of God had truly come (Matthew 12:28//Luke 11:20). There are seven separate incidents in which Jesus delivers people from demons, as well as a number of general statements that Jesus healed many who were sick and cast out many demons (e.g. Matthew 4:24). There are passages in the New Testament letters which summarize Jesus' ministry by saying that he came to defeat Satan and undo his work (e.g. 1 John 3:8).

- It is quite proper to say that combatting Satan is not just one part of the Galilean ministry of Jesus, but the focus of all of it. A. M. Hunter rightly says that "the emergent picture of the Chief Figure in the campaign, so far from being that of a high-souled teacher patiently indoctrinating[5] the multitudes with truths of timeless wisdom, is rather that of the strong Son of God, armed with the Father's power, spearheading the attack against the devil and all his works, and calling men to decide on whose side of the battle they will be."[6] But that should not be misunderstood by the modern church, as though engaging directly in spiritual warfare on the one hand, and being involved in Kingdom mission on the other, were somehow separate things. Spiritual warfare is not "one of the things" the church is called to do: it is the context for everything the church is called to do. Whenever Christians tell people the Good News of Jesus, or minister to the hungry or homeless in the name of Jesus, or pray in the name of Jesus for the sick, they are in effect engaging in spiritual warfare, and being the channels through which God takes territory from the enemy and reclaims it for his Kingdom. Directly confronting the demonic is normally necessary only in the case of people who are actually "demonized" in the way that, for example, the man in the synagogue was (Mark 1:21–26//Luke 4:33–35).

- Demons invariably recognize who Jesus is and react, often violently, against him. There are very few direct references to demonic activity in the Old Testament; but as soon as Jesus has come on earth, it is as though the powers of evil, who usually operate in darkness—which, amongst other things, means in covert ways—are, so to speak, forced out of hiding and engage in direct confrontation. Commenting on the words of the demoniac in Mark 1:24 ("Have you come to destroy us? I know who you are—the Holy One of God!") Leon Morris says, "There

---

5. Professor Hunter does not mean the word "indoctrinating" in its modern negative sense of "brain-washing"; at its most basic the word simply means "teaching."

6. Hunter, *Introducing New Testament Theology*, 18.

did not have to be any formal declaration of war. The unclean spirit recognized Jesus as 'the Holy One of God' and automatically ranked himself in opposition."[7] Without wanting to over-simplify what is obviously a complex and sensitive subject, I suggest that this is one reason why Christians today should not go looking for demons. Jesus didn't need to; in his presence, evil spirits came out of the closet and confronted him. If, as the New Testament assures us, the presence of the living Christ dwells in us by his Spirit, the same is likely to be true. Whilst Satan is no doubt the power behind all moral and spiritual temptation and evil, if people are actually demonized, or, in the popular phrase, "possessed" by a demon—though that is not the best way of expressing it: the devil does not "possess" anyone; wherever he has been able to take up residence in a person's life, he is a squatter, not an owner-occupier—the fact will soon become evident in the presence of a Spirit-filled Christian.

- There were in Jesus' day many who practiced "exorcism"; but they always did so by means of techniques, incantations, spells and the like. Jesus' way of dealing with the demonic was nothing like that: he spoke a word of authority, and the demons left; sometimes, as it were, "under protest," but they had no choice but to leave. Again, that is what makes me wary of modern practices of "exorcism" using all sorts of religious and ritualistic procedures. Jesus expelled demons "with a word" (Matthew 8:16); where Christians are dealing with a genuinely demonic presence, I am aware of no biblical reason why we cannot do the same in Jesus' name.

Right and wrong understanding of miracles

Regarding the miracles of Jesus in general, there are a number of lessons for us to note.

A large part of Jesus' ministry consisted of healing miracles.[8] But Jesus always refused to perform miracles simply to prove points, or to induce faith; in Matthew 12:38–39, we read that "some of the Pharisees and teachers of the law said to him, 'Teacher, we want to see a miraculous sign from you.' He answered, 'A wicked and adulterous generation asks for a miraculous sign! But none will be given it except the sign of the prophet Jonah.'" Later, in

---

7. Morris, *Cross in the New Testament*, 56.

8. 16.1 percent of the whole text of Luke, including all the teaching passages, between the beginning of Jesus' ministry and his final arrest, consists of healing miracles; 23.1 percent of Matthew; and 29.9 percent of Mark.

16:1–4, the Pharisees try again: "The Pharisees and Sadducees came to Jesus and tested him by asking him to show them a sign from heaven. He replied, '. . . A wicked and adulterous generation looks for a miraculous sign, but none will be given it except the sign of Jonah.'"

By "the sign of the prophet Jonah," as Jesus explained in Matthew 12:40, he meant his death and resurrection; just as Jonah was three days and three nights in the belly of the fish, so he would be three days and three nights[9] in the ground after his death, from which, like Jonah, he would emerge to new life. There are warnings here, regarding the place of miracles in the ministry of the church. As has been said, miraculous signs have a place—indeed, they should be far more "normal" than they are. But miracles are never to be performed on demand, to satisfy curiosity or to pander to a taste for the spectacular. Miracles can strengthen faith where it already exists, or be pointers to Christ for those who, even if they do not as yet have faith, are seriously seeking the way, the truth and the life. But they do not create faith where it does not exist. They are not given to convince the skeptic or to impress the spectator, but to guide the seeker.

That needs to be remembered, in a culture where there is an insatiable demand for the spectacular and the unusual, and where media-conscious Christians can sometimes seem to pander to that demand. I stand four-square with those who affirm that God works great wonders in our day; I am far less comfortable with a church culture that promotes the miraculous as a "selling-point," or forgets that what matters about a miracle is not how impressive it looks, but how it helps the person for whom it is performed. We will return to the point.

We mentioned in chapter 1 John's characteristic word "signs" to refer to Jesus' miracles. There are in fact three main nouns used in the New Testament to refer to miracles; and between them, they show the three main characteristics of miracles.

- The word "wonder" (Greek: *téras*, used sixteen times), meaning something God does which fills people with awe and causes them to marvel.
- The word "(act of) power" (Greek: *dúnamis*, which is the general word for "power," and gives us our English words "dynamo" and "dynamic"; it is used about twenty-three times in the New Testament in the sense

---

9. Some people object that Jesus was not "three nights" in the grave; if he was buried on Friday and raised on Sunday morning, he was only three days and two nights in the tomb. But "[three] days and [three] nights" is a normal Jewish way of counting days as twenty-four-hour periods, inclusively: we might phrase it as "three days or parts thereof." Even by our western ways of counting days, the other biblical phrase about the time of the resurrection, "on the third day" (1 Corinthians 15:4), means by definition "before night had fallen on the third day."

of "works of miraculous power," sometimes translated as "mighty works"), which means something that God does which displays his sheer power to intervene and to change people's lives.

- John's favorite word "sign" (Greek: *sēmeîon*, used over seventy times), which indicates that miracles are pointers to a spiritual truth about who Jesus is and the kind of life he can give.

W. E. Vine helpfully summarizes the three terms as follows: "A 'sign' is intended to appeal to the understanding, a 'wonder' appeals to the imagination, a 'power' indicates its source as supernatural."[10]

The purpose of miracles

So why did Jesus perform miracles? Granted that miracles are, as John in particular keeps reminding us, "signs," precisely what are they signs of? What lessons can we learn from the miracles of Jesus?

Signs of Jesus' compassion

We will start with the simplest and most fundamental reason for Jesus' miracles, but one which we dare not forget, namely that they are signs of Jesus' compassion with suffering humanity, and his love for people. We read in Matthew 9:35–36 that "Jesus went through all the towns and villages, teaching in their synagogues, preaching the good news of the kingdom and healing every disease and sickness. When he saw the crowds, he had compassion on them, because they were harassed and helpless, like sheep without a shepherd"; and later, in 14:14, that "when Jesus . . . saw a large crowd, he had compassion on them, and healed their sick."

Without that basic motivation of love and compassion for people in their suffering, no healing ministry can properly reflect the ministry of Jesus. There are some other motivations that are quite proper—such as the longing for people to see the power of God at work, to help them towards faith—as well as others that are far from proper, like the desire to make an impression or to make a name for ourselves, or for something to happen that will be news-worthy. But even the nobler motivations need to spring first and foremost from a deep desire to serve people at the point of their need. The starting point for a ministry of signs and wonders is not to ask God to enable us to work miracles, but to ask him to move our hearts with compassion for people.

10. Vine, *Expository Dictionary*, vol. 4, 228.

Signs of God's Kingdom

Perhaps the most essential purpose of miracles is that they are *signs that the Kingdom of God has come*; as Jesus said in Luke 11:20, "If I drive out demons by the finger of God, then the Kingdom of God has come to you." When John the Baptist in his prison cell was starting to be troubled by doubts, and sent messengers to Jesus to ask whether he was really the one who was coming to bring the Kingdom,[11] Jesus replied by referring to the miracles (Matthew 11:2-6)—they are the evidence that Jesus brings God's Kingdom. For us who live in a secular society, in which the language of "the Kingdom of God" is less meaningful to most people, we can convey the same basic truth by saying that the miracles demonstrate that God is real, that he is active in the world, and that he comes to make a difference to people's lives.

Signs of Jesus' divine nature

Miracles are also signs of who Jesus is. In the miracles, we see Jesus doing things that only God can do. It is God who makes corn grow so that we can have bread to eat, and vines grow so that we can have wine (Psalm 104:14-15): Jesus makes bread (Matthew 14:15-21) and wine (John 2:1-11) by a miracle. God alone gives men their speech or their sight (Exodus 4:11); Jesus opens the eyes of the blind (Matthew 9:27-30) and enables the mute to speak (Mark 7:32-35). The miracles demonstrate that Jesus is God in human form.

It might be objected that Jesus enabled his disciples to perform the same miracles as he, and still enables his followers to do the same, but they do not show that we have divine status. That is the importance of the works of the Kingdom being done "in Jesus' name." Jesus simply spoke a word of authority, and sickness and demons submitted to him. We speak in the

---

11. The fact that John the Baptist himself went through a period when he was plagued by doubts should greatly encourage us. First, the very fact that even the great prophet himself struggled with doubts should reassure those who have (but perhaps are ashamed to admit that they have) doubts: they are not for that reason necessarily failures. Second, John's doubts occurred at a time when he was separate from fellowship in prison. Of course his isolation was not of his own choosing; but there is a lesson here that isolation from fellowship can be the seedbed in which the weeds of doubt can best grow. People will sometimes say, "I'm not coming to church because I'm struggling with doubts"; in fact, the truth is more likely to lie the other way round. And third, John did the best possible thing with his doubts: he brought them to Jesus. We can be so ashamed of having doubts that we keep them hidden, not just from fellow-Christians, but even from the Lord. John was wiser than that; he told Jesus what he was struggling with, and Jesus responded positively and helpfully.

name of Jesus. In Acts 3, after Peter and John had "in the name of Jesus Christ of Nazareth" (verse 6) healed the crippled beggar, Peter said to the amazed crowds (verses 12–16), "Why does this surprise you? Why do you stare at us as if by our own power or godliness we had made this man walk? . . . By faith in the name of Jesus, this man whom you see and know was made strong. It is Jesus' name and the faith that comes through him that has given this complete healing to him." Works of power do not say anything about us, or what we are; they say everything about Jesus, and who he is. That places on all who minister in Jesus' name the responsibility to ensure that the way in which we pray for people always leaves them focusing on who Jesus is, not on who or what we are.

Signs of Jesus' Lordship over creation

Following on from that, the miracles can usefully be grouped in two categories: miracles of the old creation, and miracles of the new creation.[12] Miracles of the old creation (which means, of this normal human world) are the works that God does regularly in the course of nature, but which Jesus does in a special way in his miracles. For example, sick people can get better because God has created our bodies with a certain capacity for healing. Jesus' healing miracles show him doing "in close-up" and in a more dramatic way what God regularly does as Lord of creation. Every year a small amount of corn seed gives rise to a large crop and much bread—in other words, a small amount of "bread" grows into a large amount of bread. We see that every year at harvest time. When Jesus multiplies five small loaves so that they feed five thousand people, he is doing in a miraculous way (and without the normal means of the seed, soil, and corn) what God, as Lord of creation, does every year. The same is true of the changing of water into wine. Every year, God changes water into wine—water, in the form of rain, falls, and is drawn up through the roots of the vine into the plant on which grapes grow, and from those grapes people make wine. In Cana in Galilee Jesus turned water into wine in a miraculous way, without the normal channels of the rain, the vine, the grapes and the fermenting process. God controls the weather; every time a storm starts or stops, it does so because God makes it start or stop. When Jesus stills a storm, he is doing what God, as Lord of creation, does all the time.

---

12. I have borrowed this terminology, and the thinking behind it, from C. S. Lewis, who devoted two chapters in his book *Miracles* to "Miracles of the Old Creation" and "Miracles of the New Creation" (215–266). Highly recommended: and the early chapters are a brilliant argument in defense of belief in the miraculous.

Those miracles, and many others, are miracles of the old creation. They show Jesus doing in a more overtly supernatural way things that, as Lord of creation, he does all the time in the course of "nature." Of course, in his miracles Jesus goes beyond what "nature" can do unaided. But these miracles are the same *kind* of things that happen in nature.

Signs of the new creation

There are however some miracles that are different; they show Jesus doing things that do not happen in the course of life in this world, but which will be part of the new creation—the future new life in heaven. When Jesus walks on water (Matthew 14:25–33), he is doing something that does not belong in this present world. Because the whole created order is damaged by human sin, nature can sometimes be hostile or dangerous. It will not be so in heaven. The whole of the new heavens and new earth will be at peace, and we will have proper control over nature and the environment, in ways we do not have now. The times when Jesus raises dead people to life (Mark 5:35–43, Luke 7:11–17, John 11:1–44), and especially his own resurrection, are the supreme miracles of the new creation. When Jesus returns to bring about the new heavens and the new earth, all the dead will rise in a new way, like he did.

Incidentally, we need to understand that there is a vital difference between the resurrection of Jesus and all the other people whom Jesus raised from the dead. They were all restored to the same kind of life that they had had before; their "resurrections" were, in a sense, the supreme examples of miracles of healing. But Jesus rose with the new life of heaven. The people Jesus raised from death—Jairus' daughter, the widow of Nain's son, Lazarus—all had to die again; Jesus rose, never to die again (Romans 6:9). The heavenly life of the risen Jesus is the kind of life we shall all have in heaven. And the "miracles of the new creation" are instances of Jesus giving us a foretaste, a brief preview, of the glory of the new heavens and the new earth to come.

Signs of the work of God

This understanding of the miracles of Jesus as being a demonstration of the works of God in creation, but independently of the normal channels within creation through which those works are regularly done, makes the helpful point that miracles are never arbitrary. Those who dismiss the biblical accounts of miracles as "fairy-stories" show a deplorable lack of awareness of what the Bible is like—and for that matter, what fairy-stories are like. The miracles in fairy-stories are completely arbitrary and unrelated to anything that happens in the "real world": frogs turn into handsome princes when kissed, magic beans grow overnight into a stalk reaching up to a giant's palace in the clouds, at the wave of a fairy-godmother's wand mice and rats are turned into horses and coachmen for Cinderella. Anyone who can think that these tales are the same kind of thing as the biblical miracles has simply not learned to read. Things like that do not happen in the world; they are part of the literary conventions of the fantasy world of the fairy-story. Interestingly, the only mention in the New Testament of anything even remotely similar to these kinds of marvels is the devil's temptation to Jesus to turn stones into bread. That, if Jesus had done it, could justifiably be labeled as belonging in the world of the fairy-tale. But Jesus refused to do it. He would not use his authority as the Son of God to perform arbitrary acts of sheer power. In the course of nature, stones do not turn into bread, any more than frogs turn into handsome princes. But a small amount of bread (corn) does turn every year into a large amount of bread, which is what Jesus brings about when he feeds the five thousand. The miracles of Jesus clearly take place in the real world, they happen to real people, and they display, so to speak, in block capitals instances of principles that God has written into the small print of the created order: principles like fertility (multiplying the loaves), healing, and the weather alternating between calm and storm.

Signs of the awesomeness of God

That gives rise to another point, which is the rebuttal of the common accusation that people in biblical days could believe in miracles because, scientifically uneducated as they were, they did not know that such things cannot happen. In the fairy-story, no one expresses amazement when animals talk, or frogs turn into handsome princes. What according to the norms of the real world would be marvels are, in the fairy-story, quite unexceptional. When the cat first speaks to the miller's son, and asks him to get him a pair of boots, the son does not grow pale with fear, and stammer, "But . . . but . . . you can *talk*!?!" To do so would be to step outside the world of the fairy-story; it would be to show the normal human reaction to anything marvelous.

But that is invariably how people in the Gospels react to Jesus' miracles. Those miracles always provoke a reaction, and the most common reactions are amazement or astonishment (Matthew 8:27, 9:33, 12:23, Mark 1:27, 2:12, 5:42, 7:37), awe (Matthew 9:8//Luke 5:26, Luke 7:16), and fear (Mark

4:41//Luke 8:25, Mark 5:15, 5:33). The very fact that people reacted with awe, fear or amazement is clear proof that any suggestion that they "didn't known that things like that cannot happen" is nonsense: it is not necessary to have a twenty-first-century scientific education to know that men do not normally walk on water or raise the dead to life, and that cripples do not normally stand up, pick up their own stretchers and walk away; of course the people in Jesus' day knew just as well as the modern materialist skeptic that such things go beyond the norms of life in this world. And yet they saw them happening in front of their eyes. Hence their fear, their sense of being overawed by something—or rather, someone—infinitely greater than they, of whom they asked with a sense of trembling (maybe because they were already starting to suspect what the answer was?), "What kind of man is this?"

It is often said that in our society people do not believe in God any more. That is not quite true; although relatively few people are actively involved in Christian life and fellowship, a majority of people in Britain today would still claim to believe in God: thoroughgoing atheism is still relatively rare.[13] What is certainly lacking, however, is not so much belief in God as the fear of God. If we are concerned, as we should be, to see a restoration of signs and wonders to their rightful place in the mission of the Kingdom, it is vital that we also understand *why* we want to see them. It is not so that the church will look more impressive; it is not even simply to attract people's attention, though it can certainly do that. It is surely above all else that we want people who, if they think of God at all, probably think of him in quite abstract and philosophical terms—God as a concept to be debated,—to encounter the holy presence of God in a way that causes them, like those who saw Jesus heal the cripple let down through the roof in Capernaum, to be "filled with awe" (Matthew 9:8). Our evangelistic witness can give people the facts about how they can come to know God; but it is as the Spirit of Jesus works through us to perform the works of his Kingdom that they can be led to worship and revere him as the *living* God. Our words can challenge people's minds with the truth of God; but it is the Lord's works that can cause them to bow the knee before God.

---

13. It is not easy to establish reliable statistics in the area of belief and unbelief, as much depends on how questions in opinion polls are phrased. But most objective surveys over the last decade would suggest that between 15 and 20 percent of the British population are atheist or humanist; something between 50 and 70 percent would call themselves Christian, though of course for many that means that they identify themselves with the western Christian tradition (as opposed to other world religions), rather than that they are committed to practicing Christian faith.

Signs of salvation

Miracles are also signs of the nature of salvation. Jesus worked miracles at a physical level in people's bodies. But those works are also signs that Jesus can do the same things, spiritually, for all people. Jesus makes blind people see; and he can open people's "spiritual eyes" to see the truth about God. Jesus made deaf people hear; and he can open people's "spiritual ears" so that they can hear God speaking to them in their hearts. Jesus made lame and crippled people walk; and he can take damaged and crippled lives and characters and make them whole again. Jesus cleansed lepers from the uncleanness of leprosy; and he can remove from our lives anything that makes us morally unclean, like bad habits or addictions.

It has been quite common over the last few hundred years to "spiritualize" the miracles; many very well-known and highly respected Christian preachers, writers and leaders have said that, whilst we do not see physical miracles of healing today, we do see Jesus bringing spiritual healing to broken lives. In our desire to insist that we *do* see physical miracles today, and that we should expect to, it is easy to forget that miracles are also pointers to how Jesus brings spiritual salvation to people; miracles are, after all, "signs"—they point to something beyond themselves. Jesus himself makes the connection between the physical performance of a miracle and the spiritual lessons that can properly be drawn from it, when he says that his healing of the cripple let down through the roof in Capernaum is a sign to people that he has the authority to forgive sins (Mark 2:10). As well as being real and immensely worthwhile in themselves, miraculous signs are also visual aids in "natural life" of things that are true of eternal life, in the same way that parables are stories drawn from natural life which illustrate truths about the life of God's Kingdom.

Signs of heaven

Finally, the miracles are a small-scale foreshadowing of what will happen in the new heavens and the new earth. In his earthly ministry, Jesus healed a few people. One day, he will heal everybody; it is in the New Jerusalem that "there will be no more death or mourning or crying or pain" (Revelation 21:4). He raised a few people to life—one day, all the dead will be raised; Jesus said (John 5:28–29), that "a time is coming when all who are in their graves will hear his voice and come out." This is why miracles are a "sign" of the coming Kingdom. They are a small foretaste of what will one day happen in a much bigger way, perfectly and forever.

The "secrecy" of Jesus' miracles

Alongside the many remarkable accounts of miracles in the Galilean ministry, there is also a caution. Many times, especially in the earlier stages of his ministry, Jesus tells people, usually those he has healed, that they should not speak to anyone else about it, or that they should not tell people who he is.[14] There is a paradox here; miracles are "signs," they are intended to demonstrate something significant, and therefore are to be seen. And yet Jesus does not want them talked about. Why is this?

There are two connected reasons. First, Jesus does not want to be known simply as a miracle-worker. He does not want to get a reputation as someone who does spectacular things. His work as Son of God, to bring salvation and eternal life, is far more important. Jesus refused to perform miracles for those who asked for a miracle; but he did perform works of grace for those who needed grace and help.

Linked with that, Jesus does not want to be known as the Messiah so long as people have a wrong understanding of what the Messiah is. Many people thought of the Messiah as a human and political leader—someone to liberate Israel from the occupying Roman armies. Jesus does not want to be identified with those sorts of ambitions, or to encourage people to assume that his miracle-working power can be enlisted in the cause of a human and political agenda. It is only when people understand who Jesus is as the Son of God, and, in particular, what his death was about, that they can see what kind of Messiah Jesus is. In Matthew 17:9//Mark 9:9 Jesus tells his own disciples not to say to anyone what they experienced at the transfiguration "until the Son of Man had risen from the dead." In the light of the cross and resurrection, we can understand who Jesus is—not before.

Now that Christ is risen, we might think—and in a sense we are right to think—that the time for this secrecy is over; we can now "go public" with Jesus' healing power. But the Gospels would still urge caution. Jesus often worked his miracles very discreetly: he took the deaf and mute man "away from the crowd" to heal him (Mark 7:33), he led the blind man at Bethesda "outside the village" before opening his eyes (Mark 8:23), he refused to allow anyone to witness his raising of Jairus' daughter except the girl's parents and Peter, James and John (Luke 8:51). Certainly Jesus never sought to publicize or parade his works; he never went out of his way to gather a crowd to watch what he was about to do.

---

14. Examples are Matthew 8:4//Mark 1:43–44//Luke 5:14, Matthew 9:30, Matthew 12:16//Mark 3:12, Matthew 17:9//Mark 9:9, Mark 1:34//Luke 4:41, Mark 5:43//Luke 8:56, Mark 7:36, Mark 8:30.

That is what makes me wary of the modern tendency in some (not all!) extreme charismatic circles to publicize miracles using all the means that the modern world affords, like posting online video footage of meetings at which people are being prayed for to get up out of wheelchairs, or advertising "healing crusades." I have no doubt that some, maybe many, of the miracles thus promoted are genuine works of God's grace; but whilst there may truly be *signs* of God's miracle-working power in such contexts, I cannot see much of the *spirit* of Jesus' miracle-working ministry. Does anyone really think that the Jesus of the Gospels would send out mass publicity through the whole of Galilee, calling on people to turn up and see a miracle? Much of the language that is used in enthusiastic evangelical circles these days seems to reflect a desire to take the world by storm, as though our task is to conquer the earth rather than to seek to develop the meekness which, we are told on good authority, is the pre-condition for inheriting it.

Today's church needs to rediscover Jesus' ministry of signs; but we also need to learn to demonstrate those signs in the same way that Jesus did, so that they point people to, rather than distract people from, the Jesus who is above all the Savior from sin. We need the ministry of signs, but without the "hype" that so often accompanies it; and we need, whilst seeking the Lord to renew his works in our day, to be aware of the particular dangers of unwisely over-promoting miracles of healing. In our society, health has become a false god: a staggeringly high proportion of television advertisements are for beauty products, like creams to "reduce the signs of ageing"; health and fitness regimes of all kinds proliferate; alternative therapies abound, offering people the chance of a healthier life than the NHS can give them. The Roman poet Juvenal defined the ideal for which people should strive in life as *mens sana in corpore sano*—"a healthy mind in a healthy body." Today's western world seems to set rather less store by healthy minds, and very little by healthy souls; but healthy bodies are apparently the supreme good. Like many parents, when we were expecting our children, we were often asked, "Are you hoping for a boy or a girl?" Resisting the temptation to reply that we were indeed reasonably confident that it would be one or the other, we would say, quite genuinely, that we did not particularly mind. At least nine times out of ten, the person who had asked the question would respond, "Yes, so long as they're healthy, that's all that matters, isn't it?"

Well actually, no, it isn't. Of course health matters; of course we are concerned for the sick; and of course Jesus does minister to disease and suffering. But physical health is not "all" that matters, nor is it what matters the most. Character matters far more; and a relationship with God through Christ matters infinitely more. The danger of the modern "healing crusade" approach is that it can in fact pander to that idolatry of good health from which people need to be set free; it can seem to be offering people what they want for their secular happiness, rather than what they need for their spiritual wholeness. Jesus does not offer eternal youth, but eternal life. We need to minister the signs of the Kingdom in a way that gives people a thirst for that life.

Miracles and the Gospel

Those two main strands of Jesus' ministry—especially his Galilean ministry—must always go together. In the New Testament, teaching and signs, words and works, are always two sides of the same Gospel coin. Matthew stresses this very particularly: the ministry in chapters 5–9 is framed by the same summary sentence in 4:23 and 9:35: "Jesus went throughout Galilee, teaching in their synagogues, preaching the good news of the kingdom, and healing every disease and sickness." In between, there are three chapters of teaching (5–7, the Sermon on the Mount) then two chapters of miracles (8–9). When Jesus commissioned his disciples, he gave them the same charge: "As you go, preach this message: 'The kingdom of heaven is near.' Heal the sick, raise the dead, cleanse those who have leprosy, drive out demons" (Matthew 10:7–8).

The normal pattern of New Testament mission is that words and works[15] go hand in hand. Works demonstrate the reality of the Kingdom of God; and words then explain the significance of the works. That balance is as characteristic of John's Gospel as it is of the other three. Although, as we said earlier, John's emphasis is on Jesus' teaching about himself rather than on the lifestyle expected of his disciples, we see the same pattern of Jesus' works demonstrating truth and his words explaining truth. In Jesus' ministry in John 1–12, before we come to the upper room, the Last Supper and the cross, John presents us with a series of seven major discourses and seven miraculous signs;[16] and there is often a close connection between a

---

15. Of course the term "works" does not need to be confined simply to miracles; there are also works of compassion, works of charity, works of service. They too are signs of the Kingdom, alongside—but not, as some might suggest, in the place of—miraculous works of healing. It is right and proper that missionary societies should send, amongst others, doctors to parts of the world where medical care is minimal or non-existent. What is *not* right and proper is the kind of theology that says that in the New Testament the apostles performed healing miracles, but the modern church runs hospitals instead. Why can't we do both? Luke was, after all, a practicing doctor, but he was also a fellow-missionary with Paul, and he records a number of works of miraculous healing that were performed in the name of Jesus.

16. The signs are: [1] turning water into wine (2:1–11), [2] healing the nobleman's son (4:46–54), [3] healing the lame man (5:1–15), [4] feeding the five thousand

work and the teaching that arises from or leads up to it: so for example the discourse that revolves around Jesus as the light of the world is followed by his healing of a blind man, and the feeding of the five thousand leads to Jesus teaching about himself as the bread of life. In fact John 6 presents us with the clearest example of what happens when people separate Jesus' words from his works: Jesus feeds the five thousand with bread; the next day the crowd comes to find him, and Jesus says to them that they are looking for him, not because they are hungry for spiritual life, but because they had something to eat yesterday, and they are hoping for more today. They experienced the miracle, but they did not see, or at least understand, the sign. So Jesus explains the real significance of the bread: he himself is the bread of eternal life.

The church has not been good at keeping that healthy balance between Kingdom works and Gospel words. There are many good and devoted Christians who give their lives to feeding the hungry, caring for the destitute, working for the good of needy people. No one could possibly question the value of such service, nor fail to honor the heart of compassion that it demonstrates. But too often there has been no accompanying proclamation of the good news of salvation. Good works can turn poor people into rich people and hungry people into well-fed people; but they can never, in themselves, turn sinners into redeemed people. Words are needed to explain the significance of works as signs of the Kingdom: the works do not explain themselves. On the other hand, the western church has too often been very strong on words but somewhat lacking in works—certainly in works of power—and without works, there is nothing for the words to explain. In *My Fair Lady* Eliza, tired of Freddie's non-stop protestations of love, exclaims, "Words, words, words, I'm so sick of words!," and then bursts into song: "If you're in love, *show me!*" In a similar way, the unconverted world would have every right to say to the Christian church, if you say God loves me, show me.

In the book of Acts, most Gospel sermons are preached in response to questions that were asked, and those questions in their turn were prompted by something that people had seen that demonstrated the reality and the power of God. On the day of Pentecost, it was the disciples being filled with the Spirit and speaking in tongues; some people started asking (Acts 2:12), "What does this mean?" So Peter stood up and told them: it is all about

---

(6:1–15), [5] walking on water (6:16–21), [6] healing the man born blind (9:1–16), and [7] raising Lazarus (11:1–44). The discourses are: [1] the new birth (3:1–36), [2] the water of life (4:1–42), [3] the Father and the Son (5:19–47), [4] the bread of life (6:26–65), [5] the gift of the Spirit (7:1–52), [6] the light of the world (8:12–59), and [7] the good shepherd (10:1–38).

Jesus. In chapter 3, Peter and John healed a crippled beggar in the name of Jesus; when a crowd gathered, and people were expressing amazement at what had happened, Peter preached the Gospel of Christ to them. In Samaria, it was "when the crowds heard Philip and saw the miraculous signs he did" that they "paid close attention to what he said" (8:6). Peter was able to share the Gospel with Gentiles in the home of Cornelius because God gave Cornelius a vision of an angel; so Cornelius sends for Peter, gathers his friends together, and says to Peter that they are there "to listen to everything the Lord has commanded you to tell us" (10:33).

By contrast, sound evangelical preaching can sometimes seem to expect that people will listen to the message without having seen anything of the reality of God's Kingdom that can give them a reason why they should listen; it is words without works. And in the more liberal tradition of the church, there can be a very worthy commitment to addressing personal and social need, but without sharing the Gospel of the cross and resurrection; it is works without words. American schoolchildren are more familiar than their British counterparts with the phrase "show and tell," the practice of children bringing something to show to their class and talking about it to them. "Show and tell" could have been the motto of Jesus' ministry; and it should be the watchword of all Christian mission.

8

Controversy

"The Pharisees went out and plotted how they might kill Jesus"
(Matthew 12:14)

In terms of Jesus' own ministry, teaching about the Kingdom and working the signs of the Kingdom are the main threads that run though his work in Galilee. But there are two other important strands in the Galilean ministry, one of which is that Jesus repeatedly finds himself challenged by the Pharisees, who regard what he says and does as at best controversial and at worst outrageous. The things that the Pharisees take issue with are things that are also challenges for the church in our own day.

The Pharisees figure very largely, and very negatively, in the story of Jesus. The word "Pharisee" has come to imply simply a hypocrite; *Collins English Dictionary* defines the word "Pharisee," following the first meaning of "a member of an ancient Jewish sect," as "a self-righteous or hypocritical person." The term itself seems to be derived from a Hebrew word meaning "separated" or "set apart"; it refers to a group amongst the Jews who continued the tradition, from the time of Ezra, of the study of and devotion to the Old Testament law. Whereas the Sadducees saw the main focus of the law as its priestly and temple regulations, the Pharisees saw devotion to the law as consisting in complete commitment to fulfilling its ethical requirements in every area of daily life. In the Gospels they are frequently condemned by Jesus for their legalism and their hypocrisy, but Professor Cranfield is perhaps only very slightly over-stating the case when he says, "But it is important to recognize their real relative goodness. In the time of Jesus they were the real spiritual leaders of the nation . . . Jesus sides with them against the Sadducees . . . and certainly had more in common with them than with the Sadducees; and much of their theology is taken for granted in the New Testament."[1] Certainly the Pharisees stood for the authority of the Old Testament Scriptures and for a total commitment to living in obedience to God's Word; unfortunately this had led in far too many cases to a pride which made them look down on those who were less fully committed than they—in John 7:49 they dismiss the enthusiastic followers of Jesus in the words, "But this mob that knows nothing of the law—there is a curse on them"—and a legalism which had led them to think that holiness consisted in greater and greater devotion to more and more hair-splitting and petty rules. In short, the Pharisees were so set in their ways that they could not see how Jesus, who not only did not conform to all their ways, but actually showed love and grace to people who were blatant sinners, could possibly be a man of God, let alone the Messiah from God. Tragically, it would not be hard to think of parallel instances in the history of the evangelical church where commitment to the Bible has similarly degenerated into a very hard-line, unyielding exclusiveness, and sometimes to downright hypocrisy.

Controversy with the Pharisees

Throughout the Galilean ministry of Jesus he faces growing opposition from the Pharisees; and that opposition focuses on five key controversies that succeed one another throughout this first half of his ministry. The first is *Jesus' right to forgive sins* (Matthew 9:2–3//Mark 2:5–7//Luke 5:20–21). This arises out of the story of the healing of the cripple who was let down through the roof in Capernaum; Jesus heals the man's physical handicap, but first he pronounces forgiveness over his sins.[2] The Pharisees regard this as blasphemy; no one can forgive sins except God alone.

A second controversy develops soon after, because of *Jesus' associating with sinners* (Matthew 9:10–13//Mark 2:15–17//Luke 5:29–32). The Pharisees object to the fact that Jesus eats with tax-collectors and sinners; Jesus says that they are precisely the people he has come to serve and to save.

---

1. Cranfield, *Mark*, 105.

2. It is interesting that Jesus uses the phrase "the Son of Man has authority *on earth* to forgive sins": why, we might ask, "on earth"? The sense is likely to be that forgiveness is not merely to be hoped for in the future, in heaven; it can be experienced and received right here, right now. Because the Son of Man has appeared on earth, forgiveness is now available on earth.

Then there is a controversy about *Jesus and the Sabbath* (Matthew 12:1-14//Mark 2:23—3:6//Luke 6:1-11). Jesus not only rubs ears of corn between his fingers to have a snack—an action that in the Pharisees' eyes was classified as work, and therefore banned on the Sabbath—but also heals a man with a withered hand. When the Pharisees accuse Jesus of breaking the Sabbath, he responds by pointing out that the Sabbath was given to people to be a blessing, not a straitjacket, and that he is himself "Lord of the Sabbath"—a statement which, bearing in mind that all Jews knew that the Sabbath was God's institution, and was intended for God, was another unambiguous claim to divine authority.

The next issue is the so-called *"Beelzebub" controversy*.[3] The Pharisees accuse Jesus of doing his mighty works by the power of the devil (Matthew 12:24-29//Mark 3:22-27//Luke 11:14-22). In Jesus' response, he not only points out the absurdity of the suggestion—by casting out demons, he is actually undermining and overthrowing the devil's work: why would the devil himself want to do that?!—but he says two other things that have been the cause of a great deal of misunderstanding and concern to many Christians, and which for that reason deserve some comment.

The first is the so-called "strong man" saying: "No one can enter a strong man's house and carry off his possessions unless he first ties up the strong man" (Matthew 12:29//Mark 3:27//Luke 11:21-22). The phrase to "tie up," or more usually, following the wording of the Authorized Version, to "bind the strong man" has become something of a cliché in some charismatic and Pentecostal circles, in which many people are fond of saying things like "we need to bind the strong man," meaning to wage spiritual warfare against the devil in prayer. But that is to misunderstand what Jesus is saying. Satan is the "strong man," who had kept people in bondage to sin and evil. But Jesus has now come as the one who is stronger, and he has tied up the strong man, so he can release people from his influence. The fact that Jesus is casting out demons is evidence that he is already doing that—the strong man is already tied up. We do not need to "bind" him—Jesus has done it. In prayer, we can affirm the victory of the cross over all the principalities and powers of evil, and give thanks that Jesus has bound the strong man; it is on the basis of that work of Christ that we can pray for release for those who were the "strong man's" captives.

---

3. The name Beelzebub has a number of variant forms, including Baal-zebub and Beel-zebul. The original name was Baal-zebul, a Canaanite god whose name means literally "lord of the high place"; in a mocking parody of the name, the Jews changed one letter, and made it Baal-zebub, meaning "lord of the flies." By the time of Jesus this had clearly come to be used as a general name for the devil, "the prince of demons" (Matthew 12:24).

The second is the disturbing saying about the "unforgivable sin" (Matthew 12:32//Mark 3:29//Luke 12:10) which has, understandably, caused considerable anguish to many people. What does Jesus mean by "blasphemy against the Holy Spirit"? And why is it, alone amongst all sins, unforgivable? Here are four points which may shed some light on these admittedly difficult questions.

- We can be fairly sure that Jesus is not referring to a one-off comment people might make. He is speaking of a settled attitude of opposition to God and the works of God.

- He is not referring simply to a form of words. The word "blasphemy" might suggest "using a swear-word." But clearly more than that is involved. Jesus gives this warning in response to the Pharisees. They had seen Jesus doing the great work of setting people free from evil by the power of the Holy Spirit; they were claiming that he was doing it by the power of the devil. They were so blinded by their pride, and their refusal to believe that anybody except themselves could possibly be pleasing to God, that they were calling good evil and evil good. F. F. Bruce says, "If some people looked at the relief which [Jesus] was bringing to the bodies and minds of men and women and maintained that he was doing so with the help of their great spiritual oppressor, the prince of the demons, then their eyes were so tightly closed to the light that for them light had become darkness and good had become evil. The light is there for those who will accept it, but if some refuse the light, where else can they hope to receive illumination?"[4]

- We should stress that, if anyone is ever troubled that they might have committed this sin, the very fact that they are troubled about it is evidence that they haven't. They still have a conscience. The people Jesus is talking about are so convinced that they and they alone are right that they dismiss anyone who disagrees with them as a tool of the devil.

- Finally, whilst all sin is sin, and we should not think of any sin as trivial, it is important to remember that Jesus regards the spiritual pride of the Pharisees as far more serious than the moral and social sins of which the Pharisees disapproved. That is seen very clearly in the story in Luke 7:36–50 of the woman "who had lived a sinful life" (verse 37), whom Jesus forgave. The Pharisees thought she was beyond forgiveness. Jesus' words about the unforgivable sin, severe though they are, show us that the only thing that is really beyond forgiveness is being so totally convinced that you are better than everyone else that you refuse

---

4. Bruce, *Hard Sayings*, 90.

even to think that you might have any faults yourself. In effect, the only sin that is really beyond forgiveness is the stubborn refusal to accept that you yourself might actually have done anything that requires forgiveness.

That is the background to the saying about the blasphemy against the Holy Spirit. It is one thing not to realize who Jesus is, and therefore to believe and say wrong things about him ("Anyone who speaks a word against the Son of Man will be forgiven," Matthew 12:32); it is quite another to see Jesus doing in the power of the Holy Spirit mighty works that are manifestly works of good, and yet to be so consumed with pride that, because he disagrees with you, you utterly reject him and all he stands for as Satanic. It is important to realize that Jesus is not saying that all Pharisees think like that; in fact, he is not even saying that the particular Pharisees with whom he is talking have actually committed the unforgivable sin. He is however pointing out the great danger towards which their proud refusal to acknowledge that they too need God's forgiveness might tend.

The last controversial issue concerns the question, *what is authoritative for shaping the lives of God's people?* It arises when the Pharisees rebuke Jesus and his disciples for eating with ceremonially unwashed hands (Matthew 15:1-20//Mark 7:1-23). Jesus insists that the Word of God is authoritative, not the man-made traditions that the Pharisees are so keen to uphold.

Jesus' teaching here stresses that being "unclean" (that is, unacceptable in God's eyes) is not a matter of conforming or not conforming to rules and rituals. It is about the fact that we are unclean on the inside, in our hearts and characters (Matthew 15:19-20//Mark 7:20-23). Jesus makes our hearts and lives really clean on the inside. Religious ceremonies can only make us "symbolically" clean—they can teach us about the importance of being clean in God's eyes, but they cannot *make* us clean. Only Jesus can do that.

Those five points of contention are typical of things that still cause controversy amongst religious people.

Jesus' claims

The essential controversy—in many ways the one that underlies all the rest—is about who Jesus is. Those who questioned Jesus' right to forgive sins said, "Why does this fellow talk like that? He's blaspheming! Who can forgive sins but God alone?" (Mark 2:7). They were right: to forgive sins is indeed the prerogative of God. That Jesus does it can mean only one of two things: either that he is a man sinfully arrogating to himself the spurious right to be able to do what only God can do, or that he really has come into this world with the full authority of God himself. The Pharisees jump to the conclusion that the former must be the case; Jesus heals the cripple, as a sign to them that the second is true. The secular world, as well as the more liberal wing of the historical church, is happy to debate theories about Jesus the teacher, the example, the religious leader. It is when we make absolute claims for Jesus as Lord of all, as God the Son, and as the Way, the Truth and the Life, that they rebel and accuse us of being politically incorrect or narrow-minded. But whether our world likes it or not—and for the most part it does not—that is the Jesus who is presented in the Gospels, and is therefore the Jesus in whom we believe, and whom we proclaim as Lord and Savior. Whilst we must never use the fact that Jesus encountered controversy with the Pharisees to justify being deliberately or discourteously confrontational—the call to be "peace-makers" applies to our witness as well as to our pastoral care—we are certainly to avoid watering down our presentation of who Jesus is just in case some people might object.

Jesus' company

Then there is also a controversy about the people with whom Jesus associates. The comfortable church may, but the Kingdom of God does not, confirm respectable religious people in their respectable religion; rather, Jesus embraces the moral and social outcasts, the poor and needy. They were the people Jesus came to minister to. In their day John Wesley and William Booth were looked down on by, and in Wesley's case expelled from, the church because they devoted themselves to the service of the socially disreputable. Sadly, such Pharisaism has not completely died out from the western church scene. Lesslie Newbigin puts it very well:

> "Jesus could not satisfy the *vox populi*. He outraged it. He rejected the 'righteous' and accepted the 'sinners.' Or, to put the matter more accurately, the coming of Jesus is the shining of a light (1 John 1:5) in which *all* are exposed as God's enemies, and *all* are accepted as God's beloved. But the 'righteous'—the representatives of religion, of morality, of social and political order, of sacred traditions—and the 'sinners'—the 'man in the street,' the . . . crowd demonstrating outside the governor's mansion—are revealed in the final showdown as the murderers of God, and both are accepted as the beloved of God."[5]

---

5. Newbigin, *Open Secret*, 55.

This is a theme that will become prominent in the second half of Jesus' ministry, so we will reserve further comment on it until then.

Jesus' grace

Another age-old issue is the *conflict between religious rules and God's grace*. The Pharisees wanted to enforce strict religious rules (about things like keeping the Sabbath). Jesus said that God freely gives us a way of life that is for our good. Some people still want faith to be all about keeping rules; the more strictly we keep the rules, the more righteous we are.[6] One of the features of church life which proves again and again the natural tendency of human beings to start in the Spirit and end in the flesh is that many of the practices of the church which began as helpful ways in which people could live out their life in relationship with God—even such fundamental things as taking communion—can come, over a period of time, to be seen as things that we have to do because they are the proper religious thing to do; things that were originally given as helpful means to build saints become tools which saints can wield against sinners who fail to practice them properly. Jesus' litmus test for all "religious practices" is: do they liberate people to live better for God's Kingdom, or enslave people in a mass of religious regulation that they struggle to fulfill but dare not neglect?

Jesus' power

Then we come to confusion about *spiritual power*. There are those who are not comfortable with the supernatural and the miraculous, and some who will reject all such things as "from the devil." They prefer a merely human religious life. But Jesus works supernatural miracles and brings spiritual, heavenly life. There are of course counterfeit works from the devil, as Jesus said there would be (Mark 13:22). The test of an authentic Kingdom sign is not simply the nature of the sign in itself; it is the moral and spiritual fruit that accompanies and grows from it. Works of God should always lead to a greater awareness of, devotion to and faith in Jesus; where that does not occur, and in particular where the opposite occurs, we have grounds for suspecting a spiritual deception. The enemy will counterfeit Kingdom works precisely because real Kingdom works exist, just as a criminal will

---

6. It is quite common, especially in working-class communities, to hear people described as "very religious" on the grounds that they never swear, smoke or drink. Often being religious is defined in terms of things you *don't* do; Jesus' Kingdom is about living out the positive qualities of a new life.

counterfeit £10 notes because real £10 notes exist; no one ever tried to produce a fake £8 note. For Christians to fear, disbelieve in or avoid the genuinely miraculous on the grounds that there are also counterfeit miracles is to allow Satan to decide for us which parts of the Bible we will hold to; we would do better to remember the Latin proverb, *abusus non tollit usum*—"abuse does not remove [proper] use." Paul's words in 1 Corinthians 14:40 are important: addressing the abuse of spiritual gifts in worship, he says "everything should be done in a fitting and orderly way." He is quite clear: everything should be *done*—not ignored, or "not done"—but let it be done *properly*.

Jesus' authority

And finally, there is the controversy about *religious traditions versus the Word of God*. The Pharisees had traditions which they had to obey; Jesus said they ought to be obeying what God's Word says. There are still traditions in church life which dominate us; how often have people asking why a church does something in such-and-such a way been told that the answer is, "Because we've always done it this way!" And the fact that we are today part of a church that has existed for nearly two thousand years, and that most of our denominational churches have a history dating back at least a century, and in most cases several centuries, only exacerbates the problem. It was the American theologian Jaroslav Pelikan who neatly defined the difference between "tradition" and "traditionalism" in the words, "Tradition is the living faith of the dead; traditionalism is the dead faith of the living":[7] in other words, tradition, in the best sense of the word, is about the fact that we stand today in the line of those who in the past have lived out a real faith in God, and we seek by the grace of God to follow worthily in their footsteps; whereas we know we are dealing with "traditionalism" when those who themselves show little sign of any real personal experience of God still insist on doing church this way because that's the way we've always done it.

In the face of such a dictatorship of tradition, Jesus affirms that in the Kingdom of God we are governed by God's Word alone; not tradition instead of God's Word, nor God's Word as filtered through and adapted in the light of tradition. So the Galilean ministry of Jesus ends where it began, with Jesus reaffirming what he said at the beginning of the Sermon on the Mount, that he has not come to set aside the Scriptures (the Law and the Prophets),

---

7. In an interview in the American weekly magazine *U.S. News and World Report* (June 26th 1989).

but to fulfill them. In the face of these ever-present challenges to faith, the call to Christians today is to do the same.

Having said that, the modern western church needs to be careful not to court or create the wrong kind of controversy. We are all only too aware that there has been a great deal of controversy in and around the church throughout history and in our own day, but relatively little of it has anything in common with the issues that caused the Pharisees to oppose Jesus; it is far too often because of moral failings in the church that are unearthed and become newspaper headlines, or internal divisions and in-house squabblings within the church over issues like the ordination of women. Being prepared to face challenges from the world that does not like our Gospel message is not the same thing as washing our ecclesiastical dirty linen in public. Moreover, it worth remembering that Jesus' manner and behavior were morally above reproach; though the Pharisees found his claims and his Gospel unacceptable, they could find no grounds on which to accuse him of personal failings. The same is not true of those Christians who make controversial statements in a way that is self-righteous, dismissive of others, or negatively confrontational.

Jesus did not go out of his way to be controversial: he lived, proclaimed and demonstrated in his life the Kingdom of God and the Gospel of grace. Some people found that unacceptable: so be it. If people are going to criticize us, let it be because we believe in Jesus as Lord and Savior, because we show love to people whom they think do not deserve to be loved, because we seek to live by the truth of the Bible. Peter, who after all saw clearly how Jesus lived and dealt with his opponents, has a caution that we would be wise to heed; in 1 Peter 2:12, 4:14–16 he writes:

> "Live such good lives among the pagans that, though they accuse you of doing wrong, they may see your good deeds and glorify God on the day he visits us . . . If you are insulted because of the name of Christ, you are blessed . . . If you suffer, it should not be as a murderer or thief or any other kind of criminal, or even as a meddler. However, if you suffer as a Christian, do not be ashamed, but praise God that you bear that name."

Those who follow Christ are not called to be self-appointed martyrs, to moan about how badly they are treated, and certainly not to stir up controversy by their own unwise and irritating interference—by being "a meddler"—but rather to remain positive under pressure, to "praise God," and to ensure that, though others may find fault with the Gospel we believe and proclaim, they can find no grounds on which to criticize our personal lives or conduct. If we are faithful to the Jesus of the Gospels, many, not least the comfortably religious and respectable, may find the person of Christ challenging; but it is our responsibility to ensure that they do not find his people off-putting.

Controversy with the Jews

As so often, John's Gospel covers similar ground to the synoptics, but in a different way. There is in John no shortage of conflict between Jesus and the leaders of the Jews, and it centers around the fact that the latter frequently found Jesus offensive; but whereas in the synoptics the focus of controversy is the issues listed above, many of which arise from the way in which Jesus acted with other people, in John it is above all in the specific claims that Jesus makes about his own divine nature.

> "Jesus said to them, 'My Father is always at his work to this very day, and I too am working.' For this reason the Jews tried all the harder to kill him; not only was he breaking the Sabbath, but he was even calling God his own Father, making himself equal with God" (5:17–18); "At this the Jews began to grumble about him, because he said, 'I am the bread that came down from heaven'" (6:41); "'We are not stoning you for any of these [great miracles],' they replied, 'but for blasphemy, because you, a mere man, claim to be God'" (10:33).

This reminds us, first, of what we saw in some of the synoptics' controversies: that it is above all the person of Jesus himself, the Jesus who makes divine claims for himself, that people find offensive. But there is another aspect to this which relates to a major theme in John, and on which we touched when we spoke in chapter 4 of the ways in which Jesus is the fulfillment of the religious institutions of the Old Testament. Anyone who reads carefully through John can hardly fail to notice that the Jews are spoken of throughout the Gospel in ways that are, to say the least, hostile. This starts in the prologue: Jesus "came to that which was his own, and his own [that is, 'his own people,' the Jewish people] did not receive him" (1:11). There are constant references in John to "the Jews,"[8] most of which are negative or hostile: Jesus says of the Jews that they do not have the love of God in their hearts (5:42), that they do not really believe Moses (5:46–47), that they judge by human standards and lack true judgment (7:24, 8:15), that they do

---

8. The word "Jew[s]" occurs in the three synoptic Gospels a total of sixteen times, twelve of them in Jesus' title "King of the Jews"; it comes seventy-one times in John.

not keep the law, and seek to kill Jesus (7:19), that they will die in their sins (8:24), that they are slaves of sin (8:34), that they are children of the devil (8:44), that they do not belong to God (8:47), that they are liars (8:55), that they are spiritually blind and that their guilt remains (9:41). What is perhaps even more surprising is the way in which Jesus sometimes distances himself from the Jewish people, even though he was himself a Jew, indeed, the King of the Jews. Speaking to the Pharisees, he says, referring to the Jewish Scriptures (the Old Testament), "In your own law it is written . . ." (8:17)—why in "your" law, rather than in "the" law, or even "our" law?; in 8:56 he refers to "your father Abraham"—again, why "your" father, rather than "our" father?; and in 13:33, speaking to his own disciples (all of whom, like Jesus himself, were Jews) he says, "just as I told the Jews, so I tell you now . . ."

It would be completely wrong to speak of this negative portrayal of "the Jews" as "anti-Semitic," and not only because there are many positive references to the Jewish background to the Gospel in John: Jesus is indeed "the King of Israel" (1:49); John uses the Jewish title "[the] Christ" more often than any other Gospel—nineteen times in all, as many as Mark and Luke put together—and his is the only Gospel to use the transliterated Hebrew word *messías* (= "Messiah") (1:41, 4:25); Jesus himself says that "salvation is from the Jews" (4:22); the Jewish Scriptures testify to Jesus (5:39); Abraham rejoiced to see the day of Christ (8:56).[9] What we find in John is certainly not a disparagement of the Jewish people on account of their race, which would be the normal definition of "anti-Semitism"; it is rather a judgment of and maybe a warning against those Jews who, whilst claiming to be devoted to God and to the traditions and practices of Old Testament faith, reject and indeed persecute Christ, and refuse to accept him as the one sent by God. It is significant that the most severe attacks against Jesus in John's Gospel take place in the context of various "festivals of the Jews" (e.g. 7:14–24, 10:22–33): it is as though John is saying of these Old Testament ceremonies that they have become religious festivals celebrated by those who rejected and persecuted Jesus.

There may be a reason for this theme in the situation of the church in the middle and later decades of the first century. Not only was there from the start regular persecution of Christian by the Jews, but the time came

---

9. The NIV translates this admittedly strange saying as "Your father Abraham rejoiced *at the thought of seeing* my day; he saw it and was glad"; the first clause reads literally "Abraham your father was glad that he should see my day." This is most likely to mean that Abraham saw prophetically that one day the Christ would come and save God's people; perhaps this implies a special revelation from God about the significance of the promise that in his, Abraham's, seed all the nations would be blessed (Genesis 12:3).

when the Roman authorities also started to oppress Christians; but Judaism was a protected religion in the Roman Empire. It started to become clear to Jewish Christians that if they were explicit in their confession of Jesus as Savior and Lord they risked imprisonment or even death; but if they remained outwardly Jewish in devotional life, they were safe. The letter to the Hebrews was written precisely against the background of that dilemma, and its great theme is that Jesus is the fulfillment of that which is merely hinted at and prefigured in Old Testament Judaism, so that to retreat from explicitly *Christian* faith back into the formal Judaism from which it developed is to revert from spiritual substance to symbolic shadow. There is perhaps a sense in which, in this respect at least, Hebrews is the New Testament book which is, apart from the letters of John, closest in spirit to John's Gospel. In John also, there is a warning that it is only in following Christ as Savior and Lord, and in professing him as the Son of God, that there is life: "to those who received him"—that is, who accepted him on his own terms as the Son sent by the Father—"he gave the right to become children of God" (1:12). John summarizes the purpose of his book in 20:31: "These things are written that you may believe that Jesus is the Christ, the Son of God, and that by believing you may have life in his name." So reads the NIV, as do most translations; and those words might give the impression that John's purpose is evangelistic—to lead those who are not yet believers to faith. Maybe it is, at least in part. But, as was pointed out in chapter 1, it is quite likely that what John wrote was, "that you may *continue* to believe, and that by continuing to believe you may *continue* to have life in his name":[10] that would be entirely consistent with Jesus' stress on the importance of "abiding" in him (15:4–7). It is likely that John's stated purpose is to encourage Jewish Christians who might be tempted to revert to the safety of formal Jewish practice (with maybe just a hint of Christian flavoring in it?) to realize that it is by abiding in Christ, by confessing Jesus as "the Christ, the Son of God," whatever risks that may entail, that they will continue to live in the eternal life of God.

That that is a key theme in John's Gospel is confirmed by a story that comes close to the middle of the book. In chapter 9, Jesus heals a man born blind; the Jews interrogate the man, and when he continues to affirm that Jesus is sent by God, they expel him from the synagogue (verse 34). When Jesus meets the man, he asks him, "Do you believe in the Son of Man?" That is far from being a theoretical doctrinal question. If the man answers "no," or even expresses some reservations, he can be welcomed back into the family

---

10. The only Bible translation known to me that renders this verse as "continue to believe" is the *New Living Translation*; most stick to the simple verb "believe," though many, including the NIV, include in a footnote the alternative wording "continue to believe."

of formal Jewish religion, which is clearly, for anyone born into the Jewish tradition, fundamental to their sense of identity as one of God's people. But the man answers, "'Lord, I believe,' and he worshiped him" (verse 38). John's Gospel is calling on all Jews who have been or are in danger of being similarly "ex-communicated" because of their devotion to Jesus as the Son of God to continue to profess the same faith and worship the same Lord.

It would be naïve in the extreme to assume that, because pressure to revert to formal Jewish faith in order to avoid persecution is hardly an issue in our day and culture, this theme in John has no relevance for us. For all people, living faith in Jesus as Son of God and Savior has, apart from the grace of God, a natural tendency to water itself down to become formal and socially conformist religion. That is after all why Jesus encourages his people to "abide" in him: the gardener does not have to force a plant to stay rooted in the soil where it is; unless he or someone else deliberately removes it, it will "abide" where it was sown. People are not by nature like that: we do not remain rooted in Christ except by a personal and conscious decision to remain so rooted. All sorts of pressures, including political correctness and the desire for social acceptance, not to mention the major challenges that come when we take Jesus and his word at face value, can tempt believers to back away from a radical devotion to Christ as the unique Son of God, and to find refuge instead in an acceptable, moderate and safe church culture.

It is interesting, in this context, to note that the criticisms of the Pharisees for their hypocrisy and their moral and social corruption, with which we are familiar from the synoptics, are never found in John. For John, what made the Pharisees the enemies of true faith was not their moral failings, but their rejection of Jesus as Lord. Of course we must never forget or ignore Jesus' principle that "by their fruit you will recognize them" (Matthew 7:16): anyone can *say* to Jesus, "Lord! Lord!," but the test of whether they are in fact living their lives under his Lordship is the "fruit" that is seen in them, which will at least include moral righteousness. John's warning does not overthrow that principle, but needs to be set alongside it. Socially acceptable religion can seem, indeed in a sense actually *be*, very good, moral, decent; but if it denies or ignores the absolute uniqueness and centrality of Christ, it is not a form of, but rather the rejection of, the Gospel of Jesus. John is written, as he himself said (20:31), to impress upon us all that the salvation that Jesus came into the world to bring is found as we remain graciously but unapologetically committed to Jesus as "the Christ, the Son of God,"[11] and that by "continuing to believe in him you may continue to have life in his name."

11. The fact that John uses these two titles of Jesus stresses that his Gospel is intended for everybody, for the whole world: "the Christ" is an appeal to Jews to identify with their own King; and the title "Son of God" would appeal to Gentiles, who were

9

Training the Twelve

"He appointed twelve, designating them apostles" (Mark 3:14)

The other important thing Jesus does in the Galilean phase of his ministry is to choose his twelve apostles from amongst all those who are following him (Matthew 10:1–4//Mark 3:13–19//Luke 6:12–16). The last parts of the Galilean ministry focus more on Jesus' training of his disciples. They have already been with Jesus for some time, and have seen his works. He now starts to give them more personal teaching and experience of ministry.

The word "apostle" means "one who is sent." It seems to be used in the New Testament in two main ways: first, of the twelve disciples originally chosen by Jesus; and second, in a wider sense, as a term for the ministry of pioneering new works and establishing new missions and churches—in this sense, people like James, the brother of Jesus (Galatians 1:19), Barnabas (Acts 14:14), Andronicas and Junias[1] (Romans 16:7), and Silas (1 Thessalonians

---

familiar from their own religious mythology with the idea that gods have sons—this Gospel could reveal to them how Christ is in a unique way *the* Son of God.

1. It is likely that the second name should be taken as the feminine "Junia," which would suggest that "Andronicus and Junia" may have been a married couple, like Aquila and Priscilla. Those who find the very idea that the term "apostle" could be applied to a woman unacceptable sometimes suggest that "they are notable among the apostles" means, not that they are apostles, and notable ones at that, but rather that they are people who are regarded as notable *by* the apostles: that is a possible but far less likely interpretation of Paul's phrase. Many commentators and translations prefer to avoid the implication of a female apostle by keeping to the masculine form "Junias"; but to

2:6; see 1:1, which specifies that the "we" in 2:6 means Paul and Silas) are called apostles. The specific task of the original twelve was that they should be the group authorized by Jesus to establish once and for all the doctrinal content of Christian faith;[2] and in particular, they were to be witnesses of his resurrection (Acts 1:21–22). There is considerable debate in the contemporary church about whether or not there are still in any sense apostles today. Without rehearsing all the pros and cons of that argument, it is agreed by most people that the whole church is to be "apostolic" in character: believers collectively are those who are sent by Jesus into the world to live for him and serve him there. In Ephesians 4:11 Paul lists five main leadership gifts in the church, beginning with "apostles"; it is a matter of some debate amongst commentators whether he means "apostles" as a generic term—those who throughout church history are gifted by God for trans-local oversight and missionary service—or whether he means by "apostles" specifically "*the* apostles," meaning the first-generation group, the Twelve plus himself, who once for all laid the doctrinal foundation of Christian faith. What is quite clear however is that he stresses that the role of all church leaders is (verse 12) "to prepare God's people for works of service."[3] Apostles are to help the whole church to become increasingly apostolic, prophets are to help the whole church to become increasingly prophetic, evangelists are to help the

---

decide what a text must have been on the grounds of a prejudice that we are unwilling to have challenged is not the most objective approach to biblical interpretation. Having said that, this text is not sufficient in itself to establish a biblical precedent for female apostles; whilst the textual evidence strongly favors the feminine "Junia," it is not completely clear-cut. But the possibility is at least interesting.

2. Of course Paul was also a major apostolic figure whose teaching spelled out the doctrinal significance of Jesus' death and resurrection. As well as being an apostle in the more general sense of one with a trans-local ministry, Paul stands alongside the Twelve in their unique and unrepeatable role; his writings are doctrinally foundational in the same way as those of Matthew, John, and Peter. That is part of the reason why he describes himself as an apostle "abnormally born" (1 Corinthians 15:8): he is an apostle in the same way as the original Twelve, but unlike them he was called to that role only after Christ had ascended back to heaven.

3. It is important that this sentence be rightly construed. It does *not* mean that apostles (and prophets, etc.) are given to the church so that they can [1] prepare God's people, and [2] do works of service (that is, the apostles doing the works of service); it means that they are to prepare the church so that *the church* can do the works of service. Nicky Gumbel tells the story of John Wimber, who was once confronted by an irate member of his church who complained to him that, when he had come across a man in need of food and accommodation, he had tried and failed to contact any of the church leaders or their staff; so in the end, he had to look after the man himself. He protested, "'Don't you think the church should take care of people like this?' John Wimber thought for a minute and then said, 'It looks like the church did.'" (Quoted in Gumbel, *Questions of Life*, 226.)

whole church to become increasingly evangelistic, and so on. So we do not need to allow the debate about whether church leaders today are rightly labeled "apostles" to prevent us learning from the way Jesus taught the Twelve; what he taught them can help us all to be, in the real sense of the word, an apostolic people, sent by God into the world to serve his mission and his Kingdom.

The fully apostolic role of the Twelve in establishing the church was still a couple of years in the future. But in Galilee Jesus gives them a first taste of their future task. In Matthew 10:5-42//Mark 6:7-13//Luke 9:1-6 he commissions his disciples for mission, and sends them out to preach. Matthew has the most substantial instruction given to the disciples, as Jesus prepares to send them out in twos to proclaim and demonstrate the Kingdom as he has been doing. Mark and Luke also contain some of the teaching in Matthew 10, but not as much.

Matthew's Gospel is carefully structured: 4:23 is a general statement that Jesus preached and healed; and this is repeated almost word for word in 9:35. In between, in chapters 5-9, we have the Sermon on the Mount (chapters 5-7), which shows Jesus teaching; and a series of miracles in chapters 8 and 9 which show Jesus healing. Then, after the repeated general statement that Jesus taught and healed (9:35), Jesus commissions his disciples to do the same—to preach and to heal.

That in itself is a clear indication that Jesus' perception of the ministry which his disciples would exercise is as a continuation of the very same ministry that he himself had initiated. Christians can sometimes say, as though stating a self-evident fact, "Of course, we can't always do exactly the same things that Jesus did . . . ," to which, in the light of Matthew 10, we have to reply, why not? Jesus seems to think that it is the norm that we should.[4]

Of course, some of what Jesus says in Matthew 10 relates to the immediate situation which his disciples will face as they go out for their first experience of traveling around preaching. Verses 5-6 ("Do not go among the Gentiles or enter any town of the Samaritans. Go rather to the lost sheep of Israel"), 9-10 ("Do not take along any gold or silver or copper in your belts; take no bag for the journey, or extra tunic, or sandals or a staff; for the

---

4. There is a view that the reason why we should not expect to do the same works that Jesus and his immediate disciples did is that those Kingdom works were intended only for the age of the first-generation apostles, and not for subsequent ages in the church. Without at this point offering a full rebuttal of that view, it is hard to sustain in the light of Jesus' commission at the end of Matthew, where he tells his apostles to teach those whom they would later bring to faith to do all the things that he had taught them to do; in other words, the pattern of Kingdom ministry in words and works that he had taught his disciples was to be the pattern they told later generations of believers to adopt.

worker is worth his keep"), and 11 ("Whatever town or village you enter, search for some worthy person there and stay at his house until you leave") are mainly guidelines about how the disciples were to act on this particular mission trip.

- The first instruction, to go only to Jews, reflects the fact that this first half of Jesus' ministry was focused in Israel; it would later widen out to embrace Samaritans and Gentiles.

- The words in verses 9–10 about "gold or silver" etc., have at their heart the principle that the disciples should take with them only what was absolutely essential, no extras. "Sandals" probably means, do not take a spare pair of sandals: the ones you are wearing will suffice. The word translated "extra," referring to the "tunic," is in fact simply the number "two," but the spirit of that word probably governs the next words, "sandals" and "staff," as well.[5] There are probably three reasons for this simple lifestyle: first, to teach the important principle that those involved in Christian service should not be concerned about what they can gain from it, to eradicate the "profit-motive"; second, to teach them the principle he had spelled out in the Sermon on the Mount, of trusting in God to provide for their day-to-day needs; and third, because traveling preachers could reasonably expect to receive something from those to whom they ministered: hence the comment, "the worker is worth his keep."[6]

- The words in verse 11 about remaining in one house stress that these missionaries should, once they have established themselves in a community, stop being concerned about their own needs, and focus on the

5. The fact that in Mark 6:8 Jesus tells his disciples that they should take nothing "except a staff" need not be seen as a glaring contradiction. There would be times in Jesus' and the disciples' ministries when this or that item (like a staff) would be needed, and other times when they might not. That in itself should guard us against reading too much significance, especially symbolic and allegorical significance, into the specific items mentioned here as necessary or not. The essential lesson is more general: avoid unnecessary "baggage."

6. It should be stressed that Jesus is here speaking of itinerant apostles receiving practical hospitality from those amongst whom they minister: he is *not* saying that preachers and missionaries should charge a fee for their services! The issue of the right and wrong ways in which to practice paid ministry requires more substantial exploration than is appropriate or possible here; but the story in 2 Kings 5 of the healing by Elisha of Namaan, in which Elisha was insistent that he would not take any payment for his ministry, which his servant Gehazi saw as a missed opportunity to pocket a considerable reward, is a warning to those who would expect the people to whom they go as missionaries to pay them for their services. On the contrary, says Jesus, "Freely you have received, freely give" (Matthew 10:8); or, as the *New English Bible* rather neatly puts it, "You received without cost: give without charge."

Kingdom purpose for which they are there: it would be inconsistent with the spirit of their mission if, every few days, hearing that there might be a nicer house where they could stay, they were to keep moving from place to place.

However the whole chapter, including these verses, also gives us important principles about our own mission today. For example, it is important that we do not "carry baggage" (verses 9–10)—in other words, that we do not let secular things clutter up our lives and get in the way of our mission. We always engage in mission in a spirit of peace (verses 12–13), not in a confrontational or aggressive way. We should not be surprised if we face unpopularity and opposition (verses 16–31), but God promises to help us say the right thing when we are "put on the spot" in a threatening way (verses 19–20). We need always to serve out of a healthy respect for God, not to win the approval of or to court popularity with people (verses 26–28).

But for a more detailed study of the principles of Jesus' mission, we turn to Luke. In Luke 9 Jesus sent out his twelve apostles; but then in chapter 10 we are told that he appointed seventy-two others, and sent them out two by two in the same way. These seventy-two were not apostles—inasmuch as any Christian is ever "ordinary," they were "ordinary disciples"—and so we can certainly receive what Jesus says to them as being said to us also. The very fact that Jesus appoints others, besides the twelve, should encourage us to be confident that Jesus' ministry was not to be continued by the apostles alone.

The fact that he chose seventy-two is perhaps significant. Some manuscripts read "seventy," and there are Bible translations that prefer to adopt that figure, since it is a round number, and has some symbolic significance in the Bible,[7] but there may be a good reason for accepting "seventy-two" as the original figure. Jesus has already sent out his twelve apostles in six groups of two; in this second wave of mission he seems to be sending out six new teams of twelve (seventy-two being 12 × 6), each of which may have been led by a pair of the original twelve. We cannot know for certain that this is what happened; but it would fit in with the biblical pattern spelled out in 2 Timothy 2:2—"The things you have heard me say . . . entrust to reliable men who will also be qualified to teach others." And if it is true, it gives us a model for the helpful principle of always looking for the next generation

---

7. Seventy descendants of Abraham went down to Egypt (Genesis 46:27); and alongside Moses and Aaron, there were also seventy elders of Israel on the desert journey (Exodus 24:1) who were later filled with the Spirit (Numbers 11:16,24–25). Just as the twelve apostles clearly represent a New Testament equivalent of the twelve sons of Jacob, so seventy other missionaries could be seen as a New Testament equivalent of the wider leadership of Israel.

of servants and leaders. Anyone who is appointed to any ministry should always see it as part of their work to identify and help to equip those who will later take up the same ministry and continue it.

We are told in Luke 10:1 that Jesus sent these seventy-two "to every town and place where he was about to go." Like John the Baptist, they too are sent out to prepare the way for Jesus. Whenever the American president is about to go on an overseas trip, an "advance team" is sent on ahead to finalize the arrangements for his meetings. We, the Christian church, are Jesus' "advance team"; we are sent to every place in the world to which Jesus will one day return, to prepare people for his coming. And that sense of being sent into the world in the light of Jesus' future coming should always be what shapes our mission. We serve in a spirit of anticipation. Christians can engage in mission from a variety of motivations, but some of those motivations can from the outset cast a shadow over the work that will be done. Too often churches can decide that it is time to "do some evangelism" for reasons that are either duty-driven—we understand that we ought to, it is one of the things that Christians are supposed to do—or need-driven: there are so many people out there with needs, and we have to do something to try and help them. To be sure, it is nobler to be moved by the needs of others than from a sense of dry duty, but Jesus' mission, if it is to thrive, must always be Kingdom-driven: we go out and tell people the good news because Jesus is coming in glory, because there will be new heavens and a new earth, because we have a wonderful future, and we would love others to share in it.

That is one of the great lessons of the "harvest" metaphor in verse 2; it reminds us of the parables of the Kingdom in Matthew 13, and that mission, to use the theological term, is *eschatological*; that is, it is looking for the future Kingdom, the new heavens and the new earth. Our aim has always to be to draw people into a different Kingdom, not merely to enhance their lives in this world: we are not called to improve conditions in the field, but to prepare people to be gathered into God's heavenly barns. Wheat grows in a field so that it can be gathered into a barn for different use; and people live in this world so they can be gathered into God's heavenly Kingdom, for God's purposes.

In verse 2 Jesus also assures his servants that there will always be work for them to do: "the harvest is *plentiful*." There is no shortage of a harvest to reap—the shortage is in the availability of reapers. How often in this country do we hear Christians complain that there is no proper harvest, that "people aren't interested." But God-anointed harvesters will always recognize that there is a harvest out there waiting to be gathered. "No one is interested" can often be the disillusioned Christian's short-hand for "whenever we have tried our usual methods of inviting people to church, no one has come."

Whether those "methods" have much in common with Jesus' pattern for service, which we shall see in verses 5–9, is a legitimate if sometimes disturbing question. And just as in Nehemiah 4:3 Tobiah tried to discourage the Jews from rebuilding the wall of Jerusalem by pointing out that no matter what they did, it was unlikely to last, so our enemy the devil will often want us to believe that whatever we try to do by way of mission, it is most unlikely to achieve anything. Nehemiah refused to listen to Tobiah; and the wall was built. Christians are unfortunately sometimes more willing to believe the devil's negative propaganda than Jesus' positive promises; and the secret inner conviction, when we get involved in works of mission, that it won't do any good, is likely to prove to be a self-fulfilling prophecy. Those who aim at nothing will in all probability hit their target.

Furthermore, the fact that Jesus, as so often in his teaching, uses the metaphor of a "harvest" reminds us of the important lesson that mission is a slow process. Harvests do not grow overnight. Jesus' parable of the growing seed (Mark 4:26–29) shows, amongst other things, that people are at different stages along a journey: some have never yet had the seed of Gospel life sown into them; some have received a little of the message of the Kingdom, but it has not yet put down proper roots, let alone started to bear fruit. And in all cases, we are called to be like the farmer, who, James tells us, "waits for the land to yield its valuable crop, [and is] patient . . ." (James 5:7). Those who embark on Christian service expecting immediate results are doomed to immediate disappointment; mission is a process, not a quick-fix.

We need also to remember that Jesus refers to God himself in verse 2 as "the Lord of the harvest." We are farm laborers; we are not respectable gentleman-farmers who can make our own decisions about what we do with our own land. Our mission is in fact God's mission, and God himself is sovereign over his mission; mission is not something we do, it is what God is doing—and he invites us to join in with him. That essential but frequently forgotten truth is stressed by many recent writers about mission, to correct the notion that mission is a church program and a human initiative: so for example David Bosch has said, "mission is not primarily an activity of the church, but an attribute of God. God is a missionary God;"[8] and the same point was made by Lesslie Newbigin, when he wrote, "The Church is not so much the agent of the mission as the locus of the mission. It is God who acts in the power of his Spirit."[9]

In the light of that vital but too frequently forgotten truth, when Jesus in verse 3 says, "Go!," it would be wrong to see that as merely a peremptory

---

8. Bosch, *Transforming Mission*, 390.
9. Newbigin, *Gospel in a Pluralist Society*, 119.

command. It is true that we are sent by the Lord Jesus on mission; but we are not simply expected to follow orders blindly, because we're told to. God is bringing his mission in the world; to respond positively to Jesus' challenge to "go" is to accept his call to become what Paul described himself and the apostles as, namely "God's fellow workers" (1 Corinthians 3:9).

But verse 3 also raises the fact that those who go out in Jesus' name are, in a sense, vulnerable; he sends us out "like lambs among wolves." There is of course a reference here to the spiritual battle we face; that is real, but it is not the only point of the saying, and it may not even be the main point. Jesus is not simply warning us that mission is risky. It is, of course; we face enemies, both human and demonic, although we have the victory over them in Jesus' name. But he is also talking about the principle of how we live among wolves. We do not survive amongst wolves by becoming wolf-like; we do not have to show that we are as tough as they are. We are lambs, and so we are to stay lamb-like; we serve with meekness and simplicity. Too often the church has tried to win the world by force. The image of the early Catholic "missionaries" in effect conquering and colonizing South American countries, and forcing whole populations to be baptized, is perhaps an over-simplistic travesty of history; but the church as a whole has to admit, and repent of the fact that, something not all that much better has often happened. Nor is the modern evangelical church always free from blame in this respect: not all the critical stories about over-pushy evangelists browbeating vulnerable and suggestible people into "decisions for Jesus" are, unfortunately, fictional or exaggerated. Such an approach to mission could be characterized as going like wolves amongst lambs. It was not Jesus' way; and it will never advance God's Kingdom.

Jesus' cross has always to be our model. He won salvation by being vulnerable and weak. Jesus shows that gentle servanthood will win in the end; the church showing it can flex its muscles is unlikely to achieve a great deal even in the short term. So the challenge to all who seek to bring more of God's Kingdom to more of this world is to remain a lamb; do not try and become a wolf in lamb's clothing.

Jesus then repeats in verse 4 the same instructions he had given to the original twelve about not taking "excess baggage" with them on their mission. We are to trust God to supply our needs—both practical and spiritual—rather than trying to make sure that we already have everything we might need. That is not an argument against appropriate and wise preparation; it is a warning that those who try to insure themselves against every eventuality are maybe not embarking on their service for Jesus with a confidence that he is still the Lord who provides for his people.

We have already said that "do not take . . . sandals" (verse 4) may refer to taking spare pairs, rather than to literally walking bare-foot. But, apart from the practical issue of "sandals or no sandals," these words do also teach an important principle about the spirit in which we go to the world. We go as servants. "No sandals" was the sign of a slave. When the prodigal son returned home, expecting to be received and treated as a slave, the first thing the father did was to order his servants to bring sandals to put on his feet. Slaves do not wear sandals, but sons do, and the boy is still the father's son. Spiritually, we have the status of sons of God, we wear the sandals of adoption. But in relationship with the world, we go as slaves. We are there to serve the world; not, it is true, on the world's terms, but on the terms of God's Kingdom—but we still go proclaiming, as Paul said, "Jesus Christ as Lord, and ourselves as your servants for Jesus' sake" (2 Corinthians 4:5). The world is not our master—but we are the world's servants. No Christian can be a witness for Jesus who is not prepared to be a servant of others for Jesus' sake.

We are to be gentle; but also urgent. The warning in verse 4, "do not greet anyone on the road" does not mean that we are to be discourteous and ignore people; it means, don't get side-tracked. In the Middle East greetings could be long and elaborate; they could involve a serious diversion. So Jesus says, do not let anything divert you from your Kingdom task: it is too urgent.

This raises a frequent confusion: Jesus tells us to be gentle ("lamb-like") with people, but also to be urgent about our mission. Being pushy with people has all too often been justified by over-zealous preachers on the grounds that they are being urgent, that mission is a serious business. It is indeed; but Jesus says clearly that we are to be urgent about our spiritual task—it is always to be our number one priority—*and* very gracious and gentle with people; we do not deal with them in an over-insistent manner, or put pressure on them to make a response.

Verses 5–9 give us a good pattern of mission. In all our dealings with people, Jesus tells us to do four things.

1. *Bless them.* The classic eastern greeting "Peace to this house" means far more than simply saying "hello"; for the Christian, to say "peace to you" is actually to put the spiritual blessing of God's peace on their lives. Our service for people starts with praying for them and asking God to bless them with his peace. Too often our prayers for people are essentially negative: Christians can spend a lot of time in prayer bemoaning the fact that people are unbelievers and sinners, and imploring God to change them. Jesus' model was entirely positive. He invites us to pray for people by blessing them with the peace of God; and the

call to pray "peace to *this house*" gives us a model of how to pray for God to bless every part of people's lives with his peace: their families and family relationships, their work and leisure, and every aspect of their life, socially, morally, medically, financially and educationally, as well as spiritually. And it is important to remember that "peace" in the Bible never means merely tranquility, the absence of strife; it always means wholeness. It is hardly going too far to say that "peace" is more or less a synonym for "salvation." Even before people have heard the Gospel, let alone had the opportunity to respond to it in faith, Jesus calls on us to pray for the salvation of God to visit their homes, their lives and their hearts.

2. *Fellowship with them.* "Stay in that house, eating and drinking." And Jesus' disciples were to do it on their hosts' terms, rather than to impose their own preferences, just as good missionaries are told to eat whatever is the local diet, rather than insisting on arranging for their own favorites to be shipped out and made available to them. But the key lesson behind eating and drinking with people is that we meet with them, relate to them, befriend them, build social bridges with them. We are not called to try and "do mission" from a safe distance. Friendship is the best bridge across which the Gospel can walk. Some Christians can be quite dismissive of the term "friendship evangelism," and of churches that organize various social and "bridge-building" activities, fearing that this is a secular alternative to preaching the Gospel; they will protest that "Jesus did not tell us to put on church meals and invite people to come to them—he told us to preach the Gospel to them!" Indeed he did; but he first told his disciples to eat and drink with the people with whom they were hoping to share the Gospel. "Friendship evangelism" is not a safer and less challenging alternative to preaching the Gospel: it is part of the preparation for it.

3. *Perform the signs of the Kingdom.* "Heal the sick"; do those works, be they of supernatural power and/or of compassionate service, that show people what the Kingdom is like. Meet their practical needs. Works of the Kingdom are not an alternative to proclaiming the message of salvation; but, as well as meeting people's needs, they can also bring people the awareness that God is real and cares about their wellbeing, which can be the very thing that can make them more willing to listen to the message of the Gospel. In John 9, Jesus encounters a man who had been born blind; he first heals him (verses 6–7), and later (verses 35–38) talks to him about faith in the Son of Man: the response of the man born blind was "'Lord, I believe,' and he worshiped him" (verse

38). What Jesus did *not* do was to ask the man whether he believed before he would heal him. His new faith was the fruit of his experience of Jesus having touched his life with the grace of God.

4. Finally, *speak the word of the Kingdom*. "Tell them, 'The Kingdom of God is near you.'" We should note that this is step four; too many enthusiastic Christians forget the first three stages and dive straight into bombarding people with the Gospel and asking them if they are born again. But taking time to bless and to befriend people is not deferring our witness; it is laying the best foundation for it.

Jesus is always a realist. He has no intention of sending his disciples out into service wearing rose-colored spectacles. So he warns them: it will not always work. He says in verse 10, "When you enter a town and are not welcomed . . ." There will not always be a positive response. And when there is not, he urges his witnesses to leave the people with a challenge and move on. That does not mean that we write people off; but now may not be the time for them. If we have sown the seed of God's Word into their lives, we have done what we can. Our continuing to try and convert people who, at this stage, clearly do not want to be converted will not make the seed any more likely to put down roots and grow into a harvest of faith.

Jesus' words in verse 12 ("I tell you, it will be more bearable on that day for Sodom than for that town") are serious and sobering. They do not of course mean that there can never be any future hope for those who at first reject the Gospel; after all, Jesus' own brothers began by dismissing and mocking his message, but later came to be convinced that he was indeed the Messiah, and his brother James became a major leader in the Jerusalem church. But they do stress the seriousness of mission, and of what it is all about. The day is coming when God will judge the world. But with that come both a reminder and a reassurance. The reminder is that it is not about us and what people think of us. What matters is not whether people like us, agree with us, accept us; it is what they think of Jesus. So when people do not accept you, says Jesus, don't take it personally. It is not you they are rejecting, but me. Christians who feel a sense of personal affront when their witness is rebuffed seem to have forgotten that mission is not about them, but about him. And the reassurance is that we are not responsible for how people respond. Provided that we work in the positive spirit of which Jesus has been speaking, with modesty, "lamb-like," then how people respond to us is not something for which we need to take personal responsibility. Too many Christians walk around hag-ridden with guilt because someone with whom they tried to share the love and the truth of Jesus did not accept it. Our responsibility is to tell people about Jesus in the best way we can, in a way that will make it possible for people to accept; whether or not they do is their decision.

Having said that, these words clearly show that mission is a serious business. It is not something for those who are "into that kind of thing," or who have nothing better to do. Proclaiming the Kingdom is, literally, a matter of life and death.

That is also the spirit behind Jesus' words in verse 11: "Yet be sure of this: The Kingdom of God is near." That is part of the warning to those who will not accept the Gospel. Of course it is a great reassurance for us: our confidence is not that we will always be successful, but that the Kingdom is coming. Jesus is King, whether or not our mission thrives today. As Jesus was later to say to these seventy-two, "Do not rejoice that the spirits [meaning 'evil spirits' or 'demons'] submit to you, but rejoice that your names are written in heaven" (verse 20). If our confidence is in the fact that our Christian work is going well, how will we cope on the days when it does not go well? And those days will come; there may be times when the demons do not submit to us. But here in verse 11, Jesus tells his disciples to say, before they leave those who have rejected their witness, that the Kingdom is at hand whether people respond or not. So rather than engaging in an extended debate with those who, at this stage, do not want to turn to God, Jesus tells us simply to leave them with the fact that the Kingdom is coming; don't try and prove it, or plead for it, or argue about it, and certainly don't try and bludgeon people into accepting it. Just tell them. God said through Isaiah that his word would not return to him empty, but would accomplish the purpose for which he sent it forth (Isaiah 55:11); our being pushy with people will not enable that purpose to be fulfilled any more quickly. We can serve God's mission only on the basis of faith; and that includes faith in the power of God's Word to accomplish his purpose in the long-term, even if people's initial response to us as God's messengers is less than encouraging.

And even though some will not acknowledge him, Jesus is still King. And if we keep our confidence in his Kingdom, rather than in the effectiveness of our work for his Kingdom, it will help us to persevere in his mission—and that will hasten the day when his Kingdom comes in its final glory.

There is another major lesson from Jesus' sending out of his disciples on mission, which, if misapplied, could lead to problems; but that does not mean that we should forget or ignore it. How often do modern churches ask themselves the question, if we had been with Jesus in his Galilean ministry, would we have recommended sending the disciples out on active service at this stage? Surely they were nowhere near ready for such responsibilities?

After all, their understanding was, at best, patchy. After they have returned from their mission in Matthew 10//Mark 6//Luke 9, Jesus frequently has to rebuke them for their slowness to understand him and his ministry (Matthew 15:16//Mark 7:18, Mark 6:52); Luke in particular says of them that "they did not understand what this [the fact that Jesus would be betrayed into the hands of sinful men] meant; it was hidden from them . . ." (9:45), and later still that they "did not understand any of this [again referring to Jesus having predicted his death]; its meaning was hidden from them, and they did not know what he was talking about" (18:34). Worse still, their faith still left something to be desired; even after their mission trip in chapter 10, Matthew twice records Jesus rebuking the disciples for their lack of faith (14:31, 17:20), and they seem to have a talent amounting to genius for missing the point (Matthew 16:8//Mark 8:17–18). These disciples to whom Jesus had given authority to cast out demons and proclaim the Gospel can still engage in arguments about which of them is the greatest (Mark 9:33–34// Luke 9:46); indeed, in view of the fact that Luke places this argument almost immediately after the disciples' first taste of mission, on which they went around "healing people everywhere" (9:6), it is tempting to wonder whether this squabbling for supremacy may at least in part have arisen from a competitive "league-table" mind-set about what had happened on their mission ("You only healed seven people—I healed nine!").

But worst of all, these disciples, to whom Jesus entrusts the mission of the Kingdom, have not yet got their doctrine of Jesus properly sorted out; Caesarea Philippi, when for the first time Peter will declare Jesus to be the Christ, is still some way ahead. In fact, even at the time of the Last Supper, Jesus can marvel that one of the twelve, Philip, had still not grasped who he (that is, Jesus) is in relationship with the Father (John 14:9). And Jesus has to rebuke his disciples, whom he has already sent out to heal and to preach, that they are still thinking as the world thinks, not as God thinks (Matthew 16:22–23//Mark 8:33).

Most of the western Christian tradition would assume almost without question that people who are as immature as this—people who have not yet grasped the essentials of Christian doctrine, who still struggle to understand the cross, who still display worldly characteristics—are not yet ready to engage in mission and service. They need to be taught more first. When they have grown in understanding and can be seen to be mature disciples, when we've instilled all the right theology into them, then maybe we might consider them ready to serve.

Jesus thinks differently. He sends his disciples out whilst they are still raw recruits. In our western way of thinking, we assume that people learn before doing; in Jesus' way of training his disciples they learn *by* doing.

They do not study to get their theology sorted out so that they can then serve; they learn their theology by engaging in service. In the delightful film *Chicken Run*, Rocky the Rooster's way of trying to teach the imprisoned chickens to fly is by lining them up and giving them lectures on flying techniques. Jesus' training of his disciples was much more like that of the mother bird, whose way of teaching her young to fly is by pushing them out of the nest—and always being there to catch them the first few times if they don't immediately succeed.

I said that this principle, if misapplied, could be dangerous. It is easy to see why. It could seem to pander to the independent spirits of those who refuse to acknowledge that they need to learn anything, much less be in submission to anyone else; it might appear to justify those who are frankly unteachable. And it could lead to confusion if people are sent out to share the Gospel before they really know what the Gospel is, let alone the best ways of sharing it.

Because of those potential dangers, two cautions are in order. One is that we do not confuse service with leadership. The New Testament is very clear that those appointed to positions of leadership need to be known to be of mature faith and tried and tested character: "full of the Spirit and wisdom" (Acts 6:3), "above reproach ... must not be a recent convert ... they must keep hold of the deep truths of the faith with a clear conscience" (1 Timothy 3:2–10); and 1 Timothy 5:22 warns us not to appoint people too quickly, before we can be sure they are really ready to assume the responsibility of leadership. But whilst the twelve apostles would later become leaders in the church, their commissioning in Matthew 10 has more to do with the kind of Kingdom service that any believer, in principle, can exercise. Jesus is giving them an experience of Kingdom service that will be part of what prepares them for future church leadership.

The other caution is the need to preserve accountability. Although Jesus gives his as yet immature disciples a taste of mission, he does not simply thrust them out into the mission field on their own. First, he personally commissions them; they do not go on their own initiative (Matthew 10:1//Mark 6:7//Luke 9:2). Second, he sends them out in twos; no one works on his own (Mark 6:7). Third, on their return, they report back to Jesus (Mark 6:30//Luke 9:10). And fourth, after this mission, they continue to be trained and taught by him.

Those four principles need to be the model on which we encourage all believers, however new to faith, to engage in works of service. They will grow to maturity as they serve, alongside all the rest of the Bible teaching that they receive. And the fourth point is vital not only for the church's patterns of nurture for its members, but also for the mind-set which those members need to maintain. It is all too easy for people to assume, when they have seen God do the works of his Kingdom in and through them, that they have graduated as mature disciples, that they have nothing more to learn. That is not Jesus' Kingdom. We are disciples for life. No matter how many sermons we have preached or meetings we have led, or, if it comes to that, no matter how many demons we have cast out or dead people we have raised to life, we never take off our spiritual L-plates. If Christians are to remain effective servants of the Kingdom, they need to remain teachable.

But Jesus still took what we might humanly speaking call the risk of giving immature beginners direct hands-on experience of doing the works of the Kingdom, as part of their nurture in the life and faith of the Gospel. It is possible that if we made such experience, with the safe-guards of the four points listed above about proper accountability, a normal part of every new convert's nurture, we might have fewer cases of people who have been in church for years but who still seem not to have developed in their understanding or their discipleship. There is indeed a risk in exposing fairly inexperienced believers to the challenges of service; but, to quote the familiar cliché, a ship in harbor is safe—but that's not what ships are built for. Maybe we mistake the reason why we are cautious: is it really that we don't as yet trust our raw converts to be up to the tasks of service, or is it in fact that we don't actually trust the Lord of the harvest to be able to preserve and protect the trainee harvesters?

10

The Kingdom and the Gentiles

"When Jesus had finished saying these things, he left Galilee" (Matthew 19:1)

The feeding of the five thousand, which is perhaps Jesus' best-known miracle, and is the only one, apart from the resurrection itself, recounted in all four Gospels, marks the climax of Jesus' popularity amongst the Galilean crowds. Following it, the people want to make him an earthly king (John 6:15). Jesus' refusal to be that kind of Messiah sees the beginning of a decline in his popular appeal; the immediate result was that a large number of people who had been following him turned back (6:60,66)—if Jesus was not going to do the kind of things they wanted, or speak the way they liked, they saw no reason to remain with him. This is a warning for all believers: it is all too easy to be enthusiastic followers of Jesus, so long as he does what we find helpful. It is when he starts to do things, say things, or require things that suit us less that we can start to question whether or not following Jesus is in fact really what we want to do. That raises a vital challenge: that we always respond, and encourage others to respond, to Jesus on his terms, not on our own. Too often, as we invite people to follow Jesus, we can implicitly (or sometimes explicitly) seem to be bending over backwards to reassure them that Jesus will never want to lead them anywhere they do not already want to go: he will just get them there faster and more easily. We need to remember that Jesus said, "Follow me"; he did not say, "Would you like me to accompany you?"

Shortly after this, Jesus starts to travel more widely to other areas outside Galilee. This is the beginning of what we might call the second major half of Jesus' ministry. Up to now, he has been based mostly in Galilee, with a couple of trips to Jerusalem at Passover times. As he starts to move around to other non-Jewish areas, three themes dominate his ministry: first, that *the Kingdom is for the Gentiles*, not just the Jews; second, that *the Kingdom will come through the cross*; and third, that *the Kingdom is for the poor*, the outcasts, the socially despised.

It is interesting, looking at these three themes in the second half of Jesus' ministry, to note that they correspond fairly closely to the character of the three temptations that Jesus had faced in the wilderness (Matthew 4:1–11//Luke 4:1–13). One of the temptations had addressed the whole issue of Jesus' identification with the poor: "Tell these stones to become bread"; in other words, you don't need to be a starving, suffering servant, who comes to serve poor and needy people; you can use your power as Son of God to become well-fed and satisfied. Another temptation had addressed the question of Jesus' bringing the Gentiles into his Kingdom: "The devil . . . showed him [= Jesus] all the kingdoms of the world [that is, the Gentile nations] . . . 'All this I will give you,' he said"; in other words, if you are destined to inherit all the nations of the world, why not let me give you them the easy way—by worshiping me. Why do you need to go around *serving* them?! And the third temptation had addressed the key question of how Jesus will draw the world to himself: "Throw yourself down . . . for he [God] will command his angels concerning you, and they will lift you up in their hands . . ."; in other words, forget about drawing the world by going the way of the cross—do it by performing a spectacular miracle to attract attention. There is incidentally a significant difference between the ministry of angels as Satan presents it, and that which Jesus actually experienced: the devil suggests that angels are a kind of safety net to prevent us hurting ourselves; but Jesus experienced the help of angels in the Garden of Gethsemane, who strengthened him so that he might be able to go through with his call to sacrifice himself (Luke 22:43), and he specifically denied that it would be right for him to call on angels to rescue him from the cross (Matthew 26:53–54). Angels can help us face and overcome the challenges of Kingdom ministry; they are not sent to show us how to avoid them.

The fact that Satan tempted Jesus at these three points shows that he knows that they will be key themes of Jesus' ministry; and he wants to deflect him—and us—from faithfulness to those principles.

Jesus begins to travel first through the non-Jewish areas around northern Galilee: to the Phoenician area around Tyre and Sidon, north-west of Galilee (Matthew 15:21//Mark 7:24); then round to the Decapolis—the name is the Greek for "ten towns"—south-east of the Sea of Galilee, a predominantly Greek area (Mark 7:31); then finally to Caesarea Philippi, north-east of Galilee, at the south-west tip of Syria.

In these Gentile areas, Jesus demonstrates the same kind of miracles—signs of the Kingdom—that he has previously demonstrated in Galilee. In Phoenicia he heals the Canaanite woman's daughter (Matthew 15:21-28// Mark 7:24-30); in the Decapolis he heals a deaf and mute man (Mark 7:31-37). Very significantly, he performs a second miracle of multiplying loaves and fishes to feed a crowd of four thousand (Matthew 15:32-39// Mark 8:1-10). It is often pointed out that, of the two miraculous feedings of Jesus, the first (of the five thousand) was in Jewish territory, and the second (of the four thousand) was in Greek territory; this is a sign that both Jews and Gentiles can receive Jesus as the Bread of Life. And the feeding of the four thousand is followed, as was that of the five thousand, by a rebuke to those who merely seek after miracles for their own sake (Matthew 16:1-4// Mark 8:11-13)—Jesus is not only performing the same miracles, but is accompanying them by the same teaching to point people to the Kingdom significance of his works as "signs." Then finally, on his way north to Caesarea Philippi, Jesus heals a blind man at Bethsaida, on the north-eastern tip of the Sea of Galilee (Mark 8:22-26).

These signs demonstrate that the Kingdom of God is for Gentiles, not just Jews. It is for people of all nations. It is for those who are outsiders, who are not part of the existing religious establishment. And it is significant that this series of signs is given not just by Mark, but also by Matthew, who more than any other writer clearly and very positively presents Jesus as the King of the Jews; that title, and Jesus' Kingdom, Matthew shows us, are not to be understood as meaning "exclusively for the Jews," but rather "arising initially from amongst the Jews, but then going out to all the nations."

The suggestion is occasionally made that Jesus started to minister to Gentiles only after he had been rejected by his own people; that prior to that rejection, he had assumed that his ministry would and should be essentially amongst the Jewish people alone. The story of Jesus' encounter with the Syro-Phoenician woman[1] in Matthew 15:21-28//Mark 7:24-30 might seem to suggest that he was initially unwilling to help her precisely because she was not a Jew, but it is surely far more consistent with the character of Jesus to assume that his words about "throwing the children's bread to the

---

1. Mark describes her as, literally, "Greek, a Syro-Phoenician by race." So "Greek" does not mean "of Greek nationality," but is used in the frequent New Testament sense of "Gentile." "Syro-Phoenician" means that she is from the area of Phoenicia, near Tyre and Sidon, part of the modern state of Lebanon; the word was used to distinguish Phoenicians of Syria, like this woman, from those of Carthage.

dogs"[2] were a challenge to her faith: would she get on her high horse and protest that she was as good as anyone else, and that she deserved the help of Jesus just as much as any Jew, or would she humbly acknowledge that she had no claim on the help of God, but was simply appealing to his mercy? The woman passed the test with flying colors, and Jesus healed her daughter. There is a lesson there for all of us: we can never assume that we have a "right" to receive Jesus' help; we are called to recognize with humility that we deserve nothing, but at the same time to appeal to him to show us grace.

The idea that Jesus saw ministering to the Gentiles as a second best, or that it was not part of his thinking when he began his public ministry, not only indicates a rather low estimation of Jesus' awareness of what his God-given calling was, but is also in fact excluded by a number of things he had said very early in his ministry. In his first sermon in Nazareth, he had said quite explicitly that God's plan was always to encourage and bless faith amongst non-Jews (Luke 4:25–27); in conversation with the woman at the well in Sychar he had said in effect that in the future the issue of whether someone was a Jew or a Samaritan—whether they worshiped in Jerusalem or at Mount Gerizim—would be irrelevant: true worshipers would not be those of a particular race, but those who worship the Father in spirit and in truth (John 4:21–23); and from the earliest stages of his ministry Jesus had served Gentiles as well as Jews—for example, the Roman centurion (Matthew 8:5–13//Luke 7:1–10) and the man with a legion of demons (Mark 5:1–13)—and in the account of his healing of the centurion's servant Jesus says explicitly that many Gentiles would be welcomed into God's Kingdom, whilst unbelieving Jews would be rejected (Matthew 8:11–12). Indeed, I said above that Jesus' apparent initial reluctance to help the Syro-Phoenician woman was not because he was in principle unwilling to minister to Gentiles, but was a challenge to her to persist in humbly seeking his grace even though she did not "deserve" it; and it is interesting that the same issue is found in the story of the centurion's servant. In Luke's account, the Jews who

---

2. Many find Jesus' reference to non-Jews as "dogs," in contrast with the Jews who are the "children" of the household of God, somewhat offensive. It is true that the Jews frequently referred to Gentiles as "dogs"; but in fact, whereas the Jews invariably used the term for wild dogs, which is in the New Testament always a negative term referring to people who pose a threat (Matthew 7:6, Luke 16:21, Philippians 3:2, 2 Peter 2:22, Revelation 22:15), the word Jesus uses is the term for a household pet; this is the only place in the New Testament where it is found. So whilst there is a recognition of the fact that, at this stage (though not for much longer!), there is a still a distinction in spiritual status between Jews and Gentiles, Jesus' terminology is not as rude as it might appear. Living as we do in a country where household pets are often regarded as just as much part of the family as the children, the British have less reason than any to take exception to Jesus' language here!

recommend the centurion to Jesus say, "This man deserves to have you do this, because he loves our nation and has built our synagogue" (Luke 7:5–6). In effect they are saying, we know that he is not a Jew, and therefore strictly speaking you should ignore him; but because he has been helpful to us, you can regard him as deserving of your help almost as though he were one of us! In contrast to that attitude, the centurion himself says nothing to suggest he has done anything to merit Jesus' attention; on the contrary, he says, "I do not deserve to have you come under my roof"; his appeal to Jesus is based solely on the fact that, as a soldier, he can recognize authority when he sees it, and he has discerned that Jesus has authority in spiritual matters. That is why Jesus commends his great "faith"; unlike the no doubt well-meaning Jews, who thought that receiving ministry was on the basis of merit (which they had by birth, and this man had acquired by his actions), the centurion, like the Syro-Phoenician woman, recognizes his unworthiness, but trusts Jesus to help him nonetheless.

So there is no need to think that Jesus' ministry amongst the Gentiles was a reluctant "plan B," or that it was not what he at first intended. His ministry started amongst the Jews; but it was always God's plan, and Jesus' purpose, that it should move out to embrace Gentiles as well.

Within the present book, I do not propose to discuss the complex issues that revolve around the question whether in the New Testament era the Jewish people, or the modern (political) state of Israel—it is worth remembering that the two are not exactly the same—are still in any special sense the chosen people of God. That would require a separate volume all of its own,[3] and indeed, a number of such works have appeared in recent years, though they represent a variety of different views. So rather than making brief comments on what calls for much more substantial exploration of the Scriptures as a whole, I propose to draw a more general and, I hope, more widely useful lesson from Jesus' ministry amongst the Gentiles.

In Jesus' own day, it came as a shock to many Jews that he acted as though he had come for people other than or as well as them; that he was ministering in effect to the wrong people. Actually it was in the early church in the book of Acts that this "Jew-Gentile" debate really became explicit, and a strongly Jewish voice started to be heard, insisting that Gentiles could be admitted to the church, but only on Jewish terms (Acts 15). The decision of

---

3. What I will say, at the risk of being accused of dipping a toe into controversial waters and then withdrawing, as so many politicians do, behind the shelter of "No comment," is that, despite what some might claim, the answers to questions about the place of the Jewish people in the ongoing purposes of God are *not* clear-cut, black-and-white or self-evident. There are many questions to which the Bible gives straightforward and unambiguous answers; this is not one of them.

the church, and the teaching of Paul, especially in Romans and Galatians, was that this was not the case; that Gentiles could become part of God's people on exactly the same basis as Jews, namely faith in Christ. The danger for the Christian church is that we can assume that this issue is now behind us; whilst Jewish people in Jesus' day might have had a blinkered view of who the "real" people of God are, we have now got past that: we know it is the church; and the famous dictum of Saint Augustine (354–430), *salus extra ecclesiam non est* ("there is no salvation outside the church"), is invariably assumed to mean, outside the church *as we understand it* and *in the forms with which we are familiar*. And so there can be exactly the same refusal to believe that anything that happens outside the safe parameters of the established and respectable church can possibly be part of God's Kingdom.

This misunderstanding manifests itself at a couple of levels. First, for most people in our nation, "the church" always implies, or conjures up the image of, the western church. Christianity is regarded as "a western religion." Of course most people are aware that there are Christian churches all over the world; but the assumption is that the normative model of church is that of western Christendom.

It isn't. So-called "WASPs"—white Anglo-Saxon Protestants—can be as mistakenly convinced that they are the representative church in the world as first-century Jews were of thinking that only they were or could ever be the true people of God. Statistics alone give the lie to that misconception. In terms of the proportion of people who are active members of Christian churches, Western Europe is probably the *least* Christian continent. There are, it is true, a small number of individual countries with, so far as we can tell, an even smaller Christian presence than most western countries, both in terms of statistics and also of significant influence in their societies—an example would be Japan—but according to the best recent statistics, the population of Africa as a whole is now well over 50 percent Christian, with some countries like Kenya coming closer to 90 percent; Asia is over 30 percent Christian; Oceania between 65 and 70 percent. In China, where the Christian church has for decades been, and still is, severely repressed, it is estimated that upwards of 20 percent of the whole population are now committed Christians; in South Korea, it is over 30 percent. In contrast with those figures, the approximately 10 percent of the UK population who are in some meaningful sense actively involved in Christian church life seems somewhat lamentable, and makes the claim, still heard from time to time, that Britain is "a Christian country" sound rather hollow. Fifty years ago the main concentrations of "world Christianity" were, it is true, located in the west and in the northern hemisphere; today they are unquestionably in the east and in the southern hemisphere.

What is more, the life and spirit of many Third World churches can often seem to be far closer to that of the New Testament church than is often the case in the west. So it is, to say the least, unhelpful if, whenever someone hears the term "church," his first thoughts are—with no disrespect to the many excellent churches that are undoubtedly to be found around this country—of his local and rather dilapidated parish church, or of the pomp and ceremony of Westminster Abbey, or for that matter of *The Vicar of Dibley*. A far more accurate picture of what Jesus always intended "church" to be could be found in an African village congregation, or a prayer meeting in an underground fellowship in China, or a mission station in the shanty-towns of Brazil. One of the great criticisms of nineteenth- and early twentieth-century overseas mission—and it was sometimes, though not always, justified—is that western missionaries often seemed to assume that taking the Gospel to other nations had necessarily to involve exporting western culture and lifestyle as well, so that converts in Africa or Asia were not only invited to embrace faith in Jesus, but were also expected to wear western dress, sing western hymns, and erect western-style church buildings. Ironically, the reverse is badly needed in our day, though in spiritual rather than cultural terms: the western church has a lot that it needs to receive from the life and vitality of the church in the Third World.

Linked with that first challenge is a second, which takes us into the embarrassing territory of denominations. For many people in this country, the word "church" means essentially the established and institutional churches, either Anglican or Catholic. When the media want a comment about some current issue from "the church," nine times out of ten it will be a bishop who is interviewed. I do not want to be misunderstood: I have a great many very close and dear friends in the Church of England; I have no doubt that the Spirit of God is working to great effect in many of our Anglican churches up and down the land; and there are a number of aspects of the style and spirit of evangelical Anglicanism that I value and would frankly not mind seeing a bit more of in some of our Free Churches. And yet I do, I confess, find it rather irritating that again and again, whenever we talk about "the church," most people assume that we must mean the Church of England. Yes, of course, there are "other churches," but they are, it is almost taken for granted, somewhat on the unrepresentative fringe of things, the ecclesiastical also-rans. And even if people are not thinking in strictly denominational terms, they are almost always thinking of the church in its institutional form. The connotations of "church" are such things as stained glass windows, processions of robed clergy, prayer books, choirs and organs, ornate altars, feast days, hierarchies of priests, dog-collars, and historical buildings; and there are those for whom anything that calls itself a church, but lacks those things, clearly cannot be "a *real* church." Yet not one of these is ever mentioned in the New Testament as part of what God intends his church to be. That does not necessarily have to mean that they are "wrong"—if it comes to that, there is no mention in the New Testament of guitars, overhead projectors or worship groups, yet those who would question the rightness or necessity of most of the features of the established church would often regard such things as normal—but they are accidental features of the form of church that developed over the centuries in the west; they are not the essential characteristics of "the church."[4]

Just as many of the Jewish people in Jesus' day were limited by their traditional understanding of what it meant to be God's people, and as a result struggled to accept Jesus' ministry, so many in our day who have an understanding of "Christianity" that is essentially that of the established or institutional forms of western church find it very hard to cope with any spiritual life that goes beyond those boundaries.[5]

But it does. Just as Jesus is the Savior of the Jew and the Gentile, so he is the Lord who is building his Kingdom through Korean Pentecostal house meetings, African Methodists meeting under a tree in their village, and wherever else two or three are gathered in his name. I recently had the privilege of preaching in a congregation of gypsies (that is, a true Roma community) meeting in a rather dilapidated hall in a small village in a remote part of Slovakia. There was nothing in the setting that had any of the conventional connotations of "church"; but if you have ever heard "He is Lord!" sung with more genuine fervor and with a greater sense of the immediate holy presence of Jesus than I did on that evening, I can only assume that it is because, like John in Revelation 4, you were transported into the presence of the worshiping angels around God's heavenly throne. Or I think of a little group of believers whom I have visited a number of times

---

4. "Essential" and "accidental" are terms derived from the thinking of Aristotle; they are used for different properties of an object. The "essential" qualities of a "man" are those things that define what "a man" is, without which he is not a man: in other words, being an adult human male. "Accidental" qualities are secondary things that may be true of some men but not of others, such as being a plumber or a doctor, or having red hair or brown eyes. Established orders of service, liturgies, etc., are accidental features of some churches; they can be very good and helpful, but they are not the essential marks of the church of Jesus Christ.

5. I am reminded of the story of the West Indian lady who, on a visit to London, went to a service in Westminster Abbey. At one point in the liturgy something was said that she clearly appreciated, because she exclaimed in a loud and enthusiastic voice, "Praise the Lord!" Aghast at this unseemly interruption of the smooth flow of the service, two ushers at once advanced on the lady and urged her to remain quiet. "But I've got *religion!*" she declared, to which one of the ushers gravely replied, "I dare say, madam; but you didn't get it here."

in the center of Zürich: a few hundred yards away from the great cathedral where Huldrych Zwingli launched the Swiss reformation, there is a meeting, run by the Salvation Army in the first floor of what looks like a normal and somewhat run-down block of flats, attended by people who have come to faith in Jesus from backgrounds of addiction, homelessness and prostitution. If you were to stop one hundred of the citizens of Zürich and ask them where the church is in their city, at least ninety-nine would probably direct you to the cathedral. But God's people includes many whom those whose understanding of church is more limited and conventional would not expect, just as pious Jews struggled to accept that "their" Messiah would actually minister amongst Gentiles.

It might—though I would really prefer to think that it would not—be suggested that my European examples are all very well, but we live in England, where we have "proper churches." Leaving aside the minor point that both Switzerland and the country that is today Slovakia had established Protestant churches before England did, the fact is that there are now in our own country well over 2,500 churches meeting in pubs, community halls, school halls and similar informal venues, some of them catering for specific ethnic or other minority groups, including, incidentally, gypsies. Those for whom the connotations of the established church are not merely the things that they happen to be familiar with, but the defining characteristics of what anything calling itself a church ought to be, would do well to re-read the story of Peter's vision in Acts 10, in which he was told in no uncertain terms that he was not to call unclean what God had declared to be clean. If Jesus says that a group of believing teenagers worshiping in a coffee-bar is a church—and he does—then it is not for us to say that it isn't really. His frequently quoted words, that "where two or three come together in my name, there I am with them" (Matthew 18:20), are not just an encouragement to small congregations; they mean that any gathering of people who come together in the name of Jesus is a church.

Those two issues are problems of *perception* of what "the church" is; but there is also a challenge to our *expectations* of how people are received into the church. When the great debate about the place of Gentiles in the church erupted, and led to the council of Jerusalem in Acts 15, there were many who, whilst willing to allow Gentiles to be recognized as Christian believers, insisted that they could only become part of the church on Jewish terms: they had to be circumcised and made to obey the law of Moses (Acts 15:5). An analogous problem has often arisen in the churches of the west. By all means, let there be other people, different people, new people who come and join the church—but they have to do it on our terms. They have to adapt to the culture, accept the norms, live by the conventions of the church they join; they have to start to dress like us, talk like us, fit in with us.

Jesus points out in Matthew 23:15 that the Pharisees would "travel over land and sea to win a single convert." In fact the word translated "convert" is the technical term "proselyte"; proselytes were Gentiles who became affiliated to Jewish faith and chose to adopt Jewish religion and lifestyle. To "proselytize" is used in our own day as a rather dismissive synonym for evangelism, but in fact there is a significant difference between evangelism and proselytism: when we "proselytize," our aim is not merely to introduce people to our faith, but to *make them like us*. If a proselytizer heard one of his potential targets (or, as he would more probably phrase it, converts) singing, like King Louie in *The Jungle Book*, "I wanna be like you . . . I wanna walk like you, talk like you . . . ," he would be delighted: that is just what he is aiming for. The true evangelist, on the other hand, is not concerned that people become like him and his church, but that they come to Jesus. He does not seek to impose his own culture on people, or to make his converts clones of himself; rather, he wants to see them, within the terms of their own culture, become more like Jesus.

The Jews in Jesus' day found the idea that Gentiles could accept "their" Messiah as their own King hard enough to take; but the very idea that they could do so *and yet still remain Gentiles* was too much to stomach. The western Christian church has often found the same thought just as indigestible. Ironically, it is often in those churches that would be defined as non-conformist that there is the greatest stress on the need to see all converts learning to conform to their church culture, and to the most audible "tut-tutting" if, after a few weeks, they are for example still not dressing in the way that is expected when they come to church.

The apostle Paul took this a stage further still: not only did he not insist that Gentiles had to become Jews in order to become Christians; he even said that he himself became like a Gentile in order to win Gentiles, just as he became like a Jew in order to win Jews (1 Corinthians 9:20–21). The phrase "I become like a Jew" seems strange: surely Paul *was* a Jew? By nationality and background he was; but not in terms of what he allowed to shape his life. He had written off his religious heritage as so much rubbish[6] (Philip-

---

6. It is often pointed out, rightly, that the word Paul uses (Greek: *skúbala*) is actually somewhat stronger than the more delicate terms favored in most English translations: it seems to mean primarily "dung" or "excrement," and maybe also "scraps" (of food) that are left over after a meal or have gone bad. Without wishing to dwell inappropriately on the word, there is perhaps a genuine theological point here: Paul is not saying merely that religion apart from Christ is, in the popular sense of the word, "rubbish," but more specifically that *it has no nourishment in it*; the real heart of Jewish faith is consummated in Christ, whilst the rest, the cultural and ritual expressions of

pians 3:8), and now lived for Jesus alone. He was willing to go along with the norms of Jewish lifestyle when it was a help to his mission; but he was not in principle bound by them. And he was just as willing to live on Gentile terms when it helped him to benefit from opportunities to preach the Gospel to Gentiles. When in 1885 the so-called "Cambridge Seven" set off with Hudson Taylor as missionaries to China, their decision to wear Chinese dress and sport Chinese hair-styles was the cause of some amusement and not a little criticism from those who, whilst of course admiring their missionary zeal, felt that it was somewhat undignified for western Christians to be so attired; surely they ought to be "properly dressed"? But the seven were right; with the apostle Paul, they would have said, "We become like the Chinese in order to win the Chinese."

This raises the vital question of distinguishing between what is central to the Christian life and faith to which we call people, and what are the secondary and, in the Aristotelian sense, "accidental" patterns of church practice. The Jews in Jesus' day could not, as we would express it, "think outside the box"; they could not conceive of the Kingdom of God except in terms of the Jewish law with which they were familiar. Jesus' ministry to the Gentiles challenged that expectation. The western church needs to learn the same lesson: to teach the unchanging doctrines of the faith and the timeless norms of discipleship, but to refrain from making the incidental cultural expressions of church the benchmark of orthodoxy. Blaise Pascal, the great seventeenth-century scientist and Christian apologist, found it frustrating that, when it came to the question of authority, his society seemed to treat faith as if it were science and science as if it were faith. In scientific matters, where development, the continual amendment of previous thinking in the light of new discovery, should be the norm, people still regarded Aristotle as the timeless authority, and any departure from his theories as a form of heresy; but in Christian faith, the truths of which are laid down once for all in the Bible, there were parts of the church which seemed only too happy to amend their ideas about what Christianity should be to suit the present climate of social opinion. Leaving aside the question of science, Pascal might count himself extremely fortunate that he is not alive in the late twentieth and early twenty-first centuries, because our contemporary church seems to be suffering from an even more bizarre confusion. Within my lifetime, which has not lasted nearly as long as some people seem to think, I have seen, on the one hand, parts of the western Christian church almost fainting with horror at the suggestion that people might be allowed

---

Judaism, are the *skúbala*, what is left over when the Old Testament revelation has done its work and led people to feed on Christ, the bread of eternal life.

to start praying "Father in heaven, hallowed be your name" rather than "Our Father which art in heaven," and insisting that such an undermining of all that we hold dear would signal the end of Christianity and probably the imminent collapse of civilization as we know it, and on the other hand church after church deciding that in today's society it is somehow unreasonable to suggest that Christians have to believe that Jesus actually rose from the dead or that they need to acknowledge any ethical boundaries in the area of sexual relationships.

Jesus offered the Gospel to the Gentiles on the terms of the Kingdom of God, not on the terms of his Jewish contemporaries' understanding of the Kingdom of God. We have, I suggest, even fewer excuses than first-century Jews for not being able to distinguish between what is essential Christian truth and what are the accidental cultural expressions of church; we, after all, have the New Testament. What Shakespeare said of love[7]—that "Love is not love which alters when it alteration finds . . . O no! it is an ever-fixèd mark . . ."—is just as true of Christian faith. There are truths of Christian doctrine that are given in Scripture, and, though we can quite properly debate how to live in the light of them in today's world, the truths themselves are non-negotiable: for example, that Jesus is the Son of God, that he died for our sins according to the Scriptures, and that he rose from the dead on the third day. There are also norms of Christian discipleship that are just as much of an "ever-fixèd mark": principles such as forgiveness, truthfulness, servanthood, marital fidelity, prayer, dependence on God and utter devotion to Jesus as Lord. On these, we do not, in Shakespeare's language, "alter" just because we find that our culture has. But there are also church conventions; and whilst we can quite rightly respect and value them, we do not elevate them to absolute rules that we bind on all who want to join us, any more than the early church demanded circumcision of Gentile converts. To be devoted to Jesus has to mean more than remembering to kneel when everyone else kneels in church, dressing the way everyone else dresses in church or starting to eat at home the same kind of food they serve at the church garden party. And it certainly does not mean that those who join a church are obliged or should be expected to adopt the social *mores* of the average church member. A truly New Testament church would be one in which a headmaster or bank manager could sit alongside a road sweeper, where each would honor and treat the other as a brother in Christ, and where the road sweeper would never be made to feel in any way embarrassed about being working-class, but could develop as a disciple of Jesus in his own right.

---

7. In sonnet number 116, "Let me not to the marriage of true minds admit impediments."

The question is sometimes asked, if Jesus were to turn up in one of our "normal" western churches, would he fit in? The really surprising thing is the number of people who seem to assume that he would. But then, the Jews in his own day assumed that their Messiah would slot neatly into their established Jewish religious culture, which is why they were surprised and shocked when Jesus went to the Gentiles. But he did.

11

The Kingdom and the cross

"Anyone who does not carry his cross . . . cannot be my disciple" (Luke 14:27)

We now come to the turning point of Jesus' ministry: Peter's confession at Caesarea Philippi, to the north-east of Galilee, that Jesus is the Christ, the Son of God. It is following this recognition by the disciples of who he is that Jesus begins, first, to speak openly about his death, which up to now has not been mentioned to others, and second, to start to journey southwards towards Jerusalem, and towards the great climax of his life.

From this point on, there are fewer miracles recorded; most of the following chapters consist of teaching about the qualities of Christian life, in particular the call to take up our cross to follow Jesus, and preparing the disciples for the cross. This does not necessarily mean that Jesus actually performed fewer miracles; but the Gospel-writers choose from this point on to mention those aspects of Jesus' ministry which stress the nature of the life of the Kingdom, rather than those which demonstrate the power of the Kingdom.

"Who do you say I am?"

It is in Caesarea Philippi that Jesus asks his disciples, first, who people say that he is; they reply, in effect, that most people regard Jesus as standing in the great tradition of religious leaders and teachers of Israel, especially the prophets like Elijah and Jeremiah.[1] But then Jesus makes the question personal: "But what about you? Who do you say I am?" It is Peter who, acting as he so often did as spokesman for the whole group, replies, "You are the Christ, the Son of the living God" (Matthew 16:13-20//Mark 8:27-30//Luke 9:18-21). The fact that Jesus asks, "Who do you say that I am?," shows that the question matters; the essential heart of Christianity is Christ and who he is. And it is important that each person make his or her own response to that ("Who do *you* say . . . ?"), and not just go along with popular or secondhand ideas ("Who do people say . . . ?"). A familiar Christian catch-phrase is "Jesus is the answer." In fact there is a sense in which Jesus is not the answer; rather, Jesus is the question: who do you say that Jesus, the Son of Man, is? The answer is, the Christ, the Son of the living God. But Jesus poses the question: will you accept me as who I and the New Testament say that I am, or will you insist on going along with your own theories about me?

The recognition that Jesus is the Son of God is part of the whole process of becoming a Christian. Only part of it, however. Christian conversion is, as we said in speaking of the place of baptism in Christian beginnings, a rope of many strands, or a journey of discovery which includes a number of significant stages, no single one of which suffices on its own. It is impossible to pinpoint the exact moment at which we can say that Jesus' first disciples "became Christians." Was it when they first responded to his call to "follow me"? Was it here, when they first came to realize that he was the Messiah? Was it when they were convinced that he was indeed risen from the dead?—as John tells us, it was when Peter and John ran to the tomb on the first Easter morning and went inside that they "saw and believed" (20:8). Was it when they were filled with the Spirit on the Day of Pentecost? In a sense it was no single one of these, but the combination of all of them; for these disciples, and for many believers in every age, coming to faith was a process, not a one-off decision. That process started when they first began to follow Jesus; it was completed when they received the Holy Spirit. In between, it included various elements, including, here, a growing awareness of who Jesus is.

---

1. In addition to the mistake about Jesus' true identity, there seems also to be some theological confusion in the suggestion that Jesus might *be* Elijah, Jeremiah or one of the prophets. Although it could mean simply that Jesus is seen as a prophet like them, the implication is much more likely to be that some people thought that Jesus really was one of the Old Testament prophets brought back to life: Luke 9:19 says that explicitly. Such a notion is quite foreign to how God works, and has nothing to do with the biblical doctrine of the resurrection; but there is perhaps a sign here of something with which we are all too familiar in our own day, that many people find it easier to accept a superstitious, mystical or even "science-fiction" view of Jesus than the truth of who he actually is.

We must never reduce "becoming a Christian" to accepting a doctrinal truth; conversion means turning to the person of Jesus, not believing things about Jesus.[2] But on the other hand, the Jesus to whom we invite people to respond is the Jesus who is Lord. Living as we do in a non-Jewish and indeed secular society, we may feel that it is neither necessary nor helpful to stress the Messiahship of Jesus, as this is not likely to mean a great deal to most people; but we do preach the Jesus who is "the Son of the living God." Unless people have at least some degree of understanding of the fact that Jesus is Lord, the Son of God, and of some of the implications of that fact, they cannot in any biblical sense of the phrase be said to have properly embraced Christian faith, though they may of course be on a journey towards faith.

This touches on a widespread confusion which arises from the overemphasis on subjective opinion in our society, and a concomitant reluctance to accept that certain things are objective facts. The Bible, and Christian faith, affirm that Jesus *is* the Son of God. There are those who will say, "If you think of Jesus as God, and if he has the value of a God for you, then, to you, he is God." That is, frankly, nonsense. My or anyone else's thinking something does not make it true. Either Jesus is in fact the eternal Son of God who created the universe in the beginning, or he is not. If he is, then he is, even if nobody believes that he is; and conversely, if he is not, then he is not, even if the whole world believes that he is. *Peter Pan* is a great masterpiece of children's literature, but we do not in fact live in Never Never Land: saying we believe in fairies does not actually cause them to exist. And Jesus' question is not, "What do you (subjectively) think of me?," but rather, "Who do you say that I (objectively) am?" The Christian church urgently needs to resist the temptation to back down from the objectivity of Peter's declaration ("You *are* the Christ") and present instead a Jesus who can be to people whatever they decide they would like him to be. It should go without saying that we share the truth of Jesus with grace, gentleness, respect for people, and without any trace of an aggressive or "pushy" attitude. But we

---

2. It is vital to stress that conversion, that is, becoming a Christian, has to be a response to the person of Jesus himself; it is not a response to the church. Feeling drawn to the church, or even becoming a formal member of a church, does not make anyone a Christian: it is personal faith in Jesus that alone does that—as Paul told the Philippian jailor, "Believe in the Lord Jesus, and you will be saved" (Acts 16:31). This confusion is all the more widespread in view of the fact that the word "conversion" is often used these days to refer, not to how people respond to Jesus, but to a decision to change churches: a Catholic who becomes a Protestant (or *vice versa*) will often be said to have "converted." But the word "convert" is simply from the Latin for "to turn"; and in the Bible "turning," as a way of expressing "becoming a Christian," is always turning to the Lord himself (e.g. Acts 11:21).

present a Jesus who is what he says he is, and invite people to respond to him on his terms.

Jesus points out that Peter's answer is made possible only because God has revealed the truth to him. He says in Matthew 16:17, "Blessed are you, Simon, son of Jonah, for this was not revealed to you by man, but by my Father in heaven." People cannot realize who Jesus is by their own skill or intelligence, or by what other people tell them, but only when God's Spirit reveals it to them. Of course Jesus had already told his disciples, and would continue to tell them, a great deal about himself and his Kingdom; teaching and proclamation was at the heart of his ministry. Jesus is not saying that there is no human element at all in people's coming to faith; he would after all later commission his disciples to go into the world to proclaim the truth. Mission and witness, indeed all Christian ministry, has to be a shared work, in which we do what we can do, and God's Spirit does what he alone can do; that is why Paul describes himself and the other apostles as "God's fellow-workers" (1 Corinthians 3:9). Our task is to tell people about Jesus; the Spirit takes our words, reveals their truth to people's minds, and convicts their hearts of the need to respond in repentance and faith. Human proclamation and divine revelation are both involved. If we think of one only, we have a wrong understanding of mission. There have been those who have insisted that human activity in mission is unnecessary and presumptuous, since it is God's work alone; that was the response that William Carey received in 1786 when he first presented his vision for overseas mission to a group of Calvinist church leaders and asked whether it was not vital to take seriously Jesus' commission to preach the Gospel throughout the world, only to be greeted with the curt response from the chairman of the meeting, J. C. Ryland, that his suggestion was "unworthy of serious consideration," and that Carey "was a most miserable enthusiast for asking such a question."[3] Thankfully that denial of what is manifestly a central element in biblical faith—that we go into all the world and make disciples of all nations—would be rare in the church today. What is unfortunately not rare is the opposite error, of assuming that conversion is entirely a human work, which depends on us, our efforts, our skill, our ability to make people see the truth. Jesus' words to Peter here are a powerful and much-needed reminder that, although we rightly seek all possible ways to bear witness to the Gospel, it is the Father alone who can reveal its truth to people's hearts in a way that leads to a fruitful and lasting response. Human attempts to "get people to make a decision," for example by the use of increasingly loud and impassioned language, or persistent emotional appeals, may lead to people raising a hand, "coming

---

3. Stanley, *History of the Baptist Missionary Society*, 6.

forward," or whatever else the evangelist has urged them to do; whether they will lead to people entering into a life-changing relationship with God is far more debatable. It is not our task to "get people to make decisions" by hook or by crook; it is our task to tell them about Jesus, about his cross, about his offer of new life, and about the challenge of repentance and faith, and as we do so to pray and expect that the Father will send his Spirit to do what all our persuasiveness, all our eloquence, all our communication techniques cannot do, namely to touch people's hearts with a supernatural revelation of who Jesus is and a strong conviction that they need to respond to him.

It is not only the fact that Peter made this confession of Christ that is remarkable; where he made it is also of some significance. Caesarea Philippi had originally been named Panias, after the god Pan;[4] it had been renamed in honor of the Roman emperor (Caesar) and Philip the tetrarch.[5] As well as being, according to legend, the birthplace of Pan, the town boasted a huge temple dedicated to the emperor. So this town displayed prominent signs of the claims and pretensions of both pagan religion and human politics. It is in that context that Jesus is affirmed as the one true Son of God. We who live in a culture where all sorts of rival claims to authority are made by religious and political factions are here reminded that we follow and proclaim one who is *the* Son of the living God; and one moreover whose power depends not on the impressive quality of the memorials built in his name, nor on any of the pomp and paraphernalia surrounding him, but entirely on who he is in himself.

It is only following this confession that Jesus is the Christ, the Son of God, that he begins to talk openly about his coming death on the cross. Understanding who Jesus is and understanding the cross go hand in hand. So long as people see Jesus as a man, albeit a great and inspiring man, the cross can be little other than a model of undeserved suffering bravely born, or yet another troubling illustration of the fact that good people are often badly treated in this world. It is when we start to see Jesus as the Son of God that we are faced with the fact that the cross is a shocking paradox—as Charles Wesley famously wrote, "'Tis mystery all, the Immortal dies!"[6]—and can

---

4. There is today an archaeological site near the ancient city of Caesarea Philippi, in the Golan Heights, that is still known as "Banias" or "Panias."

5. A "tetrarch" was a Roman regional governor. The word is from the Greek for "rule by four [people]," and referred originally to someone who governed a fourth part of a Kingdom; the Romans came to use it more generally for the governor of any area within their empire. In the New Testament, apart from Luke 3:1, which lists three tetrarchs who were in office when John the Baptist began his ministry, it is used only of Herod (e.g. Matthew 14:1), that is, Herod Antipas, who was governor of Galilee and Perea.

6. In the hymn, "And can it be that I should gain."

begin to see with our spirits, even if we cannot fully grasp with our minds, the fact that it has a unique significance. The Scriptures are absolutely clear: only God can save, a fact stated again and again by Isaiah, as in 43:11, "I, even I, am the Lord, and apart from me there is no savior." The cross without a divine Christ cannot save us. On the other hand a divine Christ without the cross cannot save us either, because "without the shedding of blood there is no forgiveness" (Hebrews 9:22). That is why we preach Christ crucified.

"You are Peter"

Jesus' words to Peter ("You are Peter, and on this rock I will build my church . . . ," Matthew 16:18) have become some of the most controversially debated in the history of the church. The medieval Roman Catholic tradition built on them a series of doctrines which are still at the heart of a Catholic understanding of the church: the primacy of Peter, his status as the first Pope, and the definition of the "true church" as that church which acknowledges the present Pope as the successor of Peter and therefore as the supreme head of the church on earth. In their eagerness to oppose that view, Protestants have frequently claimed that Jesus' words about the rock on which he will build his church do not refer to Peter himself, but to his confession of Jesus as the Son of God: it is the fact that Jesus is Lord that alone provides the foundation on which the church can be built; and they would often say that this is confirmed in Paul's words in 1 Corinthians 3:11, that "no one can lay any foundation other than the one already laid, which is Jesus Christ." That is undoubtedly correct; the only problem is that Jesus' words here do seem to be addressed to Peter: the play on words of his name—"Peter" means "rock"—is sufficient grounds for believing that what Jesus is saying is not a universal statement that has no connection with the person to whom he happens to be uttering it.[7] The error of the Catholic view is not that Jesus is not referring to Peter—he is—but that the doctrinal edifice that the church of Rome has built on the foundation of this verse is one that the text cannot possibly bear: there is nothing here that justifies a view of papal authority,

---

7. It is true that the word Jesus uses which is translated "rock" is not absolutely the same as the form of the name "Peter." The name is the Greek masculine word *Pétros*, which is indeed a word meaning "stone," though it is never used in the New Testament as a common noun, only ever as the name of the apostle; the word translated "rock" is the cognate feminine noun *pétra*. But I think any attempt to argue that this means that Jesus did not intend his words to apply to Peter is flimsy; the two nouns are obviously so closely related that they are in effect two slightly varied forms of the same word. Nothing does more harm to a good cause—and to refute Catholic error and establish biblical truth is a very good cause—than to try and prop it up with untenable arguments.

of Peter as the first Pope, or of the position given him here by Christ being passed on to his successors in office; and all those doctrines conflict both with the spirit of the New Testament as a whole and with many specific statements within it. Peter is in a real sense the rock on which the church would be built; it was Peter who, humanly speaking, established the first church through his preaching on the day of Pentecost (Acts 2:14,37–41), who was instrumental in establishing the first truly Spirit-filled church amongst the Samaritans (8:14–17), and who through his preaching of the Gospel in the home of Cornelius established the first Gentile church (10:23–48). In the verse in Matthew that we are considering Jesus clearly says "*I* [that is, Jesus himself] will build my church"; but he usually does it through people, and the first person through whom he did it was Peter. We might say that although Peter is neither the builder nor the foundation of the church—only the Lord Jesus can be that—he was the one whose ministry first enabled people from all three of the great divisions of the ancient world, Jews, Samaritans and Gentiles, to be built on that foundation.

Where the Protestant view of verse 18 is certainly correct is in saying that the Peter who can exercise that ministry is the Peter who confesses Jesus as Son of God. The Peter of Matthew 16 is a model, not of the unique status of the bishop of Rome, but of the disciple who believes and affirms that Jesus is Lord. Two things in Matthew's Gospel militate against reading more into the text than that. One is the fact that the same power to forgive and discipline that in Matthew 16:19 is given to Peter ("whatever you bind on earth will be bound in heaven, and whatever you loose on earth will be loosed in heaven") is given in Matthew 18:18 to the church as it meets in fellowship; the wording there is more or less identical except that the verbs are in the plural: "whatever you together, the gathered church, bind or loose . . ." We cannot use Matthew 16 to teach a doctrine of the unique position of Peter, or even of Christian leadership in general; whatever authority is given to Peter in 16:19 is given to the whole church in 18:18.

The other indication that Peter is not in himself the infallible foundation of the church is found just a few verses later in 16:22–23. Peter objects to Jesus talking about going to the cross, and tries to turn him from that path, which causes Jesus to say to him "Get behind me, Satan!" Matthew is giving a very specific caution here: just moments before, Jesus was commending Peter because what he said (about Jesus as the Son of God) did not come from his or any other person's human understanding, but had been revealed to him by God the Father; and now he is saying that Satan is using Peter as his mouthpiece in an attempt to divert Jesus from his appointed path as the Suffering Servant of God. The lesson is vital: we do not receive anything as truth on the basis of the position or status of the person who said it, but only of whether what they said is or is not consistent with the Word of God. Paul says the same thing in Galatians 1:8: "Even if we [that is, those known to be apostles] or an angel from heaven should preach a gospel other than the one we preached to you, let him be eternally condemned!"[8] The authenticity of the message depends on its content, not on the status or title of the messenger. It is not only Roman Catholics who are liable to this error ("It must be true because the Pope said it!"); evangelicals can be just as lacking in discrimination ("It must be true, because I heard so-and-so on the *God Channel* say it!"). Within a few verses, Peter is described as the rock on which the church is built, *and* as the tool of Satan to prevent the church from being built. Any one of us can be a part of the church that Jesus is building, if we recognize Jesus as Lord and submit to his Lordship; or we can become a problem and a stumbling-block if we refuse to listen to Jesus and to submit to the work of the cross.

It is with this in mind that we need to understand the words in 16:19 about Peter being given "the keys of the Kingdom." As we have said, Peter was the person who, through his ministry to Jews, Samaritans and Gentiles, first enabled large numbers of people to come into the Kingdom; in that sense, Peter first held the "keys" to God's Kingdom. But he was not given absolute personal authority to admit people to the church or exclude them, as he chose. The words in verse 19 about "binding" and "loosing" have also been woefully misunderstood and misapplied in the history of the church. Three things make it clear that these words are not giving Peter, or the church in general, the power to impose authoritarian pressure on people. One is the fact that such religious dictatorship is quite contrary to the whole spirit of the New Testament; Jesus castigated the Pharisees as those who "tie up heavy loads" of religious rules for people to carry, and insisted that his disciples "do not do what they do" (23:3-4). Second, the context in Matthew 18, where the same language about "binding" and "loosing" immediately follows teaching about how to handle disagreements and disputes within the church, and the fact that the fellowship of the church as a whole is the final arbiter in matters of church discipline (verses 15-17), show that "bind"

---

8. "Eternally condemned" is a translation of the Greek word *anáthema*: Paul says of anyone preaching another Gospel, "let him be anathema!" Derived from an original term for an offering presented in a pagan temple, *anáthema* was the word used to translate the Old Testament Hebrew word *hērem*, meaning the "ban," the fact of consigning to final and absolute destruction anything permanently unclean and unacceptable to God. Paul's words are neither more nor less than the pronouncement of the curse of God on those who tamper with the Gospel. The fact that "anathema" has become a somewhat more trivial word in modern English—to say that anything "is anathema to me" normally means simply that I dislike it or disapprove of it—should not blind us to the seriousness of what Paul is saying here.

and "loose" refer primarily to the authority of the church to exercise appropriate discipline over its members. The terms "bind" and "loose" were used by Jewish Rabbis to refer to forbidding or permitting different forms of behavior. The church is here given the charge, under the authority of Jesus and in accordance with the principles of the Word of God, to teach the patterns of life that are appropriate for Christians, and to take action in the event of conduct that seriously conflicts with those principles. And it should be noted that Jesus speaks of "whatever" you bind or loose, not of "whomever"; he is referring not primarily to accepting people into or excluding them from the church (excommunication), but about teaching which modes of behavior are or are not acceptable. Of course, it is sometimes necessary as a last resort to exclude the unrepentant sinner from fellowship, as Jesus here acknowledges (verse 17; the same difficult issue is addressed in 1 Corinthians 5). It is already hard and painful to have to exercise discipline over people's conduct, but there is a real danger if the church or its leaders assume that they are called to sit in judgment on the people themselves.

And third, there may be a key to the correct understanding of Matthew 16:19 in the tenses used in the Greek verbs; literally, Matthew writes "whatever you bind on earth will be *what has been bound* in heaven, and whatever you loose on earth will be *what has been loosed* in heaven." Jesus is not giving Peter, or any other leader, or the church as a whole, a free hand to discipline anyone they choose to and promising that heaven will always endorse their verdicts; he is rather promising that God will guide his church so that the decisions they make on earth about how to handle matters of discipline in the church will be in line with the decisions God has already made in heaven about the right thing to do.

That this is how Jesus' words about "binding and loosing" are to be understood is confirmed when we recognize that, alongside the essential subject of the identity of Jesus as the Messiah, there is another theme that runs through Matthew 16:13–23, namely the difference between human understanding and truth revealed from heaven. In response to Jesus' question about who people say he is, the disciples repeat various human ideas that are circulating ("John the Baptist . . . Elijah . . . one of the prophets"); Peter's answer ("You are the Christ") is, Jesus says, the truth revealed by God. Moments later, Peter's protestation that Jesus cannot possibly go to the cross is the natural human reaction to such a terrible prospect; Jesus says that, in so responding, Peter is thinking as man thinks, not as God thinks. The same principle, that heavenly wisdom is very different from human reason, lies behind the words about "whatever you bind on earth . . .": Jesus is promising his disciples that the time will come when they are guided, not by their natural intelligence, but by the will of God in heaven; when the church will not be a human organization making decisions on the basis of human thinking, but a community of faith guided by the revealed wisdom of God. The fact that Peter here has to be rebuked for thinking as man thinks shows that the apostles have still not reached that level of spiritual maturity: but Jesus' words are the promise that they will. Maybe the modern church, which can all too often seem to make decisions according to the latest human policies and strategies, and where the criterion for choosing what we should do can often seem to be "what will work?" rather than "what is God saying?," needs to come back to taking at face value Jesus' promise that he intends to make us into a people who are shaped by God's wisdom, even though that will often be poles apart from what human understanding would advocate.

"The Son of Man must suffer"

Now that the disciples have started to understand more of who Jesus is, he begins straightaway to prepare them for the cross. The next verses, (Matthew 16:21//Mark 8:31//Luke 9:22) give us the first of three direct predictions by Jesus of his suffering; the others come in Matthew 17:22–23//Mark 9:30–32//Luke 9:44-45 and Matthew 20:17-19//Mark 10:32-34//Luke 18:31-34. Three points of interest arise from these predictions of the passion.

The Son and the Servant

One takes us back to the comments we made in the chapters on the baptism and temptation of Jesus, that he fulfills *both* the Old Testament prophecies of a conquering King who would defeat the enemies of God, *and* the prophecies of a humble and suffering servant who would die on behalf of God's people. The words of the Father over Jesus in his baptism combine those two stands of prophecy ("This is my beloved Son"—that is, the promised victorious King of Psalm 2:7—"with whom I am well pleased"—that is, the suffering servant of Isaiah 42:1). The temptations of the devil try to separate the two: "If you are the Son of God . . ."—if you are the Son, then live like the Son, and stop thinking that you have to fulfill the role of a humble servant and go the way of the cross.

We made the point earlier that the church has often failed to hold Jesus' Sonship—the fact that he is the Messiah-King—and his servanthood in proper balance, but has often stressed one and downplayed the other. Here at Caesarea Philippi, Peter seems to struggle with the same tension. He has come to see that Jesus is the Messiah—he is the promised King, who will victoriously establish God's Kingdom on earth. But Jesus now goes on to speak of his cross—the way in which he will fulfill his Messianic role is by going the way of the suffering servant; and that is what Peter cannot, at this stage, understand or accept. We should perhaps not be too hard on Peter, just because he cannot yet see how the one who is the Messiah-King can at the same time be the one who will be rejected, will suffer and die: the idea that the promised Messiah and the suffering servant could be one and the same person was unknown amongst the Jews until the time of Jesus. That is why Paul says that the message of Christ crucified is a stumbling-block, an offense, to Jews (1 Corinthians 1:23); the very phrase "Christ crucified" would seem to be an appalling contradiction: how could the same person be the Christ—the victorious Messiah—*and* the crucified one? But when Jesus, immediately following Peter's confession that he is the Messiah, goes on to speak of his suffering and death, he is clearly showing that he sees it as vital that his followers grasp that he is both the King and the crucified one, the Son and the servant. Peter had seen the first of these truths; at this stage, he cannot grasp the second, but he would later do so. In his first Christian sermon on the day of Pentecost, he affirms that "God has made this Jesus, whom you crucified, both *Lord and Christ*" (Acts 2:36); in the second, following the healing of the cripple at the Beautiful Gate, he says that "the God of Abraham . . . has glorified his *servant* Jesus" (Acts 3:13).

The pattern of the cross

Another point arising from Jesus' predictions of his cross is that, in the first at Caesarea Philippi, Jesus, having spoken of his own coming suffering, immediately goes on to speak of the cross as the pattern of service for the life of his followers: we are to take up our cross and follow Jesus, and give up our lives in order to find his new life (Matthew 16:24–25//Mark 8:34–35//Luke 9:23–24). The phrase about taking up the cross, often in the form "we all have our cross to bear!," has in our day been dreadfully trivialized; Jesus is not referring to putting up with the aches and pains of life. There are two main aspects to "taking up our cross," the first of which is that we are prepared to pay any price, endure any cost, in order to see the Kingdom of God come. For Jesus, bringing the Kingdom would mean literally carrying the cross; but he was prepared to do it, because he knew that this was what would bring salvation to the world. In that spirit, his people are told to give their lives to extend and promote Jesus' Kingdom, just as he gave his own to establish it. What that might cost will vary, and for some it will be literal martyrdom. But even where it is not, there will usually be a price to pay for serving the Kingdom: facing opposition, ridicule, hostility, being ostracized by family and friends. To take up our cross means to be ready and willing to pay that price.

This needs saying, in a western culture where it is all too easy to maintain Christian faith in a way that will not entail too much conflict with the secular world around us. Radical discipleship costs; so to avoid having to pay the cost, many will decide not to be too radical—to be as Christian as our world is prepared to accept—and often to label those whose total commitment to God's Kingdom causes them to face opposition from society as "fanatical" or "O.T.T." Representatives of respectable, comfortable and socially conformist religion need to know that by carrying our cross Jesus was not referring to wearing attractive jewelry round our necks, and that he said (Luke 6:26) "Woe to you when all men speak well of you."

The other sense of "taking up our cross" arises from the fact that the challenges of Christian life will often conflict with the appetites and preferences of our ordinary human nature: we are called to forgive people when our natural instinct would be to get our own back, or at least to ignore them; we are told to speak the truth, when the easy thing would be to invent a "white lie"; we are expected to discipline the inappropriate desires of the flesh, when all around us are urging us to indulge them. In other words, we are called, as Paul says, to be those who "have crucified the sinful nature with its passions and desires" (Galatians 5:24), to "put to death" our sinful appetites (Colossians 3:5). Anyone seen carrying a cross in Jesus' day was going to be put to death; and he is here saying that anything that belongs to our sinful nature, and is therefore incompatible with God's righteous Kingdom, must be put to death. The Holy Spirit comes, not just to fill us with charismatic gifts like speaking in tongues—though he certainly does that—but also to enable us to practice positive and joyful moral self-discipline.[9] James 3:1–12 speaks of the impossibility, humanly speaking, of taming the tongue; the real test of the Spirit-filled Christian is not just that he speaks with other tongues, but that he can control and use wisely the one he already has. To develop that degree of wise self-control will require a regular practice of "crucifying the sinful nature" and "taking up the cross."

---

9. The list in Galatians 5:22–23 of the "fruit of the Spirit" ends with the term "self-control." This does not mean, as some assume, cool, quiet and unemotional restraint—on the contrary, the Spirit fills people with great joy—but refers rather to *moral* self-control. The term Paul uses (Greek: *enkráteia*) was used by Aristotle to describe the man who, although he may have strong passions, is able to keep them under control rather than indulging them in a licentious way; Paul uses the related verb in 1 Corinthians 7:9 to say that the person who struggles to *control* his or her sexual appetite would do much better to marry.

Cross and resurrection

It is significant that in all the predictions of his passion, Jesus also says that he will be raised again on the third day. Jesus never prophesied his death without at the same time prophesying his resurrection. In that spirit, when Jesus urges his disciples to carry their cross, he accompanies that challenge with the promise that he will come again in glory at the end of the age (Matthew 16:27//Mark 8:38//Luke 9:26); being crucified with Christ now will result in our sharing his glory in the future.

In this way Jesus makes it abundantly clear that the heart of his saving work is "cross-resurrection." Anyone asking, "Which is more important, more central to Christian life and faith: the cross or the resurrection?" has clearly not grasped what Christian life and faith are. One might as well ask which wing of a plane is more important to its flying. Clearly, without both wings the plane is never even going to get off the ground, much less take anyone anywhere. Sadly, there are some within the tradition of the church who do not seem to have understood with equal clarity that unless our faith is focused in Jesus who died for our sins *and* rose again for our justification (Romans 4:25), our faith will never take off; nor that unless our life is one of taking up the cross *and* of being filled with the power, joy and vitality of Jesus' resurrection life, our lives will not be going anywhere.

The transfiguration

That presentation of the suffering and future glory of Christ is reflected in another important event in this stage of Jesus' ministry, namely his transfiguration (Matthew 17:1–13//Mark 9:2–13//Luke 9:28–36). Jesus goes up on to a mountain top with Peter, James and John, and there these three disciples for a brief moment see Jesus, not as they are used to seeing him as a man among men, but in his heavenly glory. If when the Son of God became incarnate the glory of his heavenly nature was veiled—concealed behind the curtain of his ordinary humanity—then on this mountain top the curtain was temporarily tweaked aside; they see Jesus shining like the sun, so that even his clothing becomes as brilliant white as the light (Matthew 17:2). Years later, the elderly John was to see the same again, when the glorified Jesus appeared to him on the island of Patmos (Revelation 1:9–16).

This revelation of Jesus is the climax of Jesus' disclosure to his disciples of who he is. It is significant that it follows Peter's confession at Caesarea Philippi. The disciples need to accept by faith who Jesus is before they see his glory. Seeing follows believing. The skeptical world will often ask to see proof, as when Jesus was urged to perform a miracle; "when we see, then we'll believe." God is wiser than that. He knows that unless people have a heart that is seeking him, they can see all the miracles in the world, but they still will not believe, as Jesus discovered in Korazin and Bethsaida (Matthew 11:21), and for that matter in Nazareth (13:54–57). The reverse is true: when we believe, then we will see.

The transfiguration is another example of a "miracle of the new creation." One day we will all be "changed" (1 Corinthians 15:51) from this ordinary human life to the glory of heaven, just as Jesus was for a few moments on the mountain top. The same word that is translated "transfigured" in the Gospels is the word used in 2 Corinthians 3:18 for how we are all being "*transformed* into his likeness with ever-increasing glory." That process will be completed in the new heavens and the new earth, when we will be perfectly like Jesus—the description of Jesus in his transfiguration is an indication of what we will "look like" in heaven. That is why the transfiguration immediately follows the prediction that the disciples will see the Son of Man coming in his glory (Matthew 16:28//Mark 9:1//Luke 9:27). Obviously this refers primarily to Jesus' return at the end of history. But the transfiguration is a foreshadowing of that; the disciples see briefly, for a moment, what all the world will one day see when Jesus comes again.

Moses and Elijah appear with Jesus on the mountain-top. They are the two great figures who represent the Old Testament. The Old Testament is often called "the Law and the Prophets" (Matthew 5:17, 7:12, Luke 16:16, Acts 13:15). Moses is the great law-giver: it was through Moses that God gave the people the law at Mount Sinai. Elijah was the first great prophet in Israel. So Moses and Elijah together represent "the Law and the Prophets," the Old Testament. Peter wants to build three shelters (or "shrines"), one each for Jesus, Moses and Elijah (Matthew 17:4): he sees Jesus as standing alongside or on the same level as the great saints and leaders of the Old Testament. But the voice of God from heaven corrects him. Jesus is the Son of God, so, as the Father says, "listen to him." Moses and Elijah point to Christ and testify to him, but they do not rank equally with him. That points us to a danger to which those who, like myself, stand in the strongly evangelical tradition of the church always need to be alert. In our enthusiasm for the Bible as the uniquely authoritative Word of God we can sometimes forget that the Scriptures are given to point us to Jesus, as he himself reminded the Pharisees (John 5:39–40): the Bible is not the object or focus of our faith, but the God-inspired Word that points us to Jesus, who alone *is* the object and focus of faith.

And this is where we see again the connection between the heavenly glory of Jesus, revealed in the transfiguration, and the suffering and cross of Jesus, of which he has started to speak to his disciples. Luke 9:31 says that Moses and Elijah were talking with Jesus about his coming death on the cross—literally, about the "exodus" that he was to accomplish in Jerusalem.[10] The whole Old Testament prepares God's people for Jesus and for his death. The glorified and transfigured Lord is also the one who will suffer and die; the Son of God is also the Servant of God. That is why our own lives as his disciples need to reflect both a celebration of and rejoicing in the fact that we are adopted as God's children, *and* a commitment to the call to follow him faithfully as servants, whatever it might cost.

In this connection, it is important to remember that Moses and Elijah, as well as being the representatives of the law and the prophets, had foreshadowed Jesus in a remarkable way: both were men who in their day had agonized over the sins of God's people and, although themselves not sharing in the specific evils of which the people were guilty, had identified themselves with the people as a whole (e.g. Exodus 32:31–32, 1 Kings 18:36, 19:10). Though obviously in a far more limited way than the Lord Jesus, Moses and Elijah had, like him, stood in the place of sinners, and had known the pain of being torn between the covenant love of God towards his people and the righteous anger of God who had to pronounce judgment against their sin. It is in Christ, and specifically in the cross of Christ, that God's love and justice will meet perfectly once for all, as the Father's wrath against sin is visited on Jesus in our place, and the Father's love for sinners is made effective as his Son atones for all sin and enables us to be completely forgiven and restored to God.

The Kingdom comes through the cross. There is a mistaken idea that occasionally surfaces in discussions about mission, that the New Testament presents us with two different approaches to mission: the "Kingdom" approach—doing the works of Jesus in the world—and the "Gospel" approach—telling people the message that Jesus died for their sins on the cross. Jesus' own ministry as presented in the Gospels will allow no such distinction: "what God has joined together, let man not separate." Jesus brings the Kingdom, but he can truly bring it only through the cross. It is only through coming to the cross of Jesus that we can enter the Kingdom. When people see in the life and service of the church something that

---

10. That Jesus' death is referred to as his "exodus" is full of significance for our understanding of the achievement of the cross. To mention just two main parallels: in the exodus, those who were in slavery were set free; and by the death of Christ those who are slaves to sin are redeemed and set free from condemnation. The last act of God's judgment on Egypt before the Israelites finally left Egypt was the death of the first-born sons of Egypt; and it was the death of God's Son that secured our redemption. The exodus is *the* great Old Testament "type" or foreshadowing of the salvation achieved at the cross.

captures their imagination—the Kingdom of God—and ask if and how they can become part of it, the only possible answer is to lead them to Christ crucified. There is only one door into the Kingdom, and it is cross-shaped.

12

The Kingdom and the poor

"Blessed are you who are poor, for yours is the Kingdom of God" (Luke 6:20)

In the last stage of his wider ministry leading up to the cross, Jesus spends much more of his time around the Jerusalem area. He has a "base" at the home of Mary and Martha at Bethany, a few miles to the east of Jerusalem.

Jesus and the poor

Most of the emphasis in this section is on how the Kingdom is for "unlikely people." The previous sections have shown that the Kingdom is for Gentiles, as well as Jews, and that it will come through the cross, and commits us to a lifestyle that sees the cross as its model. This section shows that the Kingdom is for sinners, outcasts and the poor, rather than the respectable and the religious. Most of this material is in Luke; he is particularly the Gospel-writer who stresses Jesus' ministry to the poor and outcasts.

It should be said that that this is not the first time that the theme of the radical social change that the Gospel brings has been raised in Luke. For example, even before Jesus was born, his mother-to-be, in her prophetic song known as the *Magnificat*, said that, in the birth of Christ, God was coming to cast down the proud and the prosperous from their thrones and to raise up the poor (Luke 1:46–55). William Barclay rightly says, "There is loveliness in the *Magnificat* but in that loveliness there is dynamite. Christianity begets a revolution in each man and revolution in the world."[1]

In the second half of Jesus' ministry, the theme of the outsider is first raised in the parable of the Good Samaritan (Luke 10:25-37). This well-known story is one of the parts of Scripture that frequently suffers from being taken out of context; it is important to heed the lesson contained in the fact that it is immediately followed by the incident at the home of Mary and Martha at Bethany, when Martha complains that her sister is sitting at the feet of Jesus instead of helping her with the domestic chores; Jesus commends Mary for having chosen "what is better" (verses 38-42). The parable of the Good Samaritan illustrates the lesson that it is not just people who have a formal religious position (like the priest and the Levite) who are acceptable to God, but those who actually live in a right way; it illustrates what it means to "love your neighbor" (verses 27-29), and demonstrates the uncomfortable truth that our "neighbor" means anyone who is in need of our help, including those with whom we might not naturally speaking feel that we have, or want to have, much in common. There was no love lost between Jews and Samaritans; yet it is the Samaritan, rather than his fellow-Jews, who comes to the aid of the muggers' victim. Jesus is quite clear: to claim that we "love God" (as the priest and the Levite no doubt would) is meaningless if we do not also love our neighbor. And that might mean that some outsiders to the religious establishment (Samaritans?) are in fact more pleasing to God than official religious leaders.[2]

But then we have the incident in the home of Mary and Martha. Whilst Martha is fussing around with lots of household chores, Mary sits at the feet of Jesus and learns from him. Jesus says that is the right thing to do. The Good Samaritan story must never be taken to mean that mere activism (being busy about good works) is in itself the best thing—Martha was after all very "active" and "busy" in the home, and Jesus tells her to calm down. We all need to spend time sitting at the feet of Jesus. But, on the other hand,

---

1. Barclay, *Luke*, 16.

2. In the 1970s the Christian theater company *Riding Lights* produced a sketch called *The Parable of the Good Punk-Rocker*; it told the story of a man on a train who was mugged by a gang of football hooligans. Amongst those who felt sorry for the victim were a social worker, whose help amounted to repeating "I really care about the kids," and a vicar, whose reaction to seeing the mugging was to lock himself in the train toilet to say a prayer for the man. It was a member of a punk rock band who actually helped the victim. (Burbridge and Watts, *Time to Act*, 78-80.) I dare say many middle-class church-goers, not to mention social workers and vicars, might have found the implications of the sketch somewhat inappropriate, if not actually offensive; but then, how do they suppose Jesus' first hearers would have reacted to being told about the good Samaritan?

sitting at the feet of Jesus must never mean being passive. It should lead to our living a life of active service to others, as exemplified by the Good Samaritan story.

Luke 12:1—13:9 then gives us a block of teaching, mostly addressed to Jesus' own disciples, on various aspects of Christian life and ministry; some of this teaching repeats themes found in other places in Matthew and Mark. But a significant proportion of it deals with the theme that will run through this whole section of Luke from chapters 12–19, namely financial and social responsibility. There is the parable of the rich fool (12:13–21), which warns people who are preoccupied with wealth that they need to pay attention to their spiritual state before God; this is followed by the teaching that we should not worry about our practical needs, but rather trust God to supply all we need (12:22–34), which repeats some of the content of the Sermon on the Mount (Matthew 6:25–34). Then the instruction in chapters 13–16, given whilst Jesus is *en route* to Jerusalem, is almost all on the theme of the Kingdom being for the poor. In 13:22–30 Jesus speaks of the urgency of entering into the life of the Kingdom, and the fact that there will be a few surprises at who is in the Kingdom and who is excluded: those Jews who were strong in national self-confidence but weak in spiritual devotion and even weaker in social compassion may well have been shocked to hear that "you [will] see Abraham, Isaac and Jacob and all the prophets in the Kingdom of God, but you yourselves thrown out. People will come from east and west and north and south, and will take their places at the feast in the Kingdom of God."

But there would be more of the same to come. In 14:1–14 Jesus begins to teach the vital lesson about humility: that disciples of the Kingdom should not only be humble themselves, but, as part of that humility, should associate with the poor and outcasts of society. The parable of the great banquet (14:15–24) reinforces the message that the Kingdom is for "the poor, the crippled, the blind and the lame" (verse 21). Then, because the Pharisees were criticizing Jesus because he was spending too much time, indeed, any time at all, with those whom they clearly regarded as morally beneath the attention of a man of God (15:1–2), Jesus tells (15:3–32) three parables about the joy in heaven over even one sinner who repents: the stories of the lost sheep, the lost coin, and the lost son. The ethos of the citizens of God's Kingdom is not to point out that sinners are sinners, nor to avoid them, nor to stress how much better than them we are, but rather to seek and save them.

Most of chapter 16 consists of teaching about the right (and wrong) use of money. The parable of the "shrewd manager" (verses 1–13) is perhaps Jesus' most puzzling parable. He appears to be commending a corrupt man as an example to follow. But the point of the story is not the rightness or wrongness of the steward's actual methods in themselves; it is that, realizing that he is in trouble, he takes steps to provide for his future. He does it in a corrupt and worldly way, but he does at least take seriously his future problem and he does something to prepare himself for it.[3] Jesus is saying, this corrupt man was willing to take steps in worldly ways to prepare himself for his worldly future. Why is it that my people so often seem unwilling to take seriously the need to prepare themselves in spiritual ways for their spiritual future? We need to use what resources we have, including our money, to do what is right in God's eyes—verse 9 speaks of "making friends for yourselves," which presumably means by generosity and almsgiving—so that we can face the coming judgment with confidence. Jesus is not speaking about salvation by works: no one can buy their way into heaven, as the whole New Testament makes clear; rather, the behavior commended is essentially that of using our money to bless others rather than storing it up for ourselves, a lifestyle which, as other parts of the Bible say, should be the fruit of faith and devotion to God. We need to see this parable alongside the parable of the sheep and the goats on the day of judgment in Matthew 35:31–46. The parable of the dishonest manager is then followed by the story of the rich man and the beggar Lazarus (Luke 16:19–31), in which the man who had spent all his life enjoying his wealth and paying no attention at all to the needs of the poor beggar at his gate finds himself, after death, being punished for his greed and sin.[4]

The story in 17:11–19 of the ten lepers healed of their leprosy continues the "outsider" theme: the only one who responded positively and came back to thank Jesus was a Samaritan. Then in 18:1–8 Jesus tells the parable of

---

3. An alternative interpretation of the steward's actions, which seeks to get round the problem of why Jesus seems to be holding up a cheat as an example to follow, is that the master's original bills had included interest, which, under Jewish law, was forbidden; and the steward was merely requiring the repayment of the original interest-free sum. Ingenious though that is, it has two obvious flaws. It requires that the hearers and readers of the story be able to read a great deal of background information into the text, which is not even hinted in the wording of the story itself; and, even more seriously, when Jesus speaks in verse 8 of the master himself commending his steward's shrewdness, he refers to the latter as the "dishonest" steward.

4. One interesting side-line in this story is the comment in verses 29 and 31. When the rich man, suffering his punishment in hell, pleads that his brothers who are still living in the world be granted a special supernatural visitation to warn them to change their ways before it is too late, he is told that they have the writings of the Bible to guide them; and Jesus adds the comment, "If they do not listen to Moses and the Prophets, they will not be convinced even if someone rises from the dead." This needs to be remembered every time people say that if they saw a miracle they would believe. Those who refuse to accept the message of the Word of God will not be changed by witnessing a miracle from God.

the persistent widow and the unjust judge, to teach the point, first, that God will act with justice to the poor, and second, that his people should persist in prayer even if they do not always receive immediate and full answers. This is another example of a parable which is not a parallel but a contrast. Many of Jesus' parables, like those in Matthew 13, say that something in this world is like, and can therefore serve as an illustration of, some aspect of God's Kingdom. But other parables, like this one about the widow and the judge, make their point by showing how different the Kingdom of God is to what happens in this world. God is *not* like the unjust judge. If in this world people can often get what they want simply by persisting in asking (even though the person they are asking doesn't care about doing the right thing), how much more can we be confident that, if we persist in prayer, God will give us what is right, because he, unlike the judge in the parable, does care very much for us.[5] The parable of the Pharisee and the tax collector (18:9–14) then repeats the warning that God's blessing is not necessarily reserved for the formally religious, and certainly not for those, like the Pharisee, whose religion is primarily a matter of outward show and an attempt to appear better than other people. It is the tax collector—the lowest level of sin to which people could sink, in the estimation of the Pharisees—who "went home justified before God"; he had humbled himself and confessed his sin, whilst the Pharisee was busy reciting the long list of his good works that made him a person far more deserving of God's favor than the tax collector.

At this point Jesus journeys from Ephraim (north of Jerusalem) through Perea (east of the Jordan), as his last period of ministry outside Jerusalem (Matthew 19:1–2//Mark 10:1). He then returns to Jerusalem via Bethany. The theme of the Kingdom being for "unlikely people" continues. Jesus receives and blesses little children (Matthew 19:13–15//Mark 10:13–16//Luke 18:15–17), and teaches that the Kingdom belongs, not to the rich and powerful, but to the child-like, a point reinforced when the rich young man decides that the demands of the Kingdom are too much for him,

---

5. There is another contrast between the judge and God, though it is obscured by a problem of translation in verse 7, which in the NIV reads "[Will he keep] *putting them off*?" The Greek verb simply means "[to be] patient," which is how it is translated in the nine other places in the New Testament where it occurs; it is often used of God's forbearance. The sense of this phrase is not easy to pin down, partly because of the grammatical complexity of the sentence; but I believe it is best to take the word in its most natural sense, namely that God is patient with his people. Unlike the unjust judge, who granted the widow's request simply to put an end to her repeated protestations, God has limitless patience with his people. In the mystery of God's providence, there may be reasons why answers to prayer are sometimes delayed; but, Jesus assures us, the reason is *never* that God has, as we might say, "had enough of us." Isaiah 40:28 assures us that "he will not grow tired or weary," and that includes the fact that he will never grow tired or weary of our persistent prayers.

and turns sadly away from Jesus (Matthew 19:16–30//Mark 10:17–31//Luke 18:18–30). Coming as it does immediately after the blessing on children and the teaching on child-likeness, this story emphasizes that those who are rich and powerful in the world's terms may not always find that the life of the Kingdom of heaven suits them.

The saying about becoming like children, and especially Jesus' words about receiving the kingdom "as a child" have been much misunderstood, especially by those who want to see in the blessing of the infants a justification for infant baptism, of which there is clearly not a trace in the story. "As a child" does not mean "during one's childhood years"—Jesus is not saying that it is in early infancy that children are to be initiated into the membership of the Kingdom—but, as the NIV rightly translates the phrase (Mark 10:15//Luke 18:17) "*like* a little child," that is, in a child-like spirit. Above all, this refers to the difference between dependency and independency; a child does not expect to have to provide for itself, to earn its living, but an adult has to take responsibility for his or her life. To receive the Kingdom in a child-like spirit means that the Christian receives the gift of God's life without even entertaining the thought that he can pay for it, earn it or work towards it, just as a child receives life, food and clothing from its parents. Our problem is that we are, even in spiritual things, painfully grown-up: we struggle with the very notion of receiving the free gift of God's grace, asking instead what we have to "do" to achieve our own salvation; our hope is that, when we eventually arrive in heaven, we will be able to burst into a loud chorus of "I did it my way!" The Bible is however quite clear: the song that is sung by the redeemed is "Worthy is the Lamb!"; the only way to enter into the Kingdom is to receive as an unmerited and unearned gift of God the life that he offers through Christ.

The parable of the workers in the vineyard (Matthew 20:1–16) again stresses the theme of God's grace to unlikely people. The "late arrivals" in the Kingdom of God get exactly the same reward as those who are the "elder statesmen" in the Kingdom. The immediate application is obviously to the Gentiles: the Jews (who have been serving God as his people for generations) will find that the Gentiles, who only now ("at the eleventh hour") have the opportunity to become God's people, will be blessed in the Kingdom in exactly the same way, and to exactly the same degree, as they are. Those who have served for decades in the church should not feel that they hold any kind of higher ranking in God's eyes than the new convert who a week ago was the twenty-first-century equivalent of a tax collector: a fact that should be remembered by those who can occasionally get on their spiritual high horse and protest at how God seems to be going out of his way to bless those who are still finding their feet in the church ("But I've been a loyal member of this church for forty years, like my parents before me!").

The last great example of Jesus' theme of the Kingdom being for the outsider, the moral and social outcast, is the story of Zacchaeus (Luke 19:1–10). As a collaborator with the Romans, Zacchaeus was despised by all his fellow-Jews; but Jesus spends time with him, eats with him (to the disgust of the crowds, verse 7), and brings him salvation when he repents.

So this whole section of Luke's Gospel in particular challenges all forms of comfortable religion. There is a perception in our country of "the church" as being at the heart of settled community life, part of the very fabric of society. But Jesus presents the Kingdom of God as being for outsiders, for those who are not part of the comfortable religious establishment; not, it is true, with the intention of explicitly excluding the members of the settled religious community, but certainly to alert them to the fact that the Kingdom of God is for others besides them, and that they are called to welcome those who may not in social terms be "like them," but who are in spiritual terms welcomed by God into his Kingdom alongside them.[6]

To summarize this theme of Jesus' moral and social teaching: Jesus has taught that the Kingdom is for the poor, the humble, the outcasts and marginalized in society, and in general for "unlikely people"—it is not specially for the respectable and socially prominent; that disciples must have a strong social concern to minister to the needs of the poor; that we must have the spirit of servants, and see ourselves as sent into the world to serve people's needs; that Christians should be ready to associate with "ordinary" and humble people, and not be concerned about moving up a social ladder; that the church needs to welcome those who are social and moral outcasts; that Christians are challenged to make good and wise use of their money in order to bless others; and that when Jesus returns, God will vindicate the poor, and comfort and reward those who had nothing in this world, whilst those who oppressed them will be punished.

---

6. The Boulting brothers' 1963 comedy *Heavens Above!* is the story of a mild-mannered working-class vicar with a strong social conscience (brilliantly played by Peter Sellers) who, through an administrative blunder, is transferred to an extremely respectable and well-heeled country parish, and who, to the horror of his flock, not only appoints a black dustman as his churchwarden, but then proceeds to fill the vicarage and its grounds with the homeless and the very far from genteel. Needless to say, there are soon moves afoot from his outraged parishioners to have him removed. To assume that such a hostile response to anyone showing charity to the wayward and undeserving could occur only in the fantasy world of the cinema would be would be nice but, sadly, naïve.

The church and the poor

In a different context, Jesus famously said, "What God has joined together, let man not separate" (Matthew 19:6). Whether the church likes it or not, God has clearly joined together the spiritual life of the Kingdom and social care for and service to the poor and the needy. The two have often been divorced in the history of the church. There have been those in the more liberal streams of the church who will willingly run night shelters for the homeless, establish food programs for the hungry and organize fund-raising activities for Third World relief agencies, but who would not see it as their role actually to talk to people about Jesus. On the other hand, until relatively recently, the evangelical churches could be very dismissive of what they labeled as "the social gospel," and would insist that our task is to evangelize; and some—thankfully, far from all—would only too willingly sit next to a vagrant on the street and tell him how to be born again, but it would not occur to them to take the vagrant to a café and buy him a meal.

"What God has joined . . ." His Kingdom is not of this world, it is a spiritual Kingdom; it is indeed about salvation from sin through faith in Christ. But part of the outworking of that salvation, for those who receive it, is clearly expected to be a commitment to serving people who find themselves on the margins of society. Ignoring Luke's Gospel and focusing solely on the other three will not allow us to dodge that challenge: Matthew says it (the parable of the sheep and the goats, 25:31–46), Mark says it (Jesus' words to the rich young man, 10:21), and even John, whose Gospel focuses more than any of the others on the spiritual nature of life in the Kingdom, at least alludes to it (13:29), as well as in his first letter specifically requiring it as an expression of the love of God (1 John 3:17). But if we believe that "all Scripture is God-breathed" (2 Timothy 3:16), then we cannot dismiss Luke as a secondary Gospel just because he talks a lot about social care. If he writes a lot about it, it is because God has a lot to say about it.

In the last couple of hundred years many Christian groups have been formed with the specific aim of promoting Christian mission amongst the poor. One of the greatest, the Salvation Army, has long since been recognized as a church denomination; others like TEAR-fund (The Evangelical Alliance Relief Fund) are registered charities. Many have the status of para-church organizations, like the London City Mission, established in 1835 by David Nasmith, and its more recent sister missions in other cities like Birmingham and Derby. These and many other excellent works are great examples of Christians fulfilling Jesus' call to serve the poor. The only concern about this multiplicity of social missions is that they can unwittingly make it easy for Christians to forget that service to the socially disadvantaged is part of what every believer is called to; it is not only the task of a few specialist organizations, leaving the rest of us free to carry on being "ordinary Christians." The Gospels leave us little doubt that compassionate service to the poor is a vital part of ordinary Christianity.

Another development in the last couple of decades in our own country has been the growth of many secular charities. The non-Christian world today can often display many of the qualities of compassion that Jesus expects to see in his church. I am writing this paragraph on the evening of the annual "Children in Need" appeal, when people all over the country will give millions of pounds to causes supporting disadvantaged children at home and overseas. It would be churlish to dismiss such works simply because their origin is secular rather than Christian, or because of the show-business hype that accompanies them; they do achieve very worthwhile things on behalf of the needy, and it may well be that the presence in the nation of a widespread spirit of charity is a residue of the days when genuine Christian faith was more widespread than it is today. I see no reason why Christians and churches should not, if they wish, contribute to such projects, and many reasons why they should be part of, rather than insisting on standing apart from, that wider national sense of civic responsibility; but that does not mean that there is no longer any need for specifically *Christian* mission to the poor. Not only will the need always outweigh the provision—as Jesus said in John 12:8, "You will always have the poor among you"—but it is still central to mission as Jesus saw and practiced it that works and words go hand-in-hand, and that works, including works of charity, be pointers to the eternal life of Christ. Christians do not have a monopoly on works of compassion, but we do have a specific calling to do those works as expressions of the love of Christ and as signs of the Kingdom of Christ. We should not dismiss or despise non-Christian charities for not sharing that vision—how could they?—and we can rightly applaud all that is good in their motivations and efforts; the fact that our works of care for the needy are done as part of our ministry of Jesus' Kingdom does not mean that we are in competition with secular charities, any more than Jesus' miracles of multiplying the loaves and fishes were intended as a snub to bakers or an attempt to put fishermen out of business.

Another trend that has become more noticeable in recent years in the church, especially amongst Pentecostal and New Church fellowships, has been that of seeking to promote Christian projects in the spirit of the world's business or entrepreneurial methods. Church leaders can seek advice on how to run their churches from managers in industry; new churches can be housed in plush office blocks, with secretaries sitting at reception desks and inquiring on an intercom whether one of the church leaders might be available to speak to a visitor who turns up without an appointment. I do not want to be thought too cynical; and I have no doubt that many churches and church projects that present that kind of image are seeking to serve people and to promote the Gospel of the Kingdom. But I cannot help wondering exactly where not being conformed to the ways of the world fits into the ethos of such churches. Is there perhaps the danger that we have come to think that, to attract the world, we have to become as impressive as the world? In the past, the church did it by building magnificent cathedrals. Today, we do it by making the church as efficient as a successful business. In the early days of what was later, under Mr Blair, to become "New Labour," when the Labour party was seeking to capture the support of much of the middle-ground of British politics, Arthur Scargill gave a speech at a Labour party conference. One might not think that Mr Scargill is exactly the person to look to for wisdom on how the church should operate, but one thing he said struck a chord with me; in that impassioned tone that had (for good or ill, depending on whether you were an unemployed miner or Mrs Thatcher) made him the public figure that he had been for some years, he declared, "I didn't join the Labour party in order to run capitalism better than the Tories!" Forget the party politics, and the left- or right-wing views. I think it is necessary in our day for evangelical Christians to say, in the same spirit, that we did not join the church to run Christianity like a more successful business than McDonald's or Starbucks. The Jesus whom we follow and serve did not establish an organized and high-tech church run by managers and grown by entrepreneurs; he washed his disciples' feet, and told us to do the same. I can find no model in the New Testament for the idea of creating business in order to make money for the church. When in Acts the rich brought the proceeds from the sale of their lands and property for distribution amongst the poor, they were not acting as those who, as Christians, had acquired lands and property in order to be able to use the proceeds for the Kingdom of God; they were people who had lived as the worldly wealthy, but, now that they had come to Christ, were determined no longer to live by that ethos, and not even to adapt that ethos to the service of the Kingdom, but to abandon it, and give away everything they had. Even if the rich young ruler found Jesus' challenge to do that difficult, the early church had many people who were up for it.

Jesus once said that those who live by the sword will die by the sword; I think it is likely to be just as true that those who live by business will die by business. Jesus did not identify himself with the socially well-placed in order to be in a position of influence to help the poor; he helped the poor by getting alongside them, and being himself. As he said in a very similar context, "Go and do likewise."

Some, understandably, are wary of appearing to stray, or actually straying, into the murky waters of politics, and it is not unknown for Christians who preach and seek to promote social justice to be dismissed as left-wing propagandists. When the Archbishop's Commission Report *Faith in the City*, an investigation into how the Church of England could play a greater role in serving the needs of Urban Priority Areas, was presented before Parliament in 1985, one MP dismissed it as "out of date, out of time, out of touch and unwelcome"; another labeled it as "pure Marxist theology," and probably not merely to distinguish it from *im*pure Marxist theology; and yet another claimed that the report proved that the Anglican Church was governed by "a load of Communist clerics." More recently, the same kind of reaction greeted the comments by Justin Welby, shortly after his enthronement as Archbishop of Canterbury, about his concern that many of the poorest in our society were being hit the hardest by the government's austerity measures; one critic accused him of following the example of his predecessor, Rowan Williams, in coming out with one left-wing political position after another. Christians might need to be prepared to bear with such criticisms, which are usually as misplaced as the Pharisees' labeling of Jesus as a glutton and a drunkard (Matthew 11:19) on the grounds that he was willing to spend time with people who enjoyed parties. If we cannot serve the poor without being called socialists, then so be it; rather than protesting[7] (which will probably do little except launch a theoretical and fruitless debate), and certainly rather than backing away from the Lord's call to care for the needy, the church of Jesus Christ should accept his assurance that "wisdom is proved right by her actions"—that God will sooner or later vindicate his children—and get on with doing what Jesus tells us to do. The same Jesus who said "you must be born again" also said "give to the poor"; what he never said was, "take your pick."

---

7. I do not want to be misunderstood: personally, I would not have a problem with being called "socialist," though I understand that some people might; but the point is not whether a Christian's political preferences lean more to the left or right. The world's misplaced criticism reveals a more fundamental error, namely that of assuming that Christians who engage in socially compassionate ministry are doing so on the basis of a socio-political agenda. Whenever Christianity is enlisted in the cause of a party political program, it always compromises or loses its distinctively Christian character. We serve the spiritual Kingdom of God, which is nothing to do with human politics and programs; and we minister to the poor as part of following Jesus, not as an expression of our agreement or disagreement with the government of the day.

The Gospel and the Gospels

"The Gospel" is not the same as "the [four] Gospels." Paul insists that his only concern is to "preach the Gospel" (e.g. Romans 1:9, 1:15, 15:19–20, 1 Corinthians 1:17); but it is noticeable that in all the records of the apostles' preaching in Acts, and in all the letters of the New Testament, there are hardly any references to the life and public ministry of Jesus. To the apostles, to "preach the Gospel" meant to proclaim the message that Christ is the one sent by God to save us from our sins by his death and resurrection; Paul says explicitly that "we preach Christ crucified" (1 Corinthians 1:23) and that, as a Gospel preacher, what he regards as being "of first importance" is the fact that "Christ died for our sins . . . that he was buried, that he was raised on the third day" (1 Corinthians 15:3–4). The public ministry of Jesus recorded in "the Gospels" is not the message which Jesus sent his disciples into the world to preach. Of course it is possible to preach "the Gospel" from "the Gospels"—George Beasley-Murray wrote a book dedicated to the lay preachers' association of London called *Preaching the Gospel from the Gospels*—but the life and teaching of Jesus is not the same thing as "*the* Gospel." We might summarize the purpose of the stories of Jesus' life in Matthew, Mark, Luke and John as two-fold.

Getting to know Jesus

First, they show us Jesus. For those who become Christians by responding to the Gospel, Jesus is the heart and focus of the whole of their life and faith; and the Gospels are written to tell them what Jesus is like, who he is, and what he did. The Jesus in whom we are invited to put our trust is not an unknown and unknowable Savior. Luke said that his purpose in writing his Gospel was "so that you may know the certainty of the things you have been taught" (Luke 1:4), and part of what he means is that those who have been told about Jesus can, in the Gospels, find out much more about the Jesus in whom they are invited to trust or have come to trust. Christian faith is not simply a leap into the dark; it is a decision to follow Jesus, when, having taken a serious look at what he is like, we conclude that he is one in whom we can put our trust with confidence.

Specifically, the Gospels show us the human Jesus. In the early Middle Ages, there was such a concentration on the heavenly, divine Christ that people often forgot the human Jesus; so Christ became a remote and almost inaccessible figure. Christ *is* the Lord of heaven; but he is also the man to whom we can relate at a human level, precisely because he came down to our level in order to relate to us.[8]

Learning to follow Jesus

Specifically, the ministry of Jesus is a pattern for us of what it means to follow him. The Gospels are not primarily intended to encourage people to become believers; they are written to instruct those who *have become* believers, to teach them about Christian life and ministry, based on and arising out of the life and ministry of Jesus himself. No one can live the Christian life until they have received it through faith in Christ, by which alone we are "born again." But when we have responded to the Gospel message about Christ, we have in the four Gospels not only a picture of the Savior who is the heart of our faith, but also a pattern of the life to which he calls us. The Gospels' accounts of the public ministry of Jesus are part of the inspired Word of God that is "useful for teaching, rebuking, correcting and training in righteousness" (2 Timothy 3:16). If the cross of Jesus shows us how God saves us, the life of Jesus shows us what he saves us *for*: it is so that we can start to live as Jesus lived, and serve the Kingdom of God as he did, by his grace and in the enabling power of his Holy Spirit. The early Christian leader Irenaeus (*c.* 130–202) wrote, "He became what we are that he might make us what he himself is."[9] Part of our "becoming what he is" means that we let his Spirit reproduce in us the same quality of life and ministry that we see in the Jesus of the Gospels. So when Christians read about the life of Jesus in the Gospels, they are not just reading about Christ, but also about the life into which Christ wants to lead them. What we see in the public ministry of Jesus is, to quote again the title of Watchman Nee's famous book, *The Normal Christian Life.*

One of the longest running television programs in the second half of the twentieth century in Britain was *This Is Your Life*; every episode famously

---

8. That medieval focus on the heavenly Christ may well be one of the reasons for the development of the unbiblical doctrine of Mary as a mediator between Christ and ourselves. The New Testament says that it is Christ who is the sole and all-sufficient mediator between God and mankind (1 Timothy 2:5). If people came to believe that we need someone to mediate between us and Christ, that suggests that they had come to think of Jesus as so far above us that we are unable to relate to him directly; whereas people found it easy to relate to Mary, not least as a "mother-figure." That is why we preach, not *just* the Christ who is Lord and God, but *also* the man Christ Jesus: people need a Savior to whom they feel they can relate.

9. In Book 4 of his work *Adversus Haereses* ("Against Heresies"); quoted in Bettenson, *Early Church Fathers*, 77.

began when Eamonn Andrews, who presented the show between 1965 and 1987, surprised an unsuspecting celebrity by appearing with his "big red book" containing the story of their life. Many Christians might be just as surprised to learn that the account of Jesus' life in the Gospels could also be entitled "this is *your* life"—not, to be sure, the story of their past, but the story of what God wants to make their life in the future, as they are, as Paul puts it in Romans 8:29, "conformed to the likeness of his Son." James says that the person who, having heard or read the word of God, then fails to live it out in practice is like a man who, having looked in a mirror, goes away and forgets what he looks like (James 1:23–24); and when we read of the public ministry of Jesus in the Gospels, we are looking both at a picture of the real Jesus, and also into a mirror to see, maybe not what we at present look like, but what it is the purpose of God to make us by his grace.

Bibliography

Barclay, William. *The Daily Study Bible: the Gospel of Luke*. Edinburgh: Saint Andrew; revised edition, 1975.
Beasley-Murray, George R. *Baptism in the New Testament*. London: Macmillan and Co., 1963.
———. *Preaching the Gospel from the Gospels*. London: Lutterworth, 1956.
Bettenson, Henry. *The Early Church Fathers*. Oxford University Press, paperback edition, 1969.
Blanchard, John (ed). *Gathered Gold*. Welwyn, Hertfordshire, UK: Evangelical Press, 1984.
Bosch, David J. *Transforming Mission*. New York: Orbis, 2001.
Brown, Raymond E. *An Introduction to the Gospel of John*. New York: The Anchor Bible Reference Library, Doubleday, 2003.
Bruce, F. F. *The Hard Sayings of Jesus*. London: Hodder and Stoughton, 1983.
Burbridge, Paul, and Watts, Murray. *Time to Act*. London: Hodder and Stoughton, 1979.
Chambers, Oswald. *My Utmost for his Highest*. London: Simpkins Marshall, 1927.
Cranfield, C. E. B. *The Gospel According to Saint Mark*. The Cambridge Greek Testament Commentary, Cambridge University Press, 1959.
Fernando, Ajith. *The NIV Application Commentary: Acts*. Grand Rapids, Michigan: Zondervan, 1998.
Forsyth, P. T. *The Cruciality of the Cross*. London: Hodder and Stoughton, 1909.
Fowler, H. W. *Modern English Usage*. Second edition, revised by Ernest Gowers. Oxford: Clarendon, 1968.
Gumbel, Nicky. *Questions of Life*. Eastbourne, UK: Kingsway, 1995.
Hilton, Walter. *The Ladder of Perfection*, newly translated by Leo Sherley-Price. Harmondsworth, Middlesex, UK: Penguin Classics, 1957.
Hunter, A. M. *Introducing New Testament Theology*. London: Student Christian Movement, 1957.
Lewis, C. S. *Miracles*. London: The C. S. Lewis Signature Edition, Collins, 2012.
———. *The Problem of Pain*. London: Collins, Fontana, 1957.
Marshall, I. H., et al (eds). *New Bible Dictionary*. Leicester, UK: Inter-Varsity Press, third edition 1996.
Morgan, G. Campbell. *The Crises of the Christ*. London: Pickering and Inglis, 1963.
Morris, Leon. *The Cross in the New Testament*. Exeter, UK: Paternoster, paperback edition, 1976.

Nee, Watchman. *The Normal Christian Life*. Fort Washington, Pennsylvania: Christian Literature Crusade, 2009.

Newbigin, Lesslie. *The Gospel in a Pluralist Society*. London: SPCK, 1989.

———. *The Open Secret: Sketches for a Missionary Theology*. Grand Rapids, Michigan: William B. Eerdmans, 1978.

Partington, Angela (ed). *The Oxford Dictionary of Quotations*. London: BCA/Oxford University Press, fourth edition, 1992.

Plass, Adrian. *The Sacred Diary of Adrian Plass (aged 37¾)*. London: Fount paperbacks, 1987.

Stanley, Brian. *The History of the Baptist Missionary Society, 1792–1992*. Edinburgh: T. and T. Clark, 1992.

Trench, Richard Chenevix. *Notes on the Parables of our Lord*. Popular edition, Grand Rapids, Michigan: Baker Book House, 1979.

Vine, W. E. *Expository Dictionary of New Testament Words*. London: Oliphants, 1940.

www.ingramcontent.com/pod-product-compliance
Lightning Source LLC
Chambersburg PA
CBHW070314230426
43663CB00011B/2120